GET

How to navigate through bankers, investors, and alternative sources for the capital your business needs

FINANCING NOW

CHARLES H. GREEN

New York   Chicago   San Francisco   Lisbon   London   Madrid
Mexico City   Milan   New Delhi   San Juan   Seoul
Singapore   Sydney   Toronto

1 2 3 4 5 6 7 8 9 10 DOC/DOC 1 6 5 4 3 2 1

ISBN 978-0-07-178031-5
MHID 0-07-178031-9

e-ISBN 978-0-07-178032-2
e-MHID 0-07-178032-7

This publication is designed to provide accurate and authoritative information in regard to the subject matter covered. It is sold with the understanding that neither the author nor the publisher is engaged in rendering legal, accounting, securities trading, or other professional services. If legal advice or other expert assistance is required, the services of a competent professional person should be sought.

—From a Declaration of Principles Jointly Adopted by a Committee
of the American Bar Association and a Committee of Publishers and Associations

Library of Congress Cataloging-in-Publication Data

Green, Charles H.
  Get financing now: how to navigate through bankers, investors, and alternative sources for the capital your business needs / Charles Green. — 1
      p. cm.
  ISBN-13: 978-0-07-178031-5 (pbk. : acid-free paper)
  ISBN-10: 0-07-178031-9 (pbk. : acid-free paper)
1. Small business—Finance. 2. Business enterprises—Finance. 3. New business enterprises—Finance. I. Title.
  HG4027.7.G737 2012
  658.15'224—dc23
                                                                      2011033383

McGraw-Hill products are available at special quantity discounts to use as premiums and sales promotions or for use in corporate training programs. To contact a representative, please e-mail us at bulksales@ mcgraw-hill.com.

This book is printed on acid-free paper.

GET
FINANCING
NOW

D

CONTENTS

A NOTE ABOUT THE TEXT

This book has many references to sources of business capital as being either lenders, funders, or investors. For clarification, the term *lenders* refers to banks or other lenders, and the use of the term is for information applicable only to debt capital providers. *Funders* refers to either lenders or investors, and the use of the term is for information applicable for either debt or equity capital. Likewise, the word *investor* is used only when referring to information applicable specifically to equity capital providers.

This publication is intended to provide readers with useful information that may assist them in financing a business using one of many strategies suggested here. This information is general in nature and is not intended to provide specific advice for any individual or business entity without qualification. While the information contained herein should be helpful to the reader, appropriate financial, accounting, tax, or legal advice should always be sought from a competent professional engaged for any specific situation.

ACKNOWLEDGMENTS

There are many people I wish to thank who contributed to the production of this book, including the friends, peers, and advisors who provided ideas and encouragement. My special gratitude goes to Stephanie and Gene, who had to endure the project with me from concept through finished book.

I appreciate many colleagues who contributed time to answer my questions, review portions of text, or set me straight on some of the finer points about their area of finance, accounting, business law, or the English language, including Barbara Benson, Marvin Bryant, Kevin Clingman, Frank Dinsmore, Barry Etra, Darryll Gillard, Michael Horton, Dar'shun Kendrick, Bill Moore, Critt Murphy, Marilyn Pearlman, Karen Rands, Erica Sandberg, Benjamin Suggs, and Kyle Walters. These consultations provided clarity and more accuracy to this work.

And I want to pay a special tribute to my dad, Joseph Henry Green (1919–2005), who taught me how to count money and the value of entrepreneurship.

INTRODUCTION

"Small" business is the category still used to classify more than 99 percent of all business entities in the United States. Representing about 40 percent of all commercial sales, 50 percent of the U.S. gross domestic product, and over 55 percent of the nongovernment workforce, small business is really *big* business.

This sector is credited for having created two out of every three new jobs in the United States for the past two decades, yet obtaining capital financing continues to be a challenge for most small business owners and entrepreneurs.

The first seven years of the new millennia were seemingly the most robust of any age for capital creation. During this period a combination of excessive financial deregulation, new product innovation, the unprecedented ease of global portability of money, and a surge of optimism created a capital market that swelled to titanic proportions.

As a result of what former Federal Reserve Chairman Alan Greenspan termed *irrational exuberance*, the financial markets simply had too much inventory for their own good. This condition evolved into a case of too much money chasing too few deals, the classic source of inflation, which metastasized around bad residential mortgages and home development during that cycle.

In their zeal to take advantage of all that funding and grow their business books, many bankers lowered borrower qualifications for people who normally shouldn't have qualified for financing (so-called liar loans). Suddenly, everybody became a real estate investor, notwithstanding the fact that many were barely able to pay for their own homes. The borrowing terms and upside reward promises seemed too good to be true. In fact, they were.

Weak loans were pooled with high-quality mortgages in a dizzying array of multitiered securities called collateralized debt obligations (CDOs), purportedly balanced between the lower and higher grades. These CDOs were sold to investors around the world enhanced with a derivative insurance called credit default swaps that were supposed to serve as a hedge for the subprime risk component.

The first wave of mortgage defaults began in 2007 when the most egregious mortgage producers started failing because they could no longer sell their loans. By the second quarter of 2008, Wall Street began teetering from a liquidity crisis as the market for CDOs dried up and major credit default claims began to unexpectedly hit insurers.

The commercial banking sector began choking on a similar variety of problems. Community banks (those with under $1 billion in assets) bet heavily on more land speculation, residential development, and commercial construction than could possibly be absorbed in one good economic cycle. Banks in Sunbelt states that had enjoyed bulging population growth, such as California, Arizona, Texas, Georgia, and Florida, were hit particularly hard.

The financial system finally crashed in September 2008 primarily under the weight of failing residential mortgages and the CDOs that funded them. Several major commercial and investment banking companies either failed or were forced into a quick sale, including Bear Stearns, Lehman Brothers, Wachovia, and the venerable Merrill Lynch. Major survivors like Morgan Stanley and American Express quickly sought refuge in the more regulated commercial banking system.

Concurrently, as new home construction and home resales fell off sharply in late 2007, a global recession emerged that affected virtually every business sector. In the United States, 15 million jobs disappeared, and the unprecedented millions of home foreclosures that followed ensured the real estate market crash would last for the foreseeable future.

After several healthy years following the 1990s S&L crisis, the crash caused hundreds of bank failures starting in late 2007. Many of the survivors were severely weakened by capital depletion from either a devalued loan portfolio or the lack of sufficient revenues. As the business sector became too weak or too timid to borrow money, most banks' primary sources of revenue were severely curtailed.

Small business capital financing evaporated almost overnight for most entrepreneurs. According to Federal Deposit Insurance Corporation chair Sheila Bair, more than $2.7 *trillion* of credit lines collapsed during this period, which made business growth and economic expansion virtually impossible.

The federal government's stimulus efforts through the Troubled Asset Relief Program (TARP), the Small Business Jobs Act, middle-class tax cuts, and the expansion of U.S. Small Business Administration (SBA) program loan limits to

$5 million have all contributed to soften the blow, but there is still much work to be done. To get the U.S. and global economies back on track to a more encouraging growth rate will require more business. Capital financing for that growth is far from certain.

Still, most entrepreneurs are yearning to monetize the opportunity they envision. Whether it's grilling steaks, selling art, developing software, or dry cleaning clothes, what they share in common is a need for business capital to launch and grow their enterprise.

To address this challenge, this book will teach readers how to navigate the more challenging and restrictive economic environment that business owners face to find capital financing. Negotiating funding is an art, and business owners should not harbor unrealistic expectations based on how easy it may have been in the past. There are new rules in effect today in every financing category.

The essential information and strategies needed to be fundable have not changed. What's different is the climate in which business owners must now search for funding, how funding sources are more sharply delineated, and how most capital providers' funding profiles have become narrower and more distinct.

Too many small business owners needing funding will unwittingly agree to outrageous terms just to acquire the money and get their business going. They enter a financing arrangement without really considering the true costs of funds. Sometimes such a leap works out well, even if it's unnecessarily expensive or restrictive. Sometimes things don't go so well.

This book encourages and helps small business owners to first look inward to better define their financial needs and clarify their business goals. It will suggest how to utilize other viable strategies or avoid costs to finance their operation without external funding.

When that is not feasible, I have clearly defined the two distinct sources of business capital, equity and debt; explained their significance and sources; and offered strategies with which to approach either. Understanding the most appropriate kind of financing according to a company's circumstances and limitations is vitally important, because it will preserve the precious time devoted to the search.

In Part 5, "Best Sources for Equity Capital," I cover the full range of options, including angel capital, venture capital, private placements, and even offer some general information about public offerings. To be clear, many of you reading this book will have few options for third-party equity due to the nature of your business and its lack of scalability. My hope is to reduce the time wasted by chasing the wrong rainbows.

But don't overlook the fact that most of Part 4, "Best Sources for Start-Up Capital," is also about equity—your own.

In Part 6, "Best Sources for Debt Capital," I provide the definitions of and keys to negotiating various debt products with many sources, including banks, government guaranteed lenders, leasing companies, and working capital finance companies. In addition, I hope to draw more attention to microlending, which might become a very important source of funding for your business due to its ability to offer higher risk gap financing as well as start-up funding.

If nothing else, I hope you will adapt better business practices and financial discipline as a distinct and effective financing tool. Finding a comfortable zone between "asleep at the wheel" and being a "spendthrift" is essential to managing your business responsibly and utilizing your resources better to realize their value and opportunity.

The lessons, suggestions, and guidance offered here are not written in the abstract by a casual observer but by an active participant in the process. My finance education continued past college through 30-plus years of experience, ranging from commercial lending to venture capital to organizing a new bank. Through the various positions I held, often I was either seeking debt or equity financing from banks or investors.

This book is an effort to share the lessons from those experiences to enable entrepreneurs to accelerate efforts to capitalize their ventures and move forward faster. My tutoring was crystallized in many diverse locales, including automotive repair garages, retail stores, construction sites, children's day-care centers, thread mills, convenience stores, chicken farms, truck terminals, restaurants, motels, marinas, testing laboratories, machine shops, and hundreds of other business facilities.

In other words, the very places in which entrepreneurs provide a variety of goods and services to our greater economy. These places are where someone employed capital, labor, and raw materials to deliver economic output to satisfy another party's economic demand.

And, there were less pleasant places that served as a classroom for my lessons about the downside risks of entrepreneurship: liquidation auctions, depositions, bankruptcy court, and even the courthouse steps on foreclosure day. I had to become familiar with writs of seizure, sheriff's sales, and the rules of dispossession.

Capital providers have not always risen to the challenges presented by the information age fast enough to provide sufficient funding for opportunities created by utilizing new technologies or meeting consumer service demands. Broad funding gaps remain as entrepreneurs pursue many service and web-based businesses. Even some small manufacturing companies still don't have reliable external funding streams.

These conditions will change soon, as the market discovers rich opportunities in meeting these credit needs, particularly as technology assists in the delivery of capital.

Finally, as we all approach the new postcrisis capital market, it's more vital than ever for business owners to get serious about gaining a greater understanding of their own financial conditions. Through most of my career, a majority of my clients could not even read their own financial statements!

How do you know whether your results are really good or really bad? Trust me, your bank balance is only one of many measurements, and it can be misleading. Your funder (or prospective funder) knows and will base its response to your requests on the metrics contained in your numbers. If you don't know what the funder will find, you may foreclose on future opportunities with it.

I have taken on this absence of business financial literacy as a mission and an opportunity in my own work, founding the Small Business Finance Institute, which aspires to create education channels to teach these kinds of skills to entrepreneurs—those who have been in business for many years or those planning to make that leap. Watch our progress at www.SBFI.org.

In this book you will find different illustrations that demonstrate how to evaluate financial results, project future activities, or create other vital information needed in the process of managing your business or finding funding. A functioning version of all of these worksheets is available at www.SBFI.org.

Part 1

Business Finance Fundamentals

WHY DO YOU NEED BUSINESS CAPITAL?

"Sorry, we can't help you." "Your expectations are out of line with our guidelines." "It's unlikely you are going to find that much money at this stage of your business."
All funders have uttered one of these three sentences on a majority of all the proposals they have ever considered, although maybe they delivered the message with gentler phrasing. Financing is strange territory for many upstart entrepreneurs, who expect that they can ask for and receive the entire sum of money they think they need for their big idea or fledgling enterprise.

Business owners frequently ask investors or lenders for an obviously inappropriate sum of capital based on either a lack of acumen to determine their real capital costs or failure to recognize the financial risk any funder is going to require that the owner share. Closing the information gap about this financing reality will advance the owners' capital search faster than any other exercise in the early business stages.

As in most of life's transactions, there's a distinct difference in business financing between what we want and what we can get. We all want world peace but often settle for a cease-fire. We want to win the big Lotto but are happy to get just a few bucks with a scratch-off card. In business it's great to imagine someone would put up all the money to pay for the pursuit of a terrific idea, but the reality is that that probably won't happen.

Capital owners employ funding within established risk parameters with the expectation of a specified return on investment. Risk is determined within stringent guidelines that are intended to avoid expensive losses of capital. The capital owners generally have the experience of previous disasters or the aversion to taking chances beyond a defined boundary with the funds they manage. These experiences and boundaries will define their appetite for risk and, as we have learned from the Golden Rule: "Those with the gold make the rules."

Business owners must recognize that the ultimate financial risk of any financing transaction is always going to be borne by them. Likewise, most of the financial rewards of a very successful enterprise will flow to the business owner as well. It's a risk vs. reward world.

Once business owners reconcile themselves to the idea that they must acclimate their capital needs to someone else's standards and accept the brunt of transaction risk for the enterprise and the capital provider, then they come around to asking themselves: Why do I really need capital?

The quick answer to that question might be "because I don't have it." More often than not, that answer is not entirely true.

Many business owners initiate efforts to acquire capital from a third party because it is perceived to be simpler and less risky than using their own resources. Depending on one's financial position, appetite for risk, and general business optimism, the personal risk is generally inversely related to the ease of accessing third-party capital.

If business owners are laden with significant cash resources relative to their capital request, the pursuit may be effortless but certainly with significant risks. If the search is a complicated process with many roadblocks to navigate, it's because the request reflects that the capital source is evaluating more risk.

Entrepreneurs often seek to use third-party capital because it seems easier to make spending decisions with someone else's money. Compare that to situations where they may have been tempted to purchase something frivolous with a credit card that they would have immediately dismissed if the purchase required payment in cash.

People seem to consider risk as a matter of possession. Spending another's money while maintaining control of one's own seems to invoke a sense of immunity from the possibility of adversity.

This pseudo immunity may be encouraged by the false presumption of reasonableness on the part of capital owners if things don't turn out as planned. Others have misperceptions or blind faith in the murky protection offered in bankruptcy and falsely believe that the courts will provide them with a universal get-out-of-jail-free card in the event of financial catastrophe. Sometimes that faith is disappointed.

Anyone operating within the reasoning described in the previous paragraph needs to do some serious soul searching before seeking business capital. The personal risks are very real, and the failure to make judicious choices can have a long-term impact on one's lifestyle, economic future, and even family.

Self-discipline, good business sense, and patience are the best attributes to exercise in order to build a successful business enterprise. Hopefully those attributes will help owners recognize the wisdom in employing their own resources where possible to avoid handing over control of their futures to third-party funders.

Tempering the amount of external funding acquired should be one of the primary goals of all small business owners. Doing so would mean that business achievements would be created with internally generated funding that ultimately eliminates external debt. Only then can businesses realize their greatest sustainability and owners truly control their own destinies.

Obviously, many businesses could not organize or function without external capital financing, and there are many good, necessary reasons to employ it for expansion and growth. However, business owners should understand the negative attributes of third-party funding and seek it only with full recognition of the potential consequences.

Define Funding Needs in Concise Terms

Once a business owner has pondered all the reasons to acquire business capital from other sources, the owner must communicate those needs to the capital source in concise terms. The definition of what is needed and why is the most important information the funder initially seeks in order to qualify interest in a deal.

Business capital is distributed by a large number of sources that individually address only a narrow set of market needs. There are investors and lenders for every purpose, including those that exclusively fund to real estate, equipment, business acquisitions, working capital, and numerous other commercial purposes. But even these broad categories are subdivided into many niche markets that continue to be defined as the economy evolves. Some niches expand due to the creation of new funding sources or to the newly developed expertise of the financiers.

For example, there are some real estate funders that choose to invest funds only in residential property mortgages. Other funders focus only on home-equity lines of credit, owner-occupied commercial properties, investor-owned properties, industrial properties, condominiums, vacation properties, restaurant properties, undeveloped land, land developments, construction projects, foreclosed properties, and even properties obtained through tax foreclosures.

Obviously it's necessary for the owner to thoughtfully define the purpose for which money is needed in as much detail as possible in order to determine the appropriate funding source. As important is the requirement to provide the funder a thorough explanation and justification as to where and when the capital needs to be disbursed.

Clearly a business seeking funding to buy a new building has an obvious business purpose needing less explanation. But additional clarity is required to define each party's expectations of the extent that funding will be injected by each participant. If both parties assume such details based only on their preferences or self-interests, there will be some confusion at the closing table when one party is surprised to learn of its greater-than-expected obligations in the transaction.

For example, do the owner and funder agree that the closing costs are to be considered part of the acquisition cost? The answer will directly impact the size of the loan from the money source and equity contribution from the owner.

Detail Every Dollar Requested

When obtaining business capital from a third party, sometimes owners have difficulty acclimating to the fact that the funder will assert restrictions as to how the funds will be used. In fact, the proceeds from most term debt financings will be spent via direct payments from closing to the agreed expenditure.

When preparing a loan proposal the owner should carefully consider the entire capital requirement to ensure that the external funding request reflects an accurate sum of the money needed. Under- or overestimating true enterprise needs can present problems for both the business and funder.

Chiefly, an inaccurate proposal signals to the funder that there could be a management issue to consider. If the owner can't get a handle on the cost of business needs, how can the funder hope to meet those needs?

Intentionally overestimating the project costs leads the lender to suspect that the business is either building a funding cushion in the transaction or not actually injecting the owner's agreed-upon portion of the funding. Either would increase the funder's risk and raise questions about the owner's projections or character.

Underestimating the cost might lead the funder to conclude that the owner is incapable of assessing the required capital budget and hence will also disappoint the funder with estimates of other deal components, such as revenues, expenses, and profits.

It's very important to carefully evaluate the true costs that need external financing and ensure the funding proposal closely mirrors these needs. Best management practices dictate that every prospective cost and expense be identified to assure all parties that the comprehensive costs of the transaction and operation have been projected as accurately as possible.

For example, purchasing a $500,000 building cannot be viewed as merely a capital cost of $500,000. The business will incur additional costs to perform due diligence and the closing transaction according to the contract conditions or financing qualifications. Hopefully all of these costs are identified not only ahead of entering into the purchase contract but definitely before seeking third-party financing.

Due diligence and real estate closings cost money. All of these expenses must be accounted for as the owner assesses the cost of owning the building before the property is actually purchased.

And what about the building costs after the acquisition? What will the business have spent to prepare the property for occupancy? Will there be architectural fees, builder's fees, or painter's fees? Certainly there will be utility deposits, telephone system installations, new stationery, movers, network designs, signage, public relations, and many other direct costs associated with relocating to the new site.

Recognizing the full costs of such a business decision on the front end enables the business owner to make better decisions and execute a strategy with more success. Providing the funder with a detailed explanation of these impact costs and how they will be covered will assure the funder that management has the acumen to plan a safe course for business operations.

This level of planning also protects the business by considering the full effect of such a decision ahead of commitment, which allows for reconsideration if financing capacity is insufficient or the business cost is too great.

A very detailed cost examination is vital, even for the most routine business strategies, to ensure the funder that management is in command of the financial impact of implementation, that the business is capable of managing operations or expansion successfully with adequate resources (subject to funding), and that the project has a strong potential to contribute to the business's success.

Do Your Homework (Your Funder Will)

Once the business owner identifies the various costs facing the business plan, it is necessary to tie down the actual figures with exact detail. Mostly for the owner's own benefit but particularly before presenting to a funder, it is important to extend the costs to know to the penny what the total costs will be.

To protect the integrity of the calculations, it is important for the owner to obtain cost quotes in writing from the various vendors, professionals, or other parties to whom such expenses will be paid. Inclusion of this kind of documentation in the financing proposal gives weight to the projections and builds others' confidence in the due diligence the owner performed.

This process is labor intensive for sure but will save much frustration once spending starts, since there is a commitment in hand. A written estimate removes ambiguity and shows the extended costs, including add-ons such as sales tax, delivery, and installation. Such hidden costs can increase the final expense 5 to 15 percent, which is disruptive if unexpected, particularly on larger cost categories.

Minimize Where Possible, Maximize When Necessary

When seeking financing, there is a tendency among business owners to ask for as much money as they can with a straight face, under the auspices of "get it while the getting is good." Other business people may challenge that notion.

Owners should start and end with the amount of funding that they alone have determined is actually needed. They should resist the temptation to accept all the money that may be thrown at them, since it may cause them to fall prey to other businesses (other funders) achieving their own objectives at the owner's expense.

Too often business owners start with "what can we get" rather than "what do we need?" There is a huge difference. One the one hand, they have a plan, and it may be more conservative to grow the enterprise deliberately with internally generated funding. Accepting external funds may (or may not) accelerate that pace, may (or may not) drive the enterprise to greater results, or may (or may not) cause owners to lose everything for a shot at faster or higher results.

Think about the different views of the word affordable. Depending on one's risk appetite and financial discipline, one party may believe something is affordable only if there is cash on hand to pay for it today. Another may take a more conservative view that affordability requires more analysis of a larger financial scope, which may assess the investment value and what return will be gained from the expense.

Still others may assess affordable as just being able to make financing payments today.

Affordability should be assessed on enterprise liquidity over and above a defined contingency reserve and the retention of earnings over time. When considering financing strategies, the financial payoff should be tangibly higher and obvious to predict.

Spending everything one earns is not a wise financial strategy. The accumulation of some portion of past success provides the financial footings for future expansion. The constant commitment of future earnings through payment obligations is management by the next dollar. This strategy leads to a crisis when the next dollar is delayed or never appears.

While fancy expenditures may impress others, unless they contribute to long-term profitability, growth, or sustainability, they are frivolous. These three attributes are essential to long-term success of any business enterprise.

Business owners should view any decision to leverage funds carefully and ensure that other resources are considered before jumping into a loan. Utilization of internal resources where possible is much less expensive and lowers the risks considerably to the future of the enterprise.

To maintain discipline and focus on the prospects for long-term business success, it is important to minimize external funding to the greatest extent possible.

❋ ❋ ❋

Sometimes a business will need capital financing for reasons that do not represent an extravagant expansion but rather a wise financial strategy. Sometimes decisions must be made fast in order to take advantage of a changing market or sudden opportunity. Sometimes a business needs more money than it may normally have an appetite to acquire.

In those circumstances where the right reasons exist to fund strategies that serve the business well and move the company's purpose forward, seeking to maximize such opportunities with third-party financing may make sense. While prudence should be maintained, financing the business is certainly not taboo.

Seeking the maximum funding leverage should be done responsibly, weighing the internal need and opportunity against the external terms and cost. Management must be comfortable with the business strategy and move forward without reservation that success is likely. Internal resources should still be utilized in a prudent proportion to the external funds. If the business risk is in an acceptable range, external funding can enable it to accelerate its success.

Because You Can, Doesn't Mean You Should

Have you ever concluded a search for business financing by "losing the battle but winning the war"? You are offered some funding that basically meets your goal, but something isn't right. Maybe the terms are too short or there's too much collateral required, or perhaps the loan covenants are overbearing. Maybe you think the funder is squeezing too hard and setting you up to fail? It happens.

Sometimes in their zeal to lower their risk, funders impose unreasonable terms, like requiring too much security or pricing the deal too high or setting repayment terms too short. Owners could be offered funding that they may be unable to repay. They shouldn't take it.

Owners also should not enter any funding transaction if they feel it's wrong for them. They should walk away from the risks. It's better to miss the opportunity than to increase the odds of failure.

During the early, high-risk stages of some businesses, owners have to beg for funding to get minimum sums on the safest terms at the highest prices. Of course once such businesses succeed and the owners don't have to rely on external funding, then the funders start begging owners to accept loans. They are quick to start offering funds when owners don't need the money.

Owners should not accept business funding unless getting it was part of their plan. Funders want to maximize their opportunity and capitalize on the business's success. What about the owners' needs? Changing course to accommodate more money that only might be needed simply because it's there does not necessarily lead to more success.

Businesses should always have a strategy, and if owners are randomly offered an unsolicited alternative, they should be wary of changing their original plans. They should avoid the risk of shortsighted, half-baked ideas and not take unsolicited money.

2

HOW (IM)MATURE IS
THE BUSINESS?

A business can be defined through a number of cycles, each having characteristics that distinguish it in chronological terms. More than a start and an end, business cycles define risk and ownership in some instances, as an enterprise may evolve from the mature cycle with one owner back into the start-up cycle for another.

Understanding how funders view these various stages helps business owners find funding channels better suited for their stage. A business in its mature stage may not sound too sexy, but equity funders are attracted to retirement-age business owners who have built successful enterprises that can be aggregated with another business. Likewise, all parties recognize the additional risk of a business in its start-up stage.

These cycles are defined in this chapter to distinguish the various stages, from big idea to exit. An early understanding of all business stages helps management graduate its strategic planning accordingly and facilitate better decisions for the business.

Big Ideas, Planning, and Organizing

The initial stage of a business actually begins prior to starting operations. This business cycle might be called the big idea, planning, or the organization stage. It exists during the period of activities leading up to the actual launch of business operations.

The length of this stage is dependent on many factors but primarily on the deliberation term or motivation of the business organizer. Either attribute can be a factor in the eventual success of the business.

Some people jump into business without sufficient preparation or research but with an exaggerated dose of motivation. Sometimes they succeed wonderfully, since their energy and drive overcome the details of organization and planning. Sometimes they just fail faster.

Other people plan for years. They create a second career of preparing for a business that never opens. They research, study, interview, read, write, discuss, and think about a business. However, they never quite get the motivation to launch it.

Both types of entrepreneurs can succeed. Perhaps the most likely success stories, though, will have some attributes of each. Planning greatly increases the odds of success or, worst case, helps avoid disaster.

During the planning stage, future business owners have the time to map out their strategies and big ideas and research the market and industry to validate their assumptions. During this early stage, the business plan should be started to aggregate this information. A business plan is a living document, so the plan should never really be viewed as "written," which may mislead management to consider that it's finished.

A business plan is never finished until the business is sold or liquidated. The plan should be updated at least annually and always reflect information from the recent past and new strategies to be employed in the near future.

The length of the planning and organization stage will depend on the degree of preparation required by the scale of business and the thoroughness of the organizer. Owners should guard against getting into business too far ahead of (or behind) the window of opportunity, the optimal time frame in the marketplace for the delivery of a particular product or service.

Is it possible to find funding in the development stage? It's difficult unless an idea can pass tougher investor qualifications and has the potential to be scaled in massive proportions: new technologies, new medical devices, or new solutions to problems that affect a broad population. Getting equity capital ahead of revenue generation is not unheard of, but it requires a strong idea that can survive the evaluation of many people.

However, most entrepreneurs in the planning stage should research conventional funding sources so as to be aware of the providers and terms under which capital financing can be obtained at the appropriate time.

Start-Up

At the time the business is actually launched—beginning with the first open door, sales call, or contract bid, the business enters the start-up stage. In some ways, start-up companies are the most fun place of the business cycle. There are fresh ideas, enthusiasm, new business cards, and so many dynamic decisions to make.

On the other hand, starting up can be a sheer fright. No customers, no revenues, a long list of financial commitments, and the high expectations of everyone who's watching. It's a very public opportunity to fall flat on your face.

Getting capital funding at the start-up phase is possible but is very restricted. Sourcing funding requires some effort and research into exactly who will fund start-up enterprises. Many factors contribute to the more restrictive market for start-up financing.

Principally, start-up businesses have new, untested, unproven ideas that may succeed but that have a higher propensity to fail. Without higher odds of success, many funders shy away from dealing with start-up situations.

Equity capital is limited to the businesses with the previously mentioned scale probability. Beyond that, only an opportunity without significant risk that could generate a defined return in a measurably short time frame to assure investors of the likelihood of exiting as planned would qualify.

The limited debt capital available is predominantly aimed at business owners wanting to finance asset acquisitions, such as real estate, equipment, or other business operations. Even more limited resources are available for some working capital financing when secured with the owner's business or nonbusiness assets.

Often new businesses are launched with very thin capitalization garnered solely from the personal resources of the organizers. Such a strategy may be slower to get going, but it's very admirable. You can be sure that owners paying for their own start-ups out of pocket don't waste much money.

Growing Places

In the middle of the flurry of rapid business growth, start-up–stage companies cross over to become growth-stage companies. No definitive official metric exists that signifies this transformation, but business owners will know when they have survived the more tenuous start-up stage with several successive months of constant sales growth, profits, and more sustainable expectations.

Growth-stage companies start to create a short success story to talk about and finally begin to develop some history. Having survived the start-up mode, they have attained a level of stable operations and successfully navigated the uncertainty and risk associated with launching a new enterprise.

Successfully entering growth-stage status does not guarantee any continued success but moves business planning to a new level. Most start-up operations hesitate to try new ideas or make any deviation from their business plans due to their limited capital and momentum, which would not be able to sustain failure.

However, the growth-stage company attains a critical mass that is sufficient to provide predictable profits and that opens the possibility to take advantage of new opportunities that may emerge. A comfort zone is created in this stage that is congenial to developing ideas to leverage success.

It's in the growth stage of a business when funders begin to seek opportunities to provide financing to move the business forward to even greater achievements. Growing businesses have the best chance of earning profits, and they continue to buy more assets, invest in new strategies, and demonstrate some level of competence and success.

Funders are attracted to these attributes, since they tend to lower the risks associated with external financing. In fact, for more successful growth-stage companies, lenders will start offering to lend more money than the businesses may want or need.

Mature—Exit Ahead?

The mature stage of a business may evolve from one of two different determinants. One is when the business's technology or popularity reaches its zenith and is no longer growing due to the availability of more efficient or preferred alternatives that provide the same product or service. Think Walmart vs. the corner five-and-dime or the smartphone vs. rotary telephone.

The second determinant could be the business ownership. Business owners age out and choose to sell the business due to wealth accumulation or the desire to simply stand down. Either way, the business has attained sufficient maturity demonstrated by its ability to be sold to a new owner who usually believes it is possible to ignite another growth stage.

Maturity defined by the former reason is simply the aging out of what built the business. In this rapidly changing information age, technological and social evolution occur with sometimes blinding speed. The ability to scale the distribution of products and ideas with viral popularity permits businesses to start, grow, and mature in relatively short periods of three to five years.

Conversion from the growth to the maturity stage by technology may take decades and even run concurrent with the emergence of competing technologies or popular alternatives. Consider eyeglasses, which continue to grow through fashion, while contact lenses grow through technology. And both face real future competition with Lasik surgery.

Other industries may come and go in a relatively short time frame, like floppy disks to store digital information. Remember when you had to "boot-up" a computer with a floppy disk? No, many of you reading this book won't, but it was required for the operation of the original personal computers built in the early 1980s. Moving that task onto the hard drive was only a matter of time, as technology quickly eliminated many steps required to compute. Growth to maturity was relatively quick.

When a business evolves to maturity due to its ownership, it's typically when the business owner nears a chosen retirement age. A successor may be another owner (partner) or a family member, but often transfer to another party is necessary through sale, or the business is simply liquidated.

Implications of maturity are many for the business enterprise. With either a legacy of success or modest survival, most mature business owners will not aggressively invest in growth or new strategies. Facing either a decline in business prospects or in the ability to manage the future, they prudently choose to preserve older wealth rather than attempt to create it again.

Access to debt capital for a mature business is usually robust, since there is lower enterprise risk for the lender when the business has a track record. Most mature businesses will rely on existing relationships that have developed over many years. Adequate financing is an important ingredient to surviving long enough to become a mature company.

Mature companies will not attract much equity capital unless there is an ownership transfer accompanied with an aggressive growth strategy. Such prospects aren't realistic if the technology has peaked or the popularity has fallen off behind newer competitors.

Legal Organization Is a Finance Issue

Business entities may operate in one of four different legal organizations, which for the most part will not affect how a lender or an investor relates to the funding request. But selecting the appropriate form of business entity is an important finance decision for the business, since each form has distinct legal and tax characteristics.

Organizing a legal entity ahead of starting operations is the best choice to make. Getting the liability protection of a legal umbrella is well worth the cost of sound advice from an attorney, and the potential tax savings will far exceed some basic work needed from an accountant—money well spent to be sure of what is necessary.

Each business form is eligible for financing from all sources.

Proprietorship

A proprietorship is a business operated by an individual who has chosen to sell products or provide services without creating a separate legal entity. The business is embodied in the efforts of the individual, who may use a distinctive business name or title, which is usually preceded with d/b/a, or (doing business as).

The business name does not carry protection from duplication by someone else, and the individual will be legally and financially liable for all acts of the enterprise. A proprietor's revenue is described as business income on Schedule C of the IRS form 1040 but becomes personal income unless it's reduced by direct expenses for producing the revenue.

There are a few good reasons for operating as a proprietor, such as simplicity and lower costs for microsize operations. However, if the plan calls for an organization to be in business for more than one year or expects revenues to exceed $10,000, an attorney should be consulted to form a legal entity for the enterprise.

Partnership

A partnership is a business organization created by two or more individuals or legal entities (or combination of individuals and legal entities) that choose to structure their business relationship in a registered partnership.

Partnerships may be defined as general or limited, each of which provides distinct levels of liability and responsibility of the individual partners. Here is a brief definition of each type partnership:

- General partnerships divide the responsibility and liability for their activities equally among the partners on a prorated ownership basis.
- Limited partnerships may limit the responsibility and liability of the limited partners for the activities of the partnership. Limited partnerships must have a general partner who accepts the personal liability for all actions of the partnership (and for that reason most general partners are partnerships, corporations, or limited liability companies). Limited partnerships must be registered with the state to create the liability veil.

Partnership income is taxed by prorating any profits or losses among the partners, as provided for in the partnership agreement and the division of ownership.

Corporation

A corporation is a business organization in which the owners, one or more share-holders, are granted certain liability protection and tax treatment as a distinct entity. Generally, shareholders cannot be held personally liable for the business of the corporation unless they purposely elect to guarantee specific liabilities.

The two different types of corporations are the C corporation and the S (sub-chapter S) corporation. Although similar, these two corporations have distinct tax attributes for their shareholders:

- A C corporation is taxed on its earnings, and the shareholders are also indi-vidually taxed on any distributions or dividends paid out by the corpo-ration. Any corporate distributions to shareholders are paid with after-tax income, thereby causing the distributions to be taxed twice.
- An S corporation is intended to provide smaller companies the advantage of a lower tax burden by passing profits or losses through to the individual shareholders on a pro rata distribution based on ownership, similar to a partnership.

Limited Liability Company

A limited liability company (LLC) combines the favorable liability protection of a corporation and the favorable taxation attributes of a partnership. LLCs are the most flexible form of legal entity, since the organizers can form it similar to a part-nership (with investments in units or interests, owners called partners, and man-agement by a general partner), a corporation (with investments in shares, owners called shareholders, and governance by a board of directors), or as a hybrid, where owners are known as members, and management is described as managing members.

Be Wary of External Factors That Affect the Business

Apart from the challenges of competing against peers and the market for success in a very competitive, fast-paced business environment, smarter business owners serve themselves well to be aware of the events in the greater world around them. Many external factors add layers of risks and barriers to success that will affect a business at any stage.

Technology delivers efficiency that can provide productivity and opportunity to most businesses, but many are also vulnerable to how technology can taketh away as well. Recent changes in Google algorithms changed how the search engine ranked various websites[1] in an effort to scuttle efforts of some rogue site operators to get an unfair visibility advantage. Unintended consequences were that many popular, successful businesses were negatively affected because of these changes.

Other risks include public policy changes that may occur on the federal, state, or local level through good intentions or at the urging of competing interests. Virtually any policies dealing with tax, labor, environment, health care, trade, education, finance, technology, or transportation will directly affect most business interests in the short or long term.

And then there are factors beyond the reach or even the effective ability of a person to control, such as globalization, immigration, and terrorism, that can create an environment or situation that directly threatens a business. Only knowledge and the use of it can arm a business owner to measure risk and lower exposure.

For example, take the financial crisis of 2008, using the common sense axiom that "if it sounds too good to be true, it is," as a business principle. When the housing bubble was approaching its recognized zenith, the Dow Jones Industrial Average was topping 14,000, and housing starts were hitting record levels each year, maybe more of us should have thought to tack in the other direction. Too few took measures to lower business risks well ahead of the crash, despite plenty of warnings of the impending collapse.

The ever-changing economy can turn on a dime, and if business owners are dependent on the nightly news for information, they're already behind. Keeping an eye on the horizon requires getting information from many sources, constantly sorting out and assessing how the business climate will fare in the big picture, and, of course, continually seeking more information, since the world continues to evolve.

A major benefit in today's technology-driven world is the fact that more free information is available to anyone than at any other time in history. One Sunday edition of the *New York Times* contains more information than the average person encountered in his entire life in the nineteenth century.[2]

Regularly published government statistics offer a plethora of indicators that provide intelligence to the entire marketplace. Cable television has spawned hundreds of niche-oriented channels, many of which provide news and business analysis. Other great sources of information on general and specific trends that

---

1. http://money.cnn.com/2011/03/08/technology/google_algorithm_change/index.htm
2. http://www.gdrc.org/icts/i-overload/infoload.html

directly or indirectly affect a business include the Internet, newspapers, industry-specific trade groups, universities, government agencies, and business associations.

Most business owners are more likely to focus on the immediate threats that negatively impact their businesses and that are easier to identify and attack. Sometimes this narrower view works fine, but sometimes it provides inadequate protection.

Mature businesses are generally less susceptible to external risks, since they have more established revenue streams and better capitalization. But they also may be less agile and harder to defend, since they may be targeted by the very factors that threaten them (for example, policies intended to lower oil consumption).

Start-up and growing businesses are generally more leveraged and are more acutely vulnerable to the financial impact of external factors. But they too could be the very target of factors that are affecting them (for example, marijuana-flavored candy manufacturers).

Either way, it's a good idea for business owners to wise up and know more about the outside world. Doing so will make it easier to defend the growth of their business, and that is an important finance strategy.

Economics 101—Micro vs. Macro

Small business owners sometimes fail to recognize their contributions to the world's gross output. There are two branches of economics: 1) macroeconomics[3] studies the performance, structure, behavior, and decision making of the entire economy; and 2) microeconomics studies how individual households and firms allocate limited resources.

The microeconomy is the division in which daily participation takes place—the village, mall, shopping center, or store. These participants are relatively small, serving a specific market. There are generally low barriers to entry, but the micro-economy limits the number of participants due to its size. The participation of some directly affects the participation of others, depending on how much is bought and sold. Individual participation in a microeconomy is definitely tangible.

The macroeconomy is defined as a broader measurement, such as the "U.S. economy," that encompasses measurement of the output and consumption of the entire nation. That macro can be broken down in countless other ways, such as the automotive industry, which would measure the sum of everything (manufacturing,

---

3. http://en.wikipedia.org/wiki/Macroeconomics

parts, sales, services, after-market, etc.) related to automobiles. Or more broadly, there is the transportation sector, which would include the automobile, airlines, rail, and shipping industries.

No single party makes or breaks the macroeconomy, but a single party can be more influential in a particular microeconomy. All U.S. microeconomic results aggregate into the sum of economic activity called the gross national product (GNP). Microeconomic participants usually have a choice of trading partners with different characteristics to match their preferences. These are the ingredients of a generally efficient economy.

Why is this information important? In the macroeconomy, regardless of revenue size or enterprise age, every business is connected in today's economy. In the digital age, consumers have more choices than ever, and when they choose a business, there is a reason. Identifying those choices and reasons becomes vital information needed to plan for business success and compete with those at the other end of countless IP addresses.

Business owners must understand their place in the microeconomy in order to develop strategic business plans. For example, consider the major grocery store in your microeconomy. Depending on the size of your town or city, you may have a larger chain store like Kroger, Super-Valu, or Safeway. These stores may appear to be giants when comparing their per-store revenues to your business (median U.S. grocery store *weekly* sales total $485,000).[4]

Their strategic advantage is obvious: everyone has to eat. Grocery stores face a brutal profitability model with fierce competition producing low margins on high volumes. The more successful stores thrive on this economic challenge and attack it by managing the vital statistics that define their success: sales per square foot, sales per labor hour, and sales per customer transaction.

Kroger has more than 2,400 stores nationwide and has successfully grown by understanding these metrics and developing growth in response to best practices learned over time. Today Kroger's average supermarket store is 75,000 square feet and represents an investment of $13 million. Kroger has grown sales volume by teaching customers to combine grocery shopping with other retail needs formerly attended to by a pharmacy and gas station.

By tracking weekly revenues and profits against operating costs and capital investment, the company focuses management on margins, labor cost, and market share—vital performance measurements that drive profits. This information identifies weaknesses more quickly, leading to corrective action. Store managers are

---

4. http://www.fmi.org/facts_figs/?fuseaction=superfact

accountable for the results and are tuned in to their operations on a per-square-foot basis.

Major grocers have a keen awareness of the demographics in each market territory (generally a 2.5 mile radius around the store) and allocate a store's floor space accordingly to maximize sales volume. For example, demographics about household incomes, family composition, ethnicity, education, and climate all impact the product mix provided by each store based on the historical buying habits of those demographics.

Economic information helps managers decide what to stock, how much to stock, and which brands are preferred. It also influences pricing and advertising strategies. No two microeconomies are exactly alike, but years of collecting data has taught these companies something about serving their markets.

What does this discussion mean for a business? Imitation is the most sincere form of flattery. Business owners who emulate some of these practices in their business can increase productivity, increase margins, and lower operating costs. Recognizing the importance of finding information that can help identify and respond to clients will provide more revenue and profits.

It's an open secret that grocery stores attract a steady stream of weekly customers to the shopping centers they occupy, and, accordingly, the rental rates for everyone else there are higher than for other nearby retail spaces. An owner who situates a business near a major grocery store does not guarantee success but does increase the probability that there will be plenty of consumer traffic.

So if a business can profit from this kind of traffic flow, wouldn't it be useful to understand which grocery store is most successful, particularly among the buyers who match the targeted demographics?

Business owners can learn much from economic information about their microeconomy. Even the statistical data from noncompetitor businesses can help them develop plans and adjust their strategy for success. Keeping an eye on the micro- and macroeconomy is good management and will help a business prosper.

3

DYNAMICS OF THIRD-PARTY FUNDING

To successfully fund their business, business owners must acclimate themselves to the dynamics of the evaluation and underwriting process. Approaching this process with realistic expectations will improve an owner's proposal and increase the chance of success.

Owners should reconcile themselves to one of the business world's basic rules, adapted from the Golden Rule: "Those with the gold make the rules."

Those requesting funding should be prepared to provide voluminous information, answer a dizzying array of questions, and be critiqued on a variety of business details. This repetitive and tedious process is not intended to be a personal challenge but is necessary for the funder to quantify risk.

The owner is asking for a service that requires subjective qualification and objective quantification. One business (the owner) is asking another business (the funder) for use of capital. The evaluation process is, out of necessity, arduous but meaningful.

Most funders see dozens of funding requests every year and must scrutinize the minute details of each opportunity to evaluate the likelihood of each one's success.

Owners must plan for funding well ahead of their needs and initiate these requests ahead of when that need is critical. Trying to rush funders through their process dampens their interest in the proposal and raises questions about whether information is being distorted or concealed, or worse, may raise questions about management. Even if eventually funded, missteps during the approval process can impact relationships, which may haunt owners later.

Information is a powerful tool to support a business funding proposal. Understanding an industry, competition, market, and the macroeconomy will enhance a business owner's quest for funding. Command of pertinent data will give the funder more confidence about the owner's ability to manage the business and return the capital.

Business owners get frustrated with funders who seem passive when considering funding proposals and the often lengthy amount of time required to work through the underwriting process. They also may get a little indignant about the conservative posture investors and bankers take when underwriting capital requests. These feelings are very common.

It's useful to recall that funders are averse to risks. Their job is to make loans or investments in situations with measured risk. In the transactions that funders elect to accept, they try to limit the risks in multiple ways, including the use of financial covenants, which are terms tied to performance metrics that may trigger default, tougher conditions, or various other options to liquidate the investment.

When funders seem too conservative, they are illuminating the limitations of their risk appetite for the subject proposal. While owners may be exuberantly confident about their prospects and capabilities, funders are naturally skeptical and will always question everything.

The funder is in business too. Investors or capital managers have a responsibility to provide a financial return for their portfolios, shareholders, or partners. Positive returns are generated by responsibly employing funds in business opportunities for a substantial return. Funders are not without their own challenges.

First, many funders must contend with their own continually changing sources of financing that affects their engagement while competing with other financiers also seeking investments. They must field aggressive but competent representatives to originate prudent financing opportunities in a rapidly changing economy. In addition, bank funders have the burden of federal or state regulators to manage.

Second, most loan officers and investors spend their entire careers concentrating on underwriting thousands of business proposals. They know a little about everything but often without specialization in anything except perhaps a narrow industry, and even then they will have only an outsider's limited perspective. They act single-mindedly to protect the interests of the institutions that employ them, as they should.

Funders evaluate transaction proposals according to the risk parameters decided on by their institutions, which are subject to change. Some of their parameters are rooted in their experiences with some great ideas that went wrong or from individuals who tried to defraud them. They have been subjected to exaggerations, ineptness, and imprudence from business owners they trusted. These experiences form a tangible degree of caution in subsequent transactions.

When seeking third-party funding, owners must educate funders on all aspects of their businesses. This process enables funders to evaluate enterprise management, performance, products or services, and prospects for success. Funders must be convinced that owners can manage their enterprises and employ the subject funds to achieve greater success.

Is the business earning money? Is its cash flow sufficient to support operations? What happened in previous periods, and what do they predict for the prospects ahead?

Debt and equity capital are made available only in situations where the likelihood of their being returned is high. Funders will always require more than one exit strategy to extract their capital, but failure to see a clear path to the production of profits will terminate their interest in a deal immediately.

The Art of Funding

Employing capital is an art but with many scientific constraints. While many established regulations, business practices, and accepted standards are involved, the practice still comes down to making qualified financial bets on unknown future outcomes.

Most unfunded requests lack key ingredients that make the capital source comfortable that the funds can ultimately be returned from operations or value generated by the business.

Funders view each financing proposal against five elementary criteria to determine whether the deal meets the basic threshold to proceed. There is no magic formula or minimum standard of these criteria for business owners. To be considered for funding, the funder has to be comfortable with the subjective strength of these criteria in the business and its owner.

While these criteria are more often cited by commercial lenders than equity investors, the principles are common to both worlds, although perhaps with different language.

If the business owner has an acute weakness in even one of these criteria, that deficiency probably will not be overcome with a stronger position in one of the remaining criteria. It depends on all of the relative strengths and weaknesses of the business and owner. These five categories are capacity, capital, collateral, credit, and character.

Capacity

The funder attempts to determine whether the business owner has the qualifications or wherewithal, the capacity, to manage the requested monies. Is the business owner operating within his abilities or attempting to accomplish something beyond his limitations?

Does the business owner's market position, industry experience, and track record give the funder confidence that the funding will be capably used to produce the projected results? Can the owner manage it?

A funder ponders whether the owner can muster the effort, resolve, and ingenuity to succeed and persevere to manage and coordinate tasks necessary to generate profitable revenues.

And prior success must be relative: if the business owner produced impressive results with $200,000 funding in an earlier deal, that accomplishment does not automatically indicate the capacity for a subsequent round of $20 million.

Sometimes owners fail this test because they are more ambitious than talented. Funders must draw conclusions from limited information and a few meetings. The owner's résumé, past accomplishments, references, and communications skills, along with some previous financial successes, contribute significantly to establishing a capacity for funding.

Capital

When funders are invited to evaluate a company, they will always quantify the size and adequacy of the owner's investment. While equity funders may give credit for intangible assets, they, like lenders, are interested in the owner having a meaningful amount of equity at risk, or skin in the game, to ensure that the owner is committed to the venture, lowering the funder's exposure to loss.

Equity is the portion of the total business cost that is contributed by the owner. Funders have varying standards for the adequacy of an original owner's degree of capitalization, depending on the use of funds and the nature of the business.

As the company's profits grow, lenders will expect the owner's equity or net worth, position to grow proportionately through retaining some of the earnings in the business. Equity investors will also limit owner withdrawals to assure long-term enterprise success rather than short-term owner lifestyle.

While this equity accumulation may cost the business owner higher tax liabilities and personal income, it's a reasonable expectation by any funder that the business contribute to financing its growth. This limitation makes good sense for the business and its owner.

Collateral

Collateral are assets offered by the owner to guarantee repayment of a loan request with the lender's lien on tangible security. These assets provide a secondary source of repayment in the event that business profits cannot repay a loan.

Lenders require that loans be supported with assets whose value is discounted to provide the lender with a safe margin to cover the time and costs of converting these assets into cash, should it become necessary.

Typically lenders require minimum discounted collateral values to be at least equivalent to the loan balance. The collateral assets always include those acquired with the loan proceeds and possibly other assets, if available or acceptable to the lender.

The discount is intended to ensure that the lender has a comfortable margin of value from which the loan can be repaid, including all of the anticipated liquidation expenses, if business operations do not provide sufficient repayment funds.

Equity funders do not use collateral per se, but they do generally require preferences (acquired through issuance of preferred stock) over any net liquidation proceeds or company assets in the event of business cession or failure. In that way, they effectively ensure that the first monies coming out of the business, if any, will go toward redeeming their investment ahead of the owner recovering anything.

Credit

Lenders evaluate an applicant's previous credit experience, which discloses whether the business or the owner has paid previous borrowings as agreed. Credit reports are also used to determine whether the business or owners have ever had difficult financial events that appear on public records. These events might include civil liability judgments, unpaid tax obligations, property foreclosures, general execution liens (FiFa), or protection under bankruptcy.

While clearly not an exclusive indicator of how well the business will perform in the future, this information relates to how the business owner has performed in the past. Negative information could disqualify the business owner from getting credit from a particular lender when it's revealed that the owner has not overcome earlier difficulties. Poor performance with previous funders may indicate either that the owner does not take repayment responsibility seriously or does not have the capacity to produce success.

Equity funders generally do not look at credit reports, but they may evaluate a prospective business owner with reference checks or a background investigation.

If negative information exists, they want to know about it and decide whether it's material to their consideration.

Character

Character may be the most important assessment the funder can make about the business owner. Regardless of other positive attributes, if the owner does not demonstrate integrity and impress the funder as trustworthy, any proposal will not go forward.

Character is the most subjective criteria. The criteria is not only difficult to define, it's difficult to assess. There is no checklist available to guide the funder's sensitivity to quantifying someone's good character, particularly when the other party is a new acquaintance.

The funder has to study the owner to evaluate her personal qualities and characteristics. Funders will watch for potential flaws that may be detected in attitude, conversation, perspective, or opinions of the business owner about business, ethics, responsibility, and commitment.

The business owner's character is important because it reveals intent. If the funder senses that the owner has an ambivalent attitude toward fulfilling responsibilities under the proposed deal, there is a character problem. Funders believe that owners should embrace commitment as a moral obligation to work toward returning the funder's capital, superseding even the legal agreement to do so.

When a funder does not feel comfortable with the owner's character, the deal is dead, and the reason will probably not be communicated to the owner. It's difficult to articulate a subjective decision without definitive proof. This ambiguity is part of the intangible matrix of underwriting business finance.

Caution: To Buy or Not to Buy *Expert* Advice

Many small business owners seeking financing have relied on professional intermediaries for advice and assistance. But many business owners have fallen victim to unscrupulous or inept loan or investment brokers who either waste valuable time to conduct a hopeless search for capital or who collect fees that are undeserved and never earned.

There are many capable, professional consultants who play an important role in today's financial marketplace through the introduction of good solutions to good companies. Entrepreneurs cannot be expected to keep track of the constantly changing financial marketplace of products and providers, and navigating it with an experienced advisor is often helpful.

Unfortunately the same entrepreneur also cannot always decide who is helpful or hurtful, and there is no standard in the business for grading these consultants. The value of these services should be measured by how quickly they assess an owner's needs, develop a funding strategy, and get the owner in front of the proposed funder. By the time an owner figures out an advisor is incompetent, the owner may have already paid for the services.

Any consultant willing to work on behalf of the business owner for several months purely on a contingency basis is either aspiring to sainthood, unsure, or not giving the client enough attention to get the deal done.

And because some owners can be fickle or coy, seasoned consultants will not make large time investments without a tangible client commitment in the form of monetary good-faith deposits. These consultants may have successfully raised many millions in financing for owners who changed their minds, resulting in no compensation for the time and considerable effort expended.

But before writing a check to engage a consultant, the owner should take the time to validate the consultant's capabilities in successfully obtaining financing. Does her track record match her confidence in accomplishing her mission? Checking references could save the owner from an elongated, expensive, and frustrating exercise in futility.

First, the business owner should require a list of references from the consultant. In contacting businesses that engaged this consultant's services, the owner can determine how well the consultant performed in the past. Here are some pertinent questions:

- Did the business obtain a financing commitment?
- If not, why not? If so, was the time frame reasonable?
- Did the consultant communicate with the business on a regular and informed basis?
- Did the consultant have a firm grasp of the owner's objectives and were they met due to the consultant's efforts?
- Did the financing offer get funded?
- Was the funding (and due diligence) cost consistent with consultant's estimate?
- Would they recommend using the consultant?

The business owner can then ask the consultant for references in the financing community. Obviously, the consultant will not permit the owner to contact any potential funder that may be the target of the subject proposal but should be open to permitting the owner to speak with other funders outside the scope of the proposed deal. Here are some pertinent questions:

- How well does the funder know the consultant or his work?
- How many transactions has the funder closed from the consultant?
- Does the funder rely on the consultant just for referrals or also on the consultant's ability to screen potential deals? (Bottom line: is the consultant only throwing a deal at the wall to see if it will stick?)

Finally, the business owner should ask whether the consultant is a member of any trade associations. Membership in such organizations as a chamber of commerce, the National Federation of Independent Businesses, or other associations may be indicative that the consultant is subject to some professional standards.

These memberships are not a qualification to finance a business but could point to the consultant's level of professionalism. These groups rarely provide references, but confirmation of any claimed membership status would be appropriate.

The business owner should remember that the consultant is not the financing decision maker. Rather the consultant provides advice about the process and recommends a funder. After selecting the funder and presenting the deal, the consultant hands over control of the deal to the funder.

Consultants are businesspeople, too. It's not unreasonable for them to request the business owner to engage their services with a written agreement and to require a retainer as an expression of commitment on the owner's part. Services and advice cannot be repossessed, and the consultant should not be penalized for changes in the business owner's situation or strategy that renders those services and advice worthless.

The business owner must take care to fully understand and agree to the compensation expectations of the consultant before work begins. The consultant's willingness to work on a contingency may sound like a good arrangement for the business owner, but it also may indicate that the owner is employing an inexperienced person. It is important to beware of people who can make a living collecting nonrefundable $250 application fees.

A good consultant will not ask for a retainer unless she is confident about successfully completing the business owner's deal. The prospects of obtaining funding cannot be reliably predicted without a thorough review of the business owner's financial statements and other pertinent data about the business.

A consultant can create value for a business by permitting the owner to concentrate on the company rather than wasting months on the wrong funding source. A willingness to pay for quality services is fine, but only when the owner takes the time to know who is capable of being engaged for this important assignment.

One other important precaution is that a business owner should make it clear that once the funder is identified and has an interest in the deal, the business owner will become the funder's principal contact for information and due diligence. If a consultant misrepresents an owner or the business, the owner can be held liable for the consultant's fraud.

Leave the Family at Home

Sometimes when negotiating a loan the lender tries to either stretch to make the deal work by enlarging the playing field or, more sinister, sees an opportunity to reduce risks by testing the idea of more personal guarantees on the loan than may be necessary. The personal guarantee of a wealthy, albeit uninvolved, family member is not easily ignored by many lenders. It's better for the business owner to just say no.

Mixing business and family is a difficult proposition when all parties are involved voluntarily. Business owners should not allow lenders to reduce them to begging a family member to borrow the money on their behalf; it is the wrong way to start a relationship. If the deal won't be approved with only the owner endorsing it, the owner should not borrow the money.

First, when a family member endorses, guarantees, or cosigns the loan, the problems are plentiful. First, it allows the lender to appoint a new director to the business. Potentially, the relative will start watching the business with much more interest, as if he suddenly had a financial stake in it (and in fact, he will). There is but one more critic to satisfy. It's not the lender's job to appoint management.

Second, even if the guarantee was offered rather than requested, there is still no way of ensuring the business gets the best deal. Some companies have failed due to meddling "investors" who do not have the business experience or ability to contribute. Landing in a deal just because a relative's net worth seems to be a good way to secure the loan is too risky.

Third, family dynamics enter the operations and organization chart of the business. Suppose the guarantor is the owner's father and the owner's training, experience, and industry instincts are leading to the implementation of a particular strategy that the father doesn't like it. His reasoning may be based on some Depression-era experience (bless his heart), or lessons he learned in an entirely different industry, position, and time.

The business owner manages his father's polite objections handily until the father assumes the role of the parent. Using names from childhood (like "son" or "sweetheart"), the debate shifts to the same tone of why the owner wasn't allowed to go to the junior sock-hop in the ninth grade. The owner has to face up to inappropriate, unfair, and emotional pressure.

It is best for a business owner to avoid these situations by not relying on family wealth and by making the business stand on its own. The business may take longer to start and grow, cost more, and be much smaller. However, the responsibility is on the business owner alone to succeed, fail, or land somewhere in the middle.

Other common family risks will be a lender's efforts to get a spouse to guarantee the loan, though the spouse has no ownership or involvement with the business. The lender has no justification to demand such a term, and, in fact, Regulation B prohibits banks from requiring a spouse with no business ownership to guarantee business loans.

An exception to that rule is only when the owner offers to secure the loan with collateral that is jointly owned. In such a case the spouse would have to sign on to perfect the collateral lien. However, even then the business owner should demand that the spouse's guarantee be limited to the ownership in that asset.

Involvement of a spouse carries the same penalties as mentioned above, except worse. The business owner lives with the spouse and usually sees him or her daily. A spouse is harder to avoid and may use the guarantee as a justification for asking questions about the business. It can ruin marriages.

And if the business owner contemplates divorce (or actually does divorce), suddenly the business loan guarantee makes the business lender a party to deliberations, further complicating them.

It's best for business owners to leave all family members who do not own part of the business out of any involvement with the business financing and find another way to secure the lender, all the while being firm about standing alone behind the deal.

Read *Before* Signing

Incredibly, many funding deals are made daily with business owners who hardly know anything about their deal except the payment amount or percentage of ownership sold. Lenders and investors routinely use boilerplate documents to define the funding terms and conditions that they assert are nonnegotiable. Business owners frequently sign them without so much as flipping through the pages.

Business owners should know about the funding terms they are negotiating. Loan and investment agreements are full of fine print that potentially provides for negative consequences that can apply even if the business meets repayment or profitability objectives. Naturally these terms protect the funder's interest.

Knowing about these terms does not mean that any of them will be changed, negotiated, or even of concern to the owner. But alternatively they may impact the owner's decision to enter the transaction or not based on whether any of the following pertain:

- The terms of the agreement and the ancillary documents represent the business owner's understanding of the transaction negotiated with the funder.
- The document terms were agreed to and are clear as to their effect on the funding relationship.
- The penalty for noncompliance with agreement terms or benchmark conditions seems inequitable or too high.
- The owner reconsiders the transaction based on the combination of conditions and costs imposed by the funder.

Worst case, understanding these terms will bring the full gravity of the funder's expectations into full view so that the owner can assess her full transaction risk.

Common Terms in Debt Financing Agreements

This section discusses some of the due diligence, documentation, and terms used to effect a commercial loan transaction.

Loan Agreement

The lender will usually define all pertinent terms of the loan transaction in a document called the loan agreement. All lender terms governing the deal should be included there, although other documents may be used to perfect specific portions of the transaction, like the promissory note, security agreement, and collateral liens.

A typical loan agreement can be dissected into several sections that convey specific definition of the transaction and its terms. While there is no universal agreement, most such documents include informally labeled sections such as declarations, precedents, terms, default, and general conditions. Some of the terms under these headings and others are described below.

Declarations

The opening section of a loan agreement may be used to announce the agreement participants along with the purpose of the agreement:

- The obligor's identity (business and/or its owner), legal organization, and state under which organized and principal address
- The lender's identity, legal organization, and state under which organized and principal address
- The purpose of the financing provided within the agreement
- Confirmation of both parties' intention to enter into a financing agreement

Precedents

The second section may be used by the parties to stipulate several facts or conditions that confirm the basic qualifications required of the borrower by the lender to enter the transaction:

- The borrower confirms that the business is organized as previously represented and is in good standing in the state under which it's organized.
- The borrower confirms that its financial condition has not changed, nor has it had any adverse changes that would likely cause the lender to cancel the loan.
- The borrower confirms the accuracy of all previous representations made to the lender and agrees to comply with the terms and conditions set forth in the loan agreement that will survive the loan closing.

Terms

Another section of the agreement defines the specific terms that are required by the lender and govern the relationship with the borrower.

Repayment Terms. The lender will detail the exact repayment terms under which the loan is provided and the lender's expectations for repayment:

- **Interest rate.** The interest rate charged for the loan is cited, usually along with a definition of how it's calculated. If the loan has a variable rate, the terms should explain the frequency of when it may change and how the change is calculated, including mention of any index that the rate may be tied to, such as prime rate or London Inter-Bank Overnight Rate (LIBOR).
- **Maturity.** The maturity of the loan is defined as the final date on which the loan is scheduled to be repaid either from sum of the periodic installments or with one final payment.

    Some factors can change the sum of the final scheduled payment. Most repayments are accounted for by first applying payments to the earned, or accrued, interest sums and the remainder to principal. If installments are made ahead of or after the scheduled date, it will change the interest calculation contemplated in the amortization table. Thus the final payment maybe higher or lower than expected.

This math may significantly increase the final loan payment if the business has frequently been late making payments.

- **Payment.** A scheduled loan payment amount will be defined in the agreement. If the payment is subject to change due to a variable interest rate, it should describe how the loan principal will amortize with the payments. Borrowers should determine whether there are level, or fixed, payments over the repayment term or whether only the principal portion of the payment is fixed and higher interest rates could mean higher payments.

Debt repayment may be scheduled, or amortized, over a longer period than the loan term, meaning the agreement will provide for lower payments that will not entirely repay the principal before the end of the agreement. Such repayment schedules require a large balloon payment at maturity.

- **Repayment period.** The loan term will be spelled out, citing either the number and frequency of installment payments or the maturity date.

Use of Proceeds Terms. The loan agreement usually specifies the exact allocation of loan proceeds approved by the lender, sometimes employing one or more of the following requirements to confirm these distributions:

- **Bank to bank.** If the loan is refinancing another loan, the lender will usually independently get a payoff sum from the other lender and pay that lender directly from the loan proceeds.
- **Budget.** If the loan is provided to finance working capital, the lender may require a preapproved budget to describe exactly how the proceeds will be employed.
- **Direct or indirect payments.** Lenders sometimes distribute loan funds directly to the approved payee or indirectly with the use of joint-payee checks issued to the borrower and the payee.
- **Payment verification.** Lenders sometimes require borrowers to provide documentation to substantiate loan disbursements or reimbursements, such as invoices, contracts, or receipts.

Collateral Terms. The loan agreement specifies the assets that are required to secure the loan and will describe conditions under which their lien be perfected. It will also spell out other obligations the borrower is expected to meet as to the protection of the collateral. Perfecting the lender's lien on assets may require use of several other documents, depending on the nature of the asset.

- **Appraisal.** Lenders will require that a property appraisal be performed to ascertain the current market valuation of the property to assure that its value is sufficient to provide the approved level of security. The nature of appraisal and qualifications of the appraiser may vary depending on the size of the loan.
- **Attorney's certificate of title.** Lenders agreeing to use real property as collateral will require that a review, or title search, be conducted of the local public records to determine whether there are any unexpected claims, or liens, on the property title. The findings of this search are documented in a certificate of title issued by an attorney conducting or reviewing the search.
- **Bulk-sales notice.** If the lender is financing the purchase of another business or certain business assets that are not titled or identified with any unique registration, the buyer and seller may have to provide the lender with compliance evidence for applicable bulk-sales notice. Such laws govern the transfer of certain assets to assure creditors that encumbered goods are not being sold and to assure buyers that there are no liens on the assets. Notices are generally made with a public notice of the pending sale.
- **Casualty insurance.** The lender will require the owner to maintain casualty insurance on any personal property used to secure a loan. This insurance is intended to replace assets or repay the loan in the event of a loss. These policies must cite the lender as loss payee and mortgagor.

  If required insurance coverage lapses, loan agreements usually provide for lender's right to force place coverage, where the lender buys coverage and the borrower is liable to pay for it. Forced coverage is very expensive, since the insurer is assuming the loss risk measured by the loan balance without underwriting the asset, usually sight unseen.
- **Dragnet clause.** A lender may include a dragnet clause when defining collateral, which will ostensibly place the lender's lien on whatever assets the borrower owns (subject to other financing liens), whether they perfect such a lien or not. This clause gives the lender standing to seek the liquidation or proceeds from liquidation of many more assets than the lender actually financed.
- **Due-on-sale clause.** Most mortgages contain a due-on-sale clause that specifies that if the property title is transferred to another party without the lender's consent, the loan maturity is automatically accelerated and immediately payable.

This provision effectively prohibits the owner from selling the property by permitting the buyer to assume the subject loan or by creating a subordinated wrap-around mortgage held by the owner.

- **Environmental assessment.** If the loan will be secured with real property that is known to have been used for commercial, industrial, or agricultural purposes, the lender will require an environmental assessment to determine the risk of contamination.

  Such assessments range from a detailed questionnaire to a title chain examination and visual inspection to evaluation of soil, water, or material samples. The presence of any environmental contamination is usually resolved by determining if regulations require further administrative action or remediation.

- **Estoppel.** Lenders with a subordinate lien on real property provide an estoppel notice to the senior lien holder, which is a declaration of loan amount where the senior lien holder's priority stops and the subordinate lender becomes the priority. It prevents the senior lender from advancing future sums and claiming to have a senior lien on them.

- **Flood insurance.** Lenders will determine whether real property used as collateral is in a 100-year flood plain and if so require flood insurance to the maximum extent available.

- **Lease assignment.** Should personal property collateral be kept in leased premises, lenders will require an assignment of the lease along with a lien waiver from the landlord. These waivers vary from simply permitting the lender to retrieve the collateral from the premises on demand to assuming the lease until they can liquidate the assets on site.

- **Lien search.** Similar to a real property title search, it's common for lenders to conduct a lien search to determine if any other liens exist on the personal assets specified to secure the loan.

- **Mortgage.** A mortgage essentially conveys a property title or the rights to convey title to a lender to secure the borrower's promise to repay a loan. Also known as mortgage deed, deed to secure debt, security deed, deed of trust, as specified by the state where property is situated.

  Failure to repay the obligation as agreed gives the lender rights under a power of sale, meaning the lender can sell the property through foreclosure to satisfy the debt. Different states have varying processes required to initiate foreclosure, ranging from 28 days to sometimes more than 12 months.

  The mortgage is a public document recorded in the local county courthouse to serve as a public notice to other creditors of the lender's priority of the property lien.

- **Negative pledge covenant.** The lender may require the borrower to agree to a negative pledge covenant, with which the borrower agrees to not do something. These often relate to an agreement not to encumber or convey a specific real or personal property asset. Such a covenant may be recorded in public records on real property and limit the owner's ability to add more financing or sell the property.
- **Personal property.** Assets that are not affixed to real property are referred to as personal property and can be identified in a variety of ways. Some equipment assets have unique serial numbers from their manufacturers, while over-the-road vehicles require a title registration with the state. Other assets (inventory, parts, etc.) cannot be distinguished from other assets of the same make.
- **Property insurance.** The lender will require the owner to maintain casualty insurance on any real property improvements or other attachments or fixtures used to secure a loan. This insurance is intended to replace improvements or repay the loan in the event of a loss. These policies must cite the lender as loss payee and mortgagor.

  On real estate policies, all lenders require that they contain the New York Standard Mortgage Clause, which requires that the mortgagor be given 30 days' notice prior to cancellation.

  If required insurance coverage lapses, loan agreements usually provide for lender's right to force place coverage, where the lender buys coverage and the borrower is obligated to pay for it. Forced coverage is very expensive, since the insurer is assuming the loss risk measured by the loan balance without underwriting the asset, usually sight unseen.
- **Real estate.** Real property ownership, or title, is evidenced by a legal document called a deed, which is generally recorded in a public record at the local county courthouse. State law governs the ownership transfer of real property to ensure process transparency and integrity.
- **Survey.** A survey is a scale drawing of real property boundaries according to the deed's legal description. It reflects all land features, structures, or improvements (buildings, garages, driveways, etc.) and easements (right-of-way, utilities, fences, etc.) within the boundary.

  Lenders may require a survey to be reviewed by the title attorney to assure that any boundary questions are identified and corrected, if necessary. Surveys may reveal encroachments from adjacent landowners or denote local zoning or restrictions that limit buildings near the boundary.
- **Title insurance.** Due to the possibility of search errors, transfer fraud, or the owners dying intestate, transferring a property title can sometimes become conflicted and the title clouded.

Title insurance is an insurance policy that protects the owner and/or lender from any problems in the chain of title and is available to settle any claims that may be asserted against it.

- **UCC-1 Financing Statement.** If the lender's collateral is transportable, called personal property or personality, such as equipment, machinery, fixtures, nontitled vehicles, accounts, or inventory, the UCC-1 Financing Statement is the document used to create a lien and public record of it.

When possible, the asset's serial number is included on the statement to identify it, but for assets with no such identification, the lender will likely attach a detailed list of the encumbered assets to be recorded in the county where the assets are located.

Other Security Terms. There are other terms that may provide repayment security for the lender in addition to or other than collateral. Some of these terms include:

- **Assignment of life insurance.** When lending to smaller companies where the principal owner is integral to the business success, lenders may require an assignment of life insurance on the owner. This insurance will assure loan repayment in the event of the unexpected death of the owner and permit successors to take over without burden of debt.
- **Offset.** When the loan is provided by a commercial bank, the bank will always provide for consent to offset any claims it has for unpaid loan payments or expenses from the deposits accounts that the borrower may maintain at the bank.
- **Personal guarantee.** Lenders extending financing loans to small, closely held businesses almost universally require the owners to provide a personal guarantee for the obligation. Such an endorsement makes the owner personally liable for loan repayment, regardless of the legal business organization.

If there is more than one guarantor, the business owner must be aware of whether the lender is requiring a joint and several guarantee. Such a status gives the lender maximum flexibility to choose exactly who to hold responsible for the *entire* loan repayment. Lenders are prone to go after the deepest pocket among the guarantors and ignore the others.

Loan Default Terms. All loan agreements will have a section that provides specific details defining events or conditions under which the lender may declare the loan in default. Here are some of the terms related to that section that define the lender's rights under these conditions:

- **Acceleration.** Most loan agreements provide for accelerated maturity in the event of the default. That means that if the owner is declared in default, the entire sum of the loan can be declared due and payable immediately.
- **Attorney's fees.** Most loan agreements provide for the business owner to reimburse the lender for any *reasonable* attorney's fees incurred while trying to collect payments or convert collateral. Depending on state law, those legal fees can be as much as 15 percent of the loan balance by statute.
- **Default rate of interest.** Many loan agreements provide for a default rate of interest. If the lender declares the loan to be in default, the interest rate will increase to a higher rate specified in the note until cured. Higher rates mean either that the payment increase or the loan will not be paid off as originally scheduled.
- **Events of default.** Most loan agreements will define a list of events or conditions that the lender may use to invoke a declaration of default. These items may include late or unpaid loan payments, unpaid insurance, unpaid property taxes, declaration of bankruptcy, or any number of other legal or financial conditions that the lender may use to exercise the right to call the loan immediately due.
- **Insecure.** Lenders sometimes will include a broadly worded provision that allows them to declare the loan in default if it becomes insecure. The intent is to allow them to initiate loan termination actions when some unexpected event, condition, or situation occurs that causes concern about their ability to be repaid as agreed. The borrower should be wary of these terms and, if required, try to negotiate as narrowly as possible.
- **Late fees.** Most loan agreements provide for a late fee if payments are not made within 10 days of the due date. These fees can be as high as 5 percent of the payment, so if a loan payment is $25,000, it could be $1,250!

General Conditions and Covenants

The next section of the loan agreement may contain any of several standard business and banking conditions and covenants that define the contract. While they are fairly common content for a broad range of contracts, the owner's familiarity with them will be useful in thinking through many what-if scenarios.

- **Arbitration.** Some loan agreements might provide for conflict resolution to be restricted to either binding or nonbinding arbitration and specify the arbitrators. Arbitration is a legal mediation process where the parties assert their claims before a neutral professional mediator. Nonbinding is optional, but binding means that other legal recourses have been waived.

The positive attribute about arbitration is that it can be faster and much less expensive than litigation. The negative attributes of binding arbitration are that the company waives the right to a jury or bench trial. Since there is no mandatory discovery, gathering evidence may be much more difficult.

Arbitration may limit a borrower's rights to due process if the borrower wants to challenge certain lender actions or the lender's interpretation of the terms. This clause may sound innocuous, but borrowers must be very wary of agreeing to essentially waiving any rights under the Constitution.

- **Authority.** The lender will require that the borrower substantiate corporate authority to enter into the loan by providing proof of legal organizational registration and a borrowing resolution from the entity's board of directors, partners, or members, as appropriate.
- **Books, records, and reports.** The lender requires the business to maintain a financial record of activities and provide copies to the lender at least annually, along with tax returns and the personal financial statements of all guarantors. Further, the lender may assert the right to inspect financial records at any time.
- **Business licenses.** The business is required to obtain and maintain whatever local or state licensing is required to legally operate in its jurisdiction.
- **Capital asset limitations.** Lenders may prohibit or limit the acquisition of capital assets in excess of a specified amount each year without prior lender approval.
- **Distributions and compensation.** Lenders prohibit owners from making capital distributions, retiring stock or partnership interests, consolidating or merging with another company, or making preferential arrangements with affiliates during the loan term without the lender's consent.

Lenders may also seek to prohibit or restrict the ability of owners to make loans, pay bonuses, or provide excessive benefits to any owner, director, officer, or employee, other than reasonable compensation during the term of the loan.

- **Entire agreement.** Many agreements will declare that the agreements executed during the loan closing exercise set forth the entire agreement and understanding of the parties and is known as the merger clause. Further, these documents will declare that the subject documents supersede all prior agreements (oral or written) and that modification, waiver of rights, or amendment to the agreement cannot be effective unless in writing and signed by both parties.

The worrisome part of this provision is that it signifies all parties' agreement that no other evidence may be introduced in court except the documents executed to represent the agreement. Correspondence or other information that are germane to an agreement ahead of the actual loan agreement may be excluded from evidence.

- **Execution.** The obligor must agree to sign, or execute, all of the required documents set forth by the lender to perfect the financing terms. Many attorneys will even ask a borrower to sign a document agreeing to re-sign any document at a later date, should an error be discovered.

- **Governing law.** Most loan agreements will define the particular state under which the agreement shall be governed, which is generally the state in which the lender is headquartered or from which the loan originated, based on which has more favorable laws for lending.

  This provision is important to the borrower, since it decides which state laws will govern either litigation or arbitration.

- **Immigration status.** Lenders generally screen business owners to determine whether they are U.S. citizens, and if they are not, lenders require verification of immigration status. This information is necessary to ascertain that any noncitizen borrower can remain in the United States long enough to repay the loan.

- **Jurisdiction.** Most loan agreements will contain a venue selection clause that defines the country, state, or county in which any case arising from the agreement will be litigated or arbitrated. If applicable, it may significantly increase the cost to dispute the agreement, particularly if the lender is in a different state.

- **Management consultants.** A lender will frequently require a business to agree not to engage a management consultant without the lender's prior approval. This provision will require that the lender get notice of any issues the business may be facing.

  Notice: The agreement will include a notice clause to define how the respective parties can deliver a legal notice to the other party in the event that a dispute or default arises. It's important to determine that the contact information is correct, particularly if a new address is being acquired post-transaction, to assure that any communication from the lender is delivered in a timely fashion.

- **Reimbursable expenses.** Lenders require the business to reimburse them for any and all expenses incurred for the loan application, closing, and collection. Borrowers must watch for and insist on including the word *reasonable* when describing these costs.

  The lender will be getting the consent of the borrower to the right to recover any future cost incurred to collect the loan, including the cost of a collection agency, asset repossession, legal fees, or bankruptcy claim.

- **Severability.** The loan agreement will have a provision asserting that should any future court precedent or law render any part of the agreement ineffective, the agreement shall continue in force without in any way invalidating or affecting the remaining provisions of the agreement.
- **Taxes.** Lenders require that borrowers agree to pay all federal, state, and local tax obligations when due and often specify that delinquent taxes or tax liens against businesses or owners constitute default.

Common Terms in Investment Agreements

This section discusses some of the agreement terms commonly used to effect an investment transaction. These terms are required by investors generally to assure enforcement of their funding offer as the business uses the investment to move toward its exit event. They can be categorized as control, economic, liquidity, or management terms, but all work to define the investor's restrictions or empowerment through future events in the business.

More often than not, equity capital investors are placing their bets on people as much as on business. They may like a business idea, but unless there is capable, committed management in place, good ideas don't go far. In earlier rounds, it's harder to require managers to sign employment contracts, because that could expose investors to contributing more funding even if things don't go as planned.

Sometimes new managers or investors join the business after the earlier funding rounds, and it's the original investor's desire to ensure that there is no ambiguity around their intentions about how future events would be sorted.

Therefore investors protect themselves with investment terms that place rights and restrictions on management as the business moves forward. Here are some of the common terms:

- **Antidilution provisions.** Investors may imbed certain terms to preserve their percentage of ownership in the event that more shares are issued to avoid dilution of their share value. It will guarantee their right to buy new shares in future financing rounds, trigger additional shares being issued (rare), or, more commonly, lower the conversion price for their shares to offset dilution. There are three ways this may be implemented:

  1. **Typical.** Usually investors are protected only in the event of a stock split, stock dividend, or similar recapitalization event.

2. **Full ratchet.** These terms provide a complete preservation of ownership percentage in all circumstances, including in a subsequent sale or merger. In cases where later shares are sold at lower prices (down round), investors may be entitled to be issued new shares or get conversion price adjustment to make up the difference.

3. **Modified ratchet.** These terms may not be applicable if additional shares were sold at lower share prices or shares were issued for employee incentives. For lower dilution, the conversion price may be adjusted with a weighted average of all shares issued.

- **Conversion rights.** These provisions allow preferred shareholders to convert their shares to common shares, as is frequently done ahead of an initial public offering (IPO).
- **Convertible debt.** Sometimes this is used to represent investments ahead of equity being issued. These notes carry a nominal interest rate that is usually deferred. The debt places investors ahead of shareholders in case of liquidation and are typically converted to equity at subsequent financing round.
- **Convertible preferred stock.** This share class is a common security for venture investors. These shares usually retain dividend rights, voting rights, and preferences over other shareholders in liquidation. They can be converted to common shares, depending on which of two categories these shares are issued under:

  1. **Participating.** These shareholders will get the preferential treatment of getting their shares bought out first but then also enjoy the participation of the conversion features. For example, if a preferred shareholder's $1 million investment owned 25 percent of the outstanding stock upon conversion with rights to be repaid first, upon a $10 million exit event, the shareholder would get $1 million paid out first and then get 25 percent of the remaining $9 million.
  2. **Nonparticipating.** These shareholders would have to choose preference between getting their shares bought first or to convert their investment to common shares, but not both. In the example cited in preceding paragraph, it would be choosing between first $1 million or $2.5 million.

- **Dividends.** These are proceeds paid to shareholders as a financial return on their investment. Generally restricted to being paid only from profits, various stock classes may have preferences or higher dividend entitlements. Dividends must be declared by the board of directors and can be paid in cash or stock. Other potential features:

1. **Cumulative.** Dividends accrue even if they are not immediately paid.
2. **Noncumulative.** Missed dividends do not accrue.
3. **Participating.** After preferred share dividends are paid, a portion of the remaining profits can also be paid as dividends to common shareholders. If preferred shares have conversion rights, they will be paid preferred dividends and common dividends as well.
4. **Nonparticipating.** Dividends are paid to preferred shareholders but not paid to common shareholders. However, preferred shareholders cannot draw dividends from the common conversion rights either.

- **Liquidation preferences.** With these rights, investors are provided with a preference on the proceeds of the company liquidation ahead of other shareholders.
- **Preemptive rights.** With these rights, investors can buy future shares on the same terms as future financing rounds that are offered to third parties. These rights would guarantee that shareholders could acquire a number of new shares necessary to maintain a pro rata share of the business ownership.
- **Protective provisions.** The company agrees to do or not to do certain things without the investor's approval that could threaten share value or company, such as amend the articles of incorporation or merge with another company.
- **Redemption rights.** Share rights that force a company to buy out the investor, generally tied to certain events or conditions.
- **Representations and warranties.** The agreement may refer to certain representations (promises) made by management to induce the investment, which could be made part of the investment agreement with management warranty.
- **Rights of co-sale.** With these rights, investors can ensure that a portion of their shares are sold on a pro rata basis with management shares at the same price and same terms, if management is selling sufficient shares that will result in a change of control. This scenario could develop during a departure of some of the management team or in a subsequent financing stage.
- **Rights of first refusal.** Investors will demand to have the priority rights to buy any shares offered by management to third parties, particularly shares owned and offered by founders or management, should they decided to sell out and leave the enterprise.
- **Takeaway provisions.** These entitle investors to penalize management for not achieving planned results by raising share conversion price or other means to dilute share value.
- **Voting rights.** These are rights that entitle all specified share classes to vote for board members and other important events that may be germane to business, such as mergers, compensation, etc. Normally common shares can

vote and preferred shares cannot. There are other conditions that may be embedded in the share rights:

1. **Full.** Permits shares to have full voting rights, even if they have not been converted to common shares.
2. **Class.** Certain share classes may be entitled to combined or exclusive rights to vote on specific matters that could come before shareholders, such as a sale or merger.
3. **Right to elect director.** Provision that provides a guaranteed right to elect one or more directors from a particular share class.
4. **Special.** With no legal limits, special rights can provide for a particular class to have specified corporate powers. Often used to assure veto rights or super-share voting requirement over certain matters such as major capital expenditures, raising more capital, selling the company, or changing the business plan, where smaller share class may be able to trump a larger share class on certain matters.

There are other terms that may appear in either a loan or investment transaction, depending on the specific transaction negotiated between the parties and the nature of the subject business needing funding. Regardless, here is some good advice to follow in any kind of funding situation:

- Never close or execute the funding agreements or transaction without reading *every* document in advance, including a statement fully accounting for the transaction costs. If you don't have time, you risk placing your business in peril.
- If there are any terms you don't understand, ask your attorney and the funder for an explanation ahead of the execution date to ensure their answer matches your understanding of what the funder agreed to do and that you are still in full agreement.
- When you are obligating your business to repay a large sum of capital or selling a large portion of your enterprise, you would be very wise to hire your own attorney to review and react to the documentation as it relates to your business and your deal.
- Remember that the funder's closing attorney is not an arbitrary participant in the closing process. The funder's attorney represents only the funder. One attorney cannot represent two parties in the same transaction. Hire your own attorney.

- Merely being aware of these terms does not change them but hopefully enlightens you to the consequences of failing to meeting the funder's expectations. Funders may waive these provisions in certain situations, even if owners don't fully comply with their agreements, but it's not a good idea to assume that you will be so lucky.
- Be aware that funders have many rights that stack dispute resolution in their favor very quickly. Know these terms before you enter into a funding arrangement with any third party to protect yourself and your business.

Protect One's Own Interests First (No One Else Will)

Don't worry about it. Those famous last words in many business negotiations are uttered by numerous funders to get beyond owner hesitation of the terms of their financing offer. Savvy business owners who understand the funder's terms must make some hard choices. Maybe everybody does it, but that doesn't mean it's automatically right for everyone.

Business owners should always think about the worst-case scenario and reflect on how the terms funders use in their agreements will impact their businesses when something unexpected happens. Sometimes funders will work with owners to resolve issues in an orderly way, allowing for more reasonable resolutions to unexpected results. Sometimes they won't, although their paperwork provides them with sufficient discretion.

Business owners must consider all the written terms and recognize that funders will be empowered to make full use of the most stringent interpretation of them. Owners may seek to forge agreements that provide more open options, but it's rare that funders will negotiate very many terms in their core agreements.

A business owner cannot afford to unwittingly put the entire company at the total mercy of a single funder, if it's avoidable. An owner must protect the business. An owner must demand, argue, and hold out for changes in the terms that will compromise the continuation of the business at the whim of the funder.

Sometimes an owner will feel forced to sign off on terms that are ripe for abuse in a take-it-or-leave-it negotiation. The need for capital may entice an owner to accept terms that are risky. The owner must be diligent about observing the offer's terms, and he must not permit the funder to abuse his rights or investment with shoddy, haphazard enforcement of terms.

Getting Third-Party Funding Is Serious Business

Many funders have had the unfortunate experience of negotiating loans with owners who used false, exaggerated, or misleading information to obtain credit. Whether or not the ploys succeeded, the effects are often felt by legitimate owners whose requests are scrutinized with even more suspicion due to the funders' negative experiences. Owners must be prepared to confirm everything.

Unless actual loan losses have been incurred, many bankers may be hesitant to prosecute loan applicants found to have used false information to obtain a loan. But when they do, they may get assistance from the federal government that insures depositors and regulates banks. Cases involving false or misleading applications for bank credit are prosecuted by a U.S. Attorney's Office, which has unlimited resources to pursue such matters.

For those individuals who are flippant about the integrity of their business dealings or who willingly try to obtain loans with fraudulent information, these actions can carry heavy penalties. It's a federal crime to submit false information in order to induce a federally regulated bank to provide business financing. If convicted, punishment can be up to 20 years of imprisonment and a fine of up to $1 million.

Many lenders now require business owners to certify in writing the accuracy and completeness of the application information they submit. These covenants acknowledge that the information is provided by the business owner in order to obtain loan approval.

Many lenders have also begun verifying each business owner's personal and business income tax returns with the Internal Revenue Service. There have been numerous frauds discovered where fictitious tax returns were submitted to lenders resulting in significant loan losses. Now most lenders confirm that the income tax returns submitted with loan applications match those filed with the IRS.

Your Funding Decision Is About You

The recognition of various business needs—capital requirements, the acquisition of funding, and the risks inherent in operating a business—is only half the effort. At this point, the business owner may be intellectually prepared to seek funding, but now must work on the actual proposal, which should include the demonstration and documentation of the answers to these questions: Who am I? What is my business about? Why do I need funding? Why should the lender fund my enterprise?

The decision day may be anticlimactic, since a large number of decisions are going to be made in the process: many by the owner, many by the funder, and many by both. The business owner must remain focused throughout the process on every decision that leads to the money for the enterprise.

An important point to remember throughout this process is the limitations of the business. While ambition and confidence may be limitless, the enterprise is not. It's all about money, but money is still only money. Business owners must take measurement of what they are getting into and the toll it will take on their businesses and on themselves.

The process of finding business capital ultimately becomes a sales challenge. Owners establish needs, find prospects, qualify, and try to close. It's one of dozens of challenges any small business faces every day, but it's not the only one. Solving money problems does not necessarily ensure success.

Money is the currency in which business owners operate, but there is a greater challenge in establishing a way to make it flow regularly through their businesses. Money doesn't end the list of challenges.

Owners need to establish some limits as to what their businesses will agree to, not agree to, and what cost (in dollars and conditions) they are willing to pay for the financing they seek. If funders ask for too much, owners should walk away from the deal, reminding themselves why they established the limits they did. They should then look for funding in other places.

4

PAYING THE FREIGHT—UNDERSTANDING FINANCING COSTS

Businesses seeking to acquire funding from third parties need to be cognizant of the cost of those funds. Understanding how funders determine and assess their costs—whether by charging interest or acquiring equity (an ownership in a business)—equips owners to better evaluate the desirability and feasibility of getting this kind of money.

Business owners should learn how interest rates and equity terms are determined in order to develop better negotiating strategies that might lower final costs. It also helps them to know when they've negotiated the best deal for themselves.

Borrowing Costs

From home mortgages to student loans to credit cards, consumers and business owners who borrow money from a bank for any reason should be aware of interest, which is the cost of using the bank's (or other lender's) money. How is interest determined? Can it be lowered? Who calculates it? Knowing the answers to these questions will help business owners manage and possibly lower their use of borrowed funding.

Interest

Interest is the rent charged to the borrower for the use of the lender's money. It's typically quoted as a percentage of the loan amount on an annualized basis. The basic formula for calculating interest is:

$$I = PRT$$
$$(\textbf{Interest} = \textbf{Principal} \times \textbf{Rate} \times \textbf{Term})$$

In practice, funders employ a variety of techniques to increase their return on financing charges, or yield, through calculation methods, payment schedules, and other associated fees. For example, most banks use a 360-day calendar to calculate interest charges on a commercial loan.

This practice employs the notion that each month, or payment period, is equivalent to 30 days: 12 payment periods a year times 30-day payment periods equals 360 days, which is substituted for 365 in calculating the daily interest charge, as is demonstrated in Figure 4.1.

To be clear, the 360-day calendar is a calculation method. When calculating the number of days' interest that will be charged, the lender will count the actual number of calendar days the funds are owed. So for a one-year loan the borrower may pay interest calculated with the 360-day rate for a cost charged for the actual 365 days. This method can be confusing.

Not surprisingly, this shorter repayment calculation results in a higher interest yield for the lender that increases the transaction costs to the business, particularly on larger, longer term loans. How much? In Figure 4.1 the daily interest charge difference between these two methods is $1.90 per day. If this loan were being amortized over a long term, that number would shrink over time as does the amount of interest as a percentage of the payment amount. But a good estimate of the difference over the first 5 years on a 25-year amortizing loan may be as much as $3,000.

FIGURE 4.1 365- vs. 360-Day Interest Yield Calculation

	365-Day Calendar	360-Day Calendar
Loan Amount	$1,000,000	$1,000,000
Interest Rate	5%	5%
Daily Interest Charge (Note 1)	$136.99	$138.89
Annual Interest Charge (Note 2)	$49,999.89	$50,694.49
Effective Yield (Note 3)	*5%*	*5.07%*

Note 1   Calculation for daily interest charge for 365 days = (($1,000,000 x .05)/365) = $136.99
                Calculation for daily interest charge for 360 days = (($1,000,000 x .05)/360) = $138.89

Note 2   Calculation for annual interest charge for 365 days = ($136.986 x 365) = $49,999.89
                Calculation for annual interest charge for 360 days = ($138.889 x 365) = $50,694.49

Note 3   Calculation for 365 day effective yield = ($49,999.89 / $1,000,000) = 5.0%
                Calculation for 360 day effective yield = ($50,694.49 / $1,000,000) = 5.07%

In the figure, the lender using a 360-day calculation method earned $694.44 more on the loan in year 1, although both loans are extended at an interest rate of 5 percent.

Lenders typically base interest rates on a number of factors, including the internal cost of funds, the loan repayment term, and a premium for the risk associated with the loan, each of which is germane to the lender's financial return.

Cost of Funds

Commercial banks traditionally obtain most of their funding from depositors, although they may augment these funds with proceeds from other sources. They are permitted to leverage their own capital by at least 94 percent, although that level will be lowered in coming years through new global capital standards referred to as Basel III. What the 94 percent means is that for every $6 of bank equity, the bank can borrow up to $94 to fund operations.

The bank's average cost of funds is a calculation that totals all of the interest costs paid to various depositors (checking, savings, and CDs) and lenders (commercial paper, etc.). The bank must carefully manage the spread between the cost of capital and the income derived from it, which is called the net interest margin.

The Federal Reserve Bank influences interest rates with monetary policy intended to control the nation's money supply as a means to manage inflation and encourage full employment. The Fed's Open Market Committee meets eight times annually to set a target Fed funds rate, the interest banks charge each other for overnight loans to meet minimum reserve requirements.

Using the Fed funds rate as a guiding index shared by all other banks, the banks will set both the rates paid to depositors and those charged to borrowers. In that way, they are able to manage their interest spreads and hopefully ensure profitable lending operations.

Risk Premium

Interest rates should reflect a premium sum determined to compensate the lender for the specific risks on the transaction. No two loans are the same, and several factors influence the loss risk to the lender, such as whether the loan is secured or not, the borrower's industry, the quality of the borrower's management, and the operating history of the business.

Since every bank will have its own view of the inherent risk of a transaction, it's difficult to compare multiple bank pricing offers, except that, generally, the lower the interest rate, the lower the risk the bank has graded the business. Evaluation of business risk is an ongoing function, which means that a lender's risk appetite can change from one month to the next for a variety of reasons: economic or industry conditions, portfolio concentration, and even banking funding concerns.

Loan Term

The repayment terms of a loan affect the borrower's risk and bank's cost of funding. The longer the repayment period, the greater exposure the lender assumes, so a 10-year loan is riskier than a 90-day note and, accordingly, will cost more.

Also influencing this calculation is the higher cost of funds for the lender, which must pay depositors higher returns to commitment to keep sums on hand for longer terms as well. Banks have to manage their assets (loans) and liabilities (deposits) carefully to ensure that they maintain a balance of the varying terms of each and therefore provide sufficient liquidity in their operations.

Variable vs. Fixed Interest Rates

Interest rates on commercial loans are either fixed—set at one level for the entire term of the loan—or variable—subject to change under certain conditions.

With regard to interest rates, a bank's overarching goal is that any rate risk shall be borne by the borrower, not the lender. Variable rates will be tied to some index that will provide an avenue for the bank to change the rates paid on the deposits that are funding loans. Fixed rates will be set at a premium over variable rates so that the bank collects a higher spread to balance out its rate exposure on the last half of the loan term.

Fixed rate loans are those set at the onset of the loan and maintained at the same level until maturity. Lenders manage loan rate spreads by pricing them over a specific source of fixed-rate liabilities with similar terms.

Fixed rates are generally priced 1 to 2 percent over the cost of a similarly priced variable rate transaction. The differential provides a hedge to lenders so that even if rates rise, they have collected a premium spread during the early part of the loan repayment period to cover that exposure.

Generally banks will fix rates only for intermediate terms, such as three to seven years, unless they are tying rates to a specific source of capital with a longer term or they have hedged the rate through a derivative transaction. Sometimes banks will specify repayment terms in a series of interim rate adjustment periods, technical maturities where the loan rate is adjusted according to a specific spread over an identified rate index.

The obvious advantage of a fixed rate to borrowers is the predictable funding cost for the life of the loan. There is no exposure to rising rate surprises that can reduce profits. The downside is that borrowers miss declining rates, which would save money or permit the loan to be repaid faster.

Here are some factors to consider when evaluating fixed rates:

- **What is the premium paid over a variable rate offer for the same loan?** Borrowers will not be offered the same rates on a variable or fixed basis. Generally fixed rates will be offered at a premium to eliminate the exposure to rising rates over the loan term. Borrowers should calculate the premium and consider whether this premium is worth that protection.
- **What is the penalty to repay this loan ahead of maturity?** Since lenders match fixed-rate loan with fixed-rate liabilities, there will often be a pre-payment penalty specified. Borrowers should get familiar with the penalty calculation before agreeing to the rate. Business conditions can change in a very short period and accordingly the loan rate may not be as attractive. Borrowers should know the cost of renegotiating or refinancing.
- **What is the business exit strategy?** The business plan over the next few years is germane to the interest-rate selection. Will the business raise more equity for expansion, be sold to new owners, or just focus on thriving in its current mode? This factor should be taken into account in deciding on an interest-rate choice.
- **What do leading economists project for the economy and how will that impact interest rates over the next 12 months and beyond?** No one will know the answer to these questions with much degree of certainty, but it's worth following the financial news in the months ahead of obtaining a loan to get an idea of what market expectations may influence interest-rate choice.

Variable interest rates are determined by specifying a margin over (or under) a particular rate index that will influence the lender's cost of funding. With this floating arrangement, the loan rate is directly tied to the lender's cost. While variable rates don't assure the borrower of future borrowing cost, the borrower gets a lower rate by tying the cost of the loan to the lender's cost of funds.

The obvious advantage of a variable rate to borrowers is that if rates decline, the borrowing cost also declines, lowering the business cost of capital. But the downside is the cost of capital can unexpectedly rise when rates increase, eating away at profits.

The three most prominent rate indexes are the *Wall Street Journal* prime rate, the Treasury rate, and the LIBOR. Each is defined in more detail a bit later.

Here are some factors to consider when evaluating fixed vs. variable rates:

- **Which index rate is to be used?** If a borrower understands the various index rates and forms an opinion about a preference, it's worth negotiating with the lender. These indexes can at times be volatile due to ever-changing events and economic expectations.
- **What is the lender's spread over the base rate and is it competitive?** If a borrower elects to use a variable rate, it's worth inquiring to other banks about competitive rate spreads, since it may clarify the lender's risk premium and how it evaluates the business.
- **How quickly will the rate adjust when its index changes?** The borrower needs to know how quickly the lender proposes that rates adjust and negotiate that point. A monthly adjustment would be advantageous in a falling environment, whereas a quarterly adjustment would provide the business more time to prepare for a change in a rising environment.

Which Is the Best Rate?

Which rate is better for the borrower? While fixed rates offer budgeting certainty and maybe some emotional comfort, they are likely to come at a higher cost. Variable rates are riskier but usually offer the borrower the lowest rate at the time of funding. In a stable rate environment the lower rate will save the borrower money while the loan balance is highest.

The borrower must consider that interest rates generally are increased when the economy is robust and the Fed is trying to cool it down to guard against inflation. It's likely that the business will also be doing well in such an environment and could afford the higher costs. As the economy slows, rates will be lowered to stimulate growth. A variable loan rate falls with it, and the borrower enjoys some relief in a period when business may be off.

Fixed rates are always more expensive on day one when the loan balance is the highest ahead of amortizing. The premium paid for the comfort of knowing that the rate will not change is huge. The borrower can't foresee the business or economic changes ahead that may impact the loan: business expansion, business sale, or owner death could all mean that the financing term might be ended early, which would trigger an even larger premium to prepay the loan.

Variable-rate financing offers a lower rate when the loan is at its highest value. On the last half of the loan amortization, even if the variable rate had risen to over the offered fixed rate, it's likely that the cash out of pocket over the life of the loan could still be lower that the fixed-rate cost over that period.

Most important, the repayment of the entire loan at any time without a penalty means that the borrower won't have to pay extra penalties for unforeseen changes in the business. If the borrower later decides that the existing loan deal is not the best available, he can refinance it with another lender at any time.

What Is the Real Prime Rate?

Everybody wants (and many expect) to get the lender's best lending rate, or its prime rate. What is really the best rate? Lenders typically use one of several interest rates as an index on which to base variable-rate lending. Each index is a reliable benchmark directly tied to current money markets that move appropriately with changes in economic conditions. Lenders generally use an index directly related to the cost of funds used for specific loan products.

The most widely used indexes to define lending rate are the prime rate, U.S. Treasury rates, and LIBOR.

Prime Rate

The most commonly used index for U.S. commercial banks is the prime rate. Traditionally defined as the interest rate offered to a bank's best corporate clients on loans maturing in less than one year, the rate has evolved to represent more of a general index for commercial and consumer lending.

Most lenders track the prime rate published daily in the *Wall Street Journal*, which reflects the base rate posted by at least 70 percent of the top 10 U.S. banks ranked by total assets. These 10 banks generally set their prime rate at approximately 300 basis points (or 3 percentage points) above the Fed funds rate.

In today's competitive market, the best corporate customer's borrowings are priced below the prime rate. Banks must compete with many other sources of corporate financing than existed when the prime rate originated.

Treasury Rate

The interest rates paid on U.S. government Treasury bonds are used to index interest rates on many loans, particularly commercial real estate transactions.

The U.S. government sells bonds to finance operations when tax collections do not cover the federal budget. There is a robust secondary market to buy and sell outstanding bonds, whose valuation inversely reflects current economic conditions. Their historically high credit rating means that these bonds are the ultimate safe haven for investors to park their funds, which earns the federal government relatively low interest rates.

Many lenders use the Treasury rates as a baseline, since the weekly bond auction is a litmus test of economic conditions and quantifies the opportunity costs of where lenders could invest funds at the lowest risk.

LIBOR

LIBOR is an acronym for London Inter-Bank Overnight Rate. The LIBOR is the British version of the U.S. Fed funds rate, the interest charged by banks to each other for overnight or longer term loans used to meet liquidity requirements.

The LIBOR is arguably the purest market rate of interest, since it's free-floating and determined without government intervention. While the prime rate and Treasury rates are directly impacted by U.S. monetary and fiscal policy, LIBOR is established by market demand and risk.

Interest Rate Spreads—It's Where the Business Will Pay

Lenders quote interest rate offers by naming the rate index along with the premium (or discount) cited as a percentage or in basis points (bps). This differential over (or under) the index is called the spread. The sum of the index plus the spread equals the cost of borrowing.

For example, the lender may quote "prime plus two," meaning it will use the prime rate as the index and add a 2 percent spread over it to determine the cost of lending. If prime were at 5 percent, the loan rate would be 7 percent (5 percent + 2 percent = 7 percent).

Some spreads are quoted as basis points, or bps, such as "LIBOR plus 350 bps." A basis point is 1/100 of 1 percent, so 100 basis points are equivalent to 1 percent. Basis points are typically used with Treasury or LIBOR rates, since both of these indexes are frequently settled in odd fractions. The prime rate is traditionally rounded to a quarter, half, or whole percentage.

Some basic ideas to consider when approaching price negotiations are as follows:

- Every fraction matters, so it's important to negotiate quarter points or bps. Over time it will be real money saved if the bank's offered rate can be lowered.
- Larger banks generally are able to get cheaper funding than smaller banks, since they have more options, resources, and reach. At the same time they

have a narrower appetite for lending to small businesses. If a business presents a lower risk, it's likely it can negotiate a better rate with a larger bank.

- Smaller banks, particularly newer banks, are more aggressive lenders because they generally have fewer investment options. That being said, they also have higher funding costs, so with the associated higher risks their rates will be higher than those of more mature, larger banks.

- Before negotiating a loan a business owner should know what the business can afford. The owner must do some realistic profit/loss and cash-flow planning to have a firm idea of what rate is unaffordable.

Pay Attention to Other Fees and Closing Costs

Business owners will face a barrage of various costs to obtain debt financing. They must be prepared to pay costs ranging from 3 to 6 percent of the transaction to close the loan. Some fees are simply not negotiable, while others may offer some wiggle room.

Loan Fees

On most commercial loans, borrowers are charged a loan fee by the lender to recapture the costs associated with the loan application, underwriting, and processing. These fees generally are ½ to 1 percent of the loan amount and are essentially subtracted from the loan amount. Naturally these fees add plenty to the lender's transaction yield.

The borrower may pay the fee out of pocket, but in reality the borrower and lender are just exchanging checks. If the lender is making a $1,000,000 loan and charging a $10,000 fee, the borrower is getting a loan for $990,000 with the obligation of paying back $1,000,000 plus interest.

Using the same scenario described in Figure 4.1 (and leaving the 365/360 comparison), Figure 4.2 demonstrates how bankers can drive their financial yields upward with loan fees. The figure shows a single pay loan for $1,000,000 for 12 months (365 days) at an interest rate of 5 percent plus a 1 percent fee.

Closing Costs

A frequent complaint from small business borrowers is about the cost of loan closings. Lenders seem indifferent, and the professionals involved seem callous. But the reality is that most of these costs are inherent to the deal and can't be avoided.

FIGURE 4.2 Loan Fee and Interest Yield Calculation

	365-Day Calendar	360-Day Calendar
Loan Amount	$1,000,000	$1,000,000
Loan Fee	$10,000	$10,000
Net Loan Proceeds	$990,000	$990,000
Interest Rate	5%	5%
Annual Interest Charge	$49,999.89	$50,694.49
Total Loan Fee and Interest	$59,999.89	$60,694.49
Effective Yield (Note 1)	*6.06%*	*6.13%*

Note 1   Calculation for 365 day effective yield = ($59,999.89 / $990,000) = 6.06%
            Calculation for 360 day effective yield = ($60,694.49 / $990,000) = 6.13%

Accepting these expenses as a cost of doing business may be easier by putting them in perspective and recognizing their value. Whether any costs can be reduced or eliminated depends on the transaction and sometimes on the borrower's efforts. Some of the most common loan closing costs are listed below followed by ideas for how to lower them:

- **Attorney fees.** Commercial loans are usually closed by an attorney representing the lender, particularly where collateral is involved and always when that collateral is real property. To assure that the collateral liens are perfected correctly and to get a second set of eyes on the closing documents, lenders rely on professional assistance.

   The cost of the lender's legal counsel is passed directly on to the borrower along with other due diligence costs of the transaction.

   These fees may vary widely depending on the market, size of the firm, and the exact nature and extent of the attorney's involvement, ranging from flat hourly rates up to a fixed percentage of the transaction. Plus the borrower will have to pay for all out-of-pocket expenses, including title insurance, administrative costs, etc., if applicable.

   Note: An owner should never discard an old title insurance policy and always buy an owner's policy to cover the gap between the lender's coverage and the property costs.

   It's important to recognize that much of the attorney's work directly benefits the borrower too, particularly when providing assurance of a clear public record and absence of claims against assets.

- **Appraisals.** Lenders require that collateral assets be appraised to confirm their fair market value before closing the loan. An appraisal is an evaluation prepared by a certified professional seeking to identify an asset's value based on current conditions using various methodologies such as market value, cost approach, and income approach.

Most commonly associated with real estate, appraisals are also performed for equipment, vehicles, and operating businesses. Appraisal costs vary widely depending on the type of report, relative value of the subject assets, and certification of the appraiser.

Note: An owner should never discard an old appraisal and should always insure property improvements for a minimum of the values cited in the latest appraisal.

- **Environmental assessment.** Real property used as collateral must be screened for potential past or present environmental contamination. Lenders that don't make reasonable efforts to ascertain a property's condition could become liable for its cleanup cost. Additionally, they must assess the financial impact that any identified problems pose to the transaction.

 The existence of contamination does not necessary render a site unsafe or unsuitable but the information must be determined and evaluated by the buyer, user, and lender to make informed decisions.

 Note: An owner should never discard an old environmental assessment. It may be needed someday to protect the business's interests if the property formerly owned later becomes contaminated.

- **Survey.** A survey is a scaled diagram of the boundary lines of a real estate tract that includes a visual representation of any improvements, easements, encroachments, or natural elements within its borders. The survey will be drawn to represent the legal description of the property as recorded with the local county and described in the owner's deed.

 Additionally the survey will cite local property or zoning codes that may impose setback lines or any other restrictions on how improvements can be situated on the site.

 Lenders require surveys on larger loans but they are also needed to obtain a title insurance policy *without exceptions.* Without a survey, a title report will cite it as an exception for "matters that may be revealed by a survey."

 Surveys are generally not expensive and should always be obtained by the buyer prior to purchasing property. The cost of a survey is generally determined by the size of the property, improvements, and number of conditions on it.

 Note: An owner should never discard an old survey. It may provide guidance to future surveyors who need past reference points when surveying properties with changing physical characteristics.

Managing or lowering due diligence expenses can be done if the business owner employs the following tactics:

1. Ask for a written fee estimate (which may have to be done through the lender). Feel free to negotiate with service providers to lower fees or at least cap them.
2. When similar (legal, appraisal, or environmental) work has been performed in the recent past, provide the information to the service providers, which may reduce their work and accordingly their fees.
3. Be responsive to whatever information is requested during the process. Repetitive requests by the service providers costs them more time and the borrower more fees. Volunteering information beyond their questions may enhance their understanding of the situation, which should prove beneficial.

- **Recording costs and taxes.** Many counties and states assess fees and document recording taxes upon the transfer of a real property title or placement of mortgage liens on them. These recorded documents serve as the official public record of the transfer or encumbrance of property and therefore are required to perfect a lender's lien on collateral. Fees may vary from state to state but they are not negotiable.

Return on Equity

Many business owners have the option to finance their enterprises using funding from private sources: equity capital. Equity comes from investors who agree to provide specific sums to a business in exchange for a portion of ownership.

Private investors are not lenders—they do not expect the nominal return on their investments typically available from interest on loans. Investors seek a larger kind of return that comes from owning businesses and selling them.

While many business owners may envision operating an enterprise for years, investors typically envision using capital to accelerate a company's progress from one stage to another in a finite time frame and then liquidating their investment. Their reward is based on enterprise success, as measured by the business's value growth.

That value growth will not necessarily be reflected by the company's net worth so much as the market value of the business to an acquirer or to another round of investors who want to take it to an even higher stage. Early-stage investors usually liquidate their investment through a sale of their interest in the business for a premium.

Rather than measuring their reward with a fixed percentage, their opportunity is open-ended and without a limit. Accordingly, they are willing to accept more risks than lenders who accept lower returns.

Based on these factors, many business owners are attracted to the idea of finding investors to fund their enterprises. The problem is that most small businesses will never provide the kinds of financial returns required by investors in a suitable time frame. The kinds of businesses investors consider, how they value a business, and the returns they expect are covered in Chapter 13.

Part 2

Basics to Becoming Fundable

5

PREPARE TO
DISCLOSE EVERYTHING

When seeking financing from a third party, business owners are often surprised by the extensive amount of information that funders require. This information is needed to provide the funder with a complete dossier of the business, its owners, operating history, and financial capacity.

The size of the funding proposal will not necessarily affect the list of needed information. For the funder it's the need to understand the business and the owner's situation, financial condition, and prospects for repayment or return, whether the funding is for thousands or millions of dollars.

The degree of scrutiny may seem greater on larger transactions because the funder's exposure is proportionately greater. But in reality there is generally more information to examine for a larger enterprise, and the funder's parameters are certainly tighter when more risk is at stake. Regardless, the business owner's command of this information is important for the management of the business, whether or not the owner is seeking money.

There is no comprehensive list of required application information. The list of suggested information presented in this chapter is extensive. Depending on the situation of a particular company owned by a particular individual, this list might be either too inclusive or too exclusive for many items that could be needed for a particular request.

No two deals are alike—the funder, owner, business, and situation are all unique in every transaction. Therefore, recognize that the funder is basically starting from scratch with each consideration of a new proposal.

Literally hundreds of variables can alter the information requirements demanded by the funder. Even the funder will not know all that is needed until the process is initiated and until the information begins to map out the business's situation, from which the funder will determine if the business qualifies under its funding criteria.

This chapter examines many of the items usually requested by funders, describes exactly what the funder is looking for, and why this information is pertinent to evaluate the transaction.

Attention to detail during this process will enhance the chances of being funded and accelerate the response. By anticipating what's needed and any possible questions, the owner will be better prepared to respond more quickly, more accurately, and in a manner more likely to achieve the desired result.

Most of the information, documents, and records needed by the business owner are detailed here, organized in specific categories and in the logical order for discussing these topics with the funder when the owner presents the funding proposal.

Although the business owner must compile a voluminous set of information, the funding proposal should be introduced to the funder personally. The business will benefit from the most effective and persuasive technique for obtaining funding approval—the impressive selling skills of the owner.

Merely delivering a large bundle of raw information is ineffective, since there is no certainty that it was ever reviewed. Even a brief oral presentation will provide the funder with a better context in which to evaluate a proposal.

A most important but simple document is a written summary of a proposal to specify exactly how much funding the business is seeking, how it will be used, and how it will be repaid or returned. The funder can then refer to the more detailed information to begin answering its own questions once it has an idea of exactly what the owner wants.

The owner's level of preparation and cooperation will quickly inform the funder whether the owner would be a desirable client or partner. If it's difficult to get responses to questions or document requests before the funding is closed, the funder might assume it could be even worse afterward.

Responsive, cooperative owners demonstrate good management skills and a certain sense of respect—after all, they are asking to use someone else's money. Such basic courtesies are necessary to facilitate timely consideration of the proposed funding, and failure to display this common sense will be self-defeating.

Much of the data suggested in this chapter may not exist in the form of a document, but for purposes of transferring information to a funder, it is important for business owners to get accustomed to creating memos or other written forms to communicate. With all the facts, figures, and other information a lender needs, it's always best to put this type of communication in writing to reduce errors and misunderstanding. Emphasis should be on providing information that is complete, concise, logically sequenced, and accurate.

Submitting information to promote the business is undermined when there are careless grammatical errors, misspelled words, and incoherent ideas. With the availability of high-quality word processing software, most of these errors can be eliminated. There is no excuse for poorly written information communicated incorrectly and haphazardly.

When supplying information to the funder the owner should assume that the funder does not understand the industry jargon or abbreviations. Technical terms and methodologies should be explained to ensure that the funder can follow the reasoning of the loan proposal.

The owner should assume that the funder has no familiarity with the specific industry in which the business owner is involved. Accordingly, the application needs to communicate the business owner's strategy in exact detail and project how the results will impact the owner's business.

The business owner must be aware that the funder will check the company's credit history, appraise the collateral, check references, verify accounts, and test the reasonableness of financial projections of the company's future performance. These tests are conducted in order to quantify the risk associated with providing capital.

Before starting the evaluation process for funding, it's vital for the owner to know in detail the contents of all the information provided to the funder. The owner will be expected to promptly answer questions about the information, thereby greatly enhancing the chances of success by anticipating what the funder's analysis will conclude.

The business owner should be prepared to discuss anything submitted to the funder and even provide additional supporting documentation, if necessary. Best practice is to respond to any questions with a written response—even if it's a follow-up to a conversation on the topic. The memo will reinforce the explanation and provide more clarity, particularly when other decision makers become involved.

The funder will need information from several distinct categories. Although there is no official format, the owner's data submission should be organized to assist the funder to catalog this information more efficiently so it can find whatever is needed quickly. This compilation method is more efficient and better sequenced than submitting information in a business plan.

Categorized organization of information will permit the funder to absorb information at its own pace, depending on the direction and priorities of its review.

Due to the typically large volume of material, it's more useful to arrange the information in a series of large, open-ended folders, rather than using ring binders, clamps, or color-coded tabs. This system permits the funder to reach and replace each section easier. Some of the information will be copied for various uses in the review process, which can be done easily if the documents are not bound.

It's smarter to provide clean, clear document copies that are legible. Everything should be reviewed prior to submission to eliminate incorrect compilation, incomplete pages, poor copy reproductions, or out-of-sequence documents. These logistical errors will confuse the reviewer and distract from the evaluation of the proposal.

Original documents, such as the company's financial statements, should not be submitted unless several original copies exist. Any copied document may be authenticated, if necessary, with a dated original signature on the cover page.

Finally, if the owner cannot produce a particular document or other requested information, an explanation of the delay and the time frame for when the information will be available serves the owner well.

An owner should not blame any missing information on another party—this will only make the owner look foolish. If the owner can't manage to gather necessary information from the other party, who is being paid to provide it, what will the funder think about the owner's ability to generate revenues or return its capital?

If information is not available due to reasons that cannot be immediately resolved, then the owner should consider delaying the funding request.

Everybody Wants a Business Plan

How do companies use business plans? Too often business owners put a business plan together only when seeking external financing from lenders or investors. Business plans should provide information on the short- and intermediate-term strategies for accomplishing long-term goals. Business plans should detail how financial, operational, marketing, and human resources will be converted into a successful and profitable venture. Business plans should be used as a road map to determine the destination and then measure results against projections.

Many people are obsessed with business plans—particularly those who charge exorbitant fees to prepare them. Business plans are very good tools that can assist business owners and managers to plan better and target results better. And when an existing business is seeking to obtain additional financing, a business plan can be a very good document to communicate how the company plans to build on the results it has already compiled to that point in its operating history. But the plan itself is not a sufficient substitute for everything else needed by the lender.

If an owner has put together a business plan merely to justify financing, then it has limited utility or value for both the owner and the lender. If the lender requires a business plan, then the owner probably hasn't made a clear case about what the business goals are. That being the case, the owner should invest the time to produce a plan. But it would also be in the owner's interest to continue to use and regularly update the plan after the financing is obtained.

What Information Is Really Needed and Why?

The business owner should produce information for the funder that clearly sets forth the exact proposal for financing. Along with the proposal, the owner should provide supporting information that documents every representation made about the business, its owners, and the proposal.

Figure 5.1 includes information that should be readily available to management at any time regardless of the pending financing proposal. Each item documents specifications of business resources, operating results, asset records, or financial details. (More information on this figure can be found in Chapters 6 and 7.)

While the list may seem staggering at first glance, it's merely a comprehensive summary of information used by the owner during the life of the business. It's important to the funder because it's important to the business.

The list is intended to prevent business owners from overlooking the obvious components, but it cannot be all-inclusive due to the unique features of the business. There may be obvious or not-so-obvious aspects to the business that define the need for additional information, which the owner should be prepared to provide when compiling a loan proposal.

The thoroughness of the funder's request compared to the suggested information in Figure 5.1 may vary due to the size, sophistication, and market of the business or funder. Nonetheless, regularly reviewing and being familiar with the entire set of suggested information can only strengthen a loan proposal.

Many items needed for the funder's due diligence that are prepared by third-party professionals, such as an appraisal, are not included in the list. There are also some obvious differences in the information required by a lender as opposed to an investor. Some specialty lenders will also focus more heavily on the collateral information than other lenders will.

Information about specific asset financing situations (i.e., securities, notes, inventory, etc.) is not included in the list because it impacts fewer business owners.

FIGURE 5.1 Financing Proposal: Basic Information

Basic Transaction Information
Proposed Financing Amount
Purpose of Funding
Proposed Deal Structure
Detailed Use of Proceeds
Proposed Collateral

Business Details
Legal Business Name
Trade Business Name, if any
Address (all locations)
Business Ownership
Employer Identification Number
Date Established
Number of Employees
Name of Depository Bank
Business History
Organizational Chart
Key Employee Résumés

Legal Entity Documents
Articles of Incorporation, Limited Partnership
  or LLC
Bylaws, Partnership Agreement, or LLC
  Operating Agreement

Business Financial Information
Business Financial Statements (3 yrs.)
Business Tax Returns (3 yrs.)
Interim Financial Statement (within 60 days)
Reconciliation of Net Worth (if req'd.)
Receivable Aging (at interim stmt. date)
Inventory Aging (at interim stmt. date)
Payables Aging (at interim stmt. date)
Business Liability Schedule (at interim stmt. date)
Profit / Loss Projections (2 yrs.)
Business Cash-Flow Projections (12 mos.)
Schedule of Lease Agreements
Financial Report Analysis

Business Marketing Information
Describe Business Profile
Describe Business Products or Services
Describe Business Operations
Describe Customer Profile
Competition Analysis
Describe Marketing Campaign

Miscellaneous Business Information
Collateral Information
Affiliated Business Information
Franchise Business Information

Owner Details
Full Owner Name(s)
Current/Previous Address(es)
Date of Birth
Social Security Number
Credit Authorization, (if applicable)
Place of Birth (SBA only)
Citizenship (SBA only)
Military Service (SBA only)
Affiliated Interests

Owner Financial Information
Personal Financial Statement
Personal Tax Returns (3 yrs.)

Derogatory Personal Information
Bankruptcy
Litigation
Divorce
Bad Decisions
Bad Health
Bad Credit
Explanation of Derogatory Personal Information

A brief explanation of each of these items follows. At a minimum, a financing proposal should include the basic information found in the list.

Basic Information to Prepare a Financing Proposal

As crazy as it sounds, many business owners will prepare a mountain of documents to deliver to the funder but never provide a clue as to what the funder is being asked to do. A financing proposal must contain a specific proposal that sets forth exactly what the owner wants: how much, for what purpose, for how long, the method to be repaid, and at what expense.

Proposed Financing Amount

A business owner should begin the conversation about funding by laying out the amount of money needed right away. No guesswork, no big introductions, no surprises: "I am here to see you about $2 million for my business."

The owner may save time by learning that the funder has absolutely no interest in the business or that it is eager to do business. But either way, the owner's first sentence needs to get the funder's attention, and this declaration is how it's done.

Purpose of Funding

The funder has to understand why the business needs money in an exacting level of detail. Writing a concise statement of exactly why the owner wants the funds ensures that both parties are focused on the same goal. Further, it's advisable for the owner to provide a detailed schedule that breaks down every expense line: where the funds will be spent and when.

The funder will ask the owner to provide a thorough explanation to justify all capital expenses. It wants to hear the business case for new investments as assurance that the proposal is merited for the sake of business success. It behooves the owner to help the funder recognize the importance of such choices and demonstrate point-by-point how these investments will generate additional revenues and sufficient profits to repay funding or accelerate enterprise value.

Proposed Deal Structure

The owner should propose the ideal funding structure at the beginning of the conversation. The word *structure* refers to the terms and conditions that outline how the funding will be paid back to the funder and when. The deal structure will be formed through roughly a six-step process for a loan transaction or an equity capital to find agreement between the business and the funder to get to the closing table (see Figure 5.2 and Figure 5.3 for loan process and equity capital process, respectively).

Specifically, the six steps for a loan transaction can be described as:

1. Borrower presents business plan and makes full information disclosure.
2. Lender screens borrower's capacity, capital, collateral, credit, and character.
3. Lender gathers data, interviews borrower, and checks independent references.

4. Lender analyzes data and underwrites loan transaction.
5. Lender offers borrower commitment with specific pricing and repayment terms.
6. Final due diligence is performed and loan is funded.

The six steps for an equity capital can be described as:

1. Owner presents business plan and makes full information disclosure.
2. Investor screens business for concept, management, and scalability.
3. Investor gathers data, interviews borrower, and checks independent references.
4. Investor and business reach agreement on future valuation and exit event.
5. Investor offers term sheet with investment offer and transaction expectations.
6. Final due diligence is performed and investment is funded.

The business owner has the best opportunity to influence the loan structure at the initial negotiation. By introducing the company's preferences from the

FIGURE 5.2 Six Steps to a Business Loan

beginning, the owner sets the expectations for discussions and is likely to get a better deal by steering discussion toward those terms.

The terms suggested by the owner may be the same structure that would have been offered later by the funder anyway, but putting them forth first should signal that the owner has done the necessary homework and knows what the business can handle.

Funders usually will not provide funding to cover the owner's desire to hold cash reserves, particularly when those reserves are funded by borrowed money. If an owner ventures into this area, most funders will grow concerned about the owner's confidence in the business plan and not be willing to add the risk of the expensive costs of reserves.

The funder will always have the ultimate leverage in determining the loan terms (remember the Golden Rule). Nevertheless, the business owner's proposal of reasonable terms should be asserted, particularly when backed up with solid number projections to make the case compelling.

Components of the deal structure should include:

- **Loan / investment amount.** Specify exactly how much money the business needs and defend it with supporting information, making sure to factor in

FIGURE 5.3 Six Steps to Equity Capital

any lender's proportional equity requirement or investor's equity valuation calculus.

- **Funding term.** Define the period over which to amortize the loan repayment or liquidate the investment. Maximum loan terms are affected by regulatory and market risk factors. Be prepared to get a longer amortization but a shorter-term call provision on conventional financing. Investors don't go far beyond three years.

- **Interest rate.** Ask for a very favorable interest rate but be realistic about how much risk the deal presents to the lender. Real estate loans are generally safer than equipment loans, and equipment loans are generally safer than working capital loans. The interest rate should be a function of the lender's risk.

- **Collateral.** Establish limits as to what collateral sufficiently secures the transaction, taking into account the discount a lender must make to create a safe margin for liquidation costs and the distressed nature of sale. Resist the lender's effort to mortgage everything.

- **Endorsements.** Except for large real estate development transactions or companies that are publicly owned, almost every small business loan requires the personal endorsement or guarantee by the owner. That commitment assures the lender the owner will stand behind the repayment of the debt even if the business cannot. Resign to the fact that this term is very important to the lender but resist efforts to involve family members who are not in the business. According to Regulation B, a bank cannot require a spouse to endorse a loan if that spouse has no ownership in the business.

The business owner should be sure to figure out how to calculate loan payments using the loan amount, interest rate, and repayment term requested *before* initiating negotiations about the loan structure. Being able to accurately determine the payment is essential in order to ensure that the payment requirements are workable in the business income and cash flow projection model. An owner never should agree to terms under which the business cannot perform.

There are several financial software applications, such as Microsoft Excel, that provide loan amortization calculations. Alternatively, the business owner may choose to buy a business calculator to accomplish this task.

Detailed Use of Proceeds

The business owner's loan proposal must include a specific schedule that defines how the funding will be used. If the owner doesn't specify these details, the funder too often makes decisions based on limited, inaccurate information or assumptions, which often reduces the funding offer.

Funders deserve to know precisely where every dollar goes. When the business is purchasing assets, this number is easy to define. However if the funds are needed to provide working capital, precisely mapping where these funds will be applied is a little more difficult.

The owner should produce an accurate worksheet that details how the funding will be used. He should be prepared for the funder to request that he verify the planned uses of all proceeds in advance, for example by providing copies of notes being paid off (along with the original loan settlement statement and security agreement), purchase contracts, bills of sale, construction contracts, price quotes or other documents that confirm the use of funds.

If there is working capital in the transaction, the owner should prepare a schedule of where these funds will be applied. Most funders require business owners to provide paid receipts to justify working capital expenditures and will prefer to restrict disbursements to reimburse the business after the costs are incurred. If a borrower requests to finance a loan's transaction costs, the owner should find out from the lender exactly what these costs will be before completing the proposal.

The owner should also produce a detailed month-to-month cash flow projection for working capital funding, predicting how and when the cash proceeds will be used and describe the expected expenses or purchases that will be paid. It's easier for the owner to restrict the use of these particular proceeds for larger ticket items, such as inventory, services, or other major costs that the funder can identify without as much documentation.

Proposed Collateral

The business owner should define what assets are available to reasonably secure a requested loan. Collateral is important to a lender because it defines a tangible alternative to the normal liquidation of a loan. The lender will typically require coverage for 100 percent of the loan with assets valued on a discounted basis.

For example, if the owner is purchasing a building with the loan proceeds, the lender will discount the property value in order to determine its "collateral value." If the lender's loan policy defines an advance rate of 75 percent on commercial real estate, the lender will reduce the value of the business owner's real property by 25 percent to calculate the maximum advance rate. On that basis, the lender will lend the business owner up to 75 percent of the cost of the building.

Should the business owner require a larger loan, the lender may consider increasing the loan if the owner has additional assets to pledge to secure the higher sum. Most lenders margin commercial real estate in the wide range of 65 to 85 percent, according to their risk appetite, type of property, and market conditions. Here are some of the different property categories from a lender's perspective:

- **Single purpose.** Generally, properties with a single-purpose improvement present a larger risk to the lender, since the asset only has one specific use and cannot be easily adapted to other commercial businesses. These factors limit the resale of the property in the future to a smaller set of buyers. Examples of single-purpose property are a bowling alley, convenience store, or motel.
- **Limited use.** Limited-use properties are less risky, since the building may be used for a few different commercial activities based on little or no modification. The resale market is therefore open to a larger number of potential buyers. Examples of limited-use properties are restaurants, medical buildings, or some day-care centers.
- **Multiuse.** Finally, all lenders like multiuse properties, which are generic and can be used for an unlimited number of purposes. The resale market for these properties is open to many different industries and businesses. Examples of multiuse property are office buildings, commercial/industrial buildings, and warehouses.
- **Unimproved.** Also influencing the lender's leverage on real estate will be its internal loan policy and the current local real estate market conditions. Unimproved real estate, or raw land, is usually margined at 50 percent.

Lenders vary on equipment loans but often will finance new equipment purchases at 100 percent of cost, depending on the prepurchase cash flow, repayment terms, and their appetite for the specific type of equipment.

Transactions involving previously used equipment generally value those assets at 25 to 50 percent of costs (depending on equipment and usage) and generally value furniture and technology at $0. Lenders see little or no value in leasehold improvement or fixture investments unless the underlying real estate also secures the loan.

Traditionally, accounts receivable and inventory (current assets) are of little value to most lenders unless these assets are monitored daily. Current assets can disappear too fast to be considered as a dependable secondary source of repayment unless they are under supervision and control of the lender. Other specialty lenders have the capability of providing this supervision and do fund business-to-business receivables. Chapter 18 contains more information about working capital financing.

6

BUSINESS DETAILS

Funders require much administrative information about the subject business to ensure that they have an accurate understanding of with whom they are getting into business. This information confirms that the subject is legally organized, qualified to do business in the jurisdiction, free of lurking problems, and a good investment opportunity for the funder.

The information covers a broad range of facts that are pertinent to the owner's business identity and eligibility for financing. While this discussion may sound trivial, it's the starting point for all proposal evaluations because it provides the funder with grounding, describing how the business is organized and the nature of its operation.

- **Legal business name.** The funder needs to know the exact legal name under which the business is legally registered. This information applies to all businesses that operate under legal registration or agreement (corporation, partnership, or limited liability company). Such entities are generally registered through a state filing with limited protection of the business name in that jurisdiction.
- **Trade business name.** The funder needs to know any trade or d/b/a (doing business as) names under which the company operates. If the business is known to its customers in a name different from that name under which it's legally organized, both names need to be identified to the funder. Such trade name registrations are typically registered with the local superior court.
- **Address.** The funder needs to know the mailing address, the principal street location, and the registered address of the business. In addition the funder

will want the addresses of other offices, stores, plants, warehouses, or other sites used by the business in the course of normal operations. The owner must remember to provide other communication modes, such as the telephone number, facsimile number, and e-mail address of the principal contact.

- **Business ownership.** The funder needs a complete list of the individual owners of the business with names, addresses, and the exact percentage of ownership. This list should denote any varying stock classes or partnership categories among the ownership.
- **Employer's identification number.** Funders need the taxpayer's identification number information for verification of the business identification, tax compliance, and possible reporting of the transaction details to a government agency (SBA).
- **Date established.** The business owner should confirm the date on which the business was established to give the funder a time reference in which to understand the business stage and growth trajectory.
- **Number of employees.** The funder should be provided with details of how many persons the company employs, including in any subsidiary companies. In addition, the owner should be prepared to estimate the number of employees that will be added, if any, if the proposed financing is approved.
- **Name of depository bank.** The funder should be provided with details of the name and address of the principal depository bank used by the business. The funder may seek a reference to confirm that all relations have been conducted satisfactorily.
- **Business history.** The funder will need a quick history of the business, which is made simpler if the owner prepares a narrative about the business's origins and the major achievements that defines its progress.

  Some relevant information may include the company's:

  ○ Purpose or inspiration to start up
  ○ Development of any products or services
  ○ Geographic growth, if any
  ○ Principal employees and their contributions
  ○ Significant dates in its history
  ○ Milestone accomplishments in revenue growth

- **Organizational chart.** Production of an organizational chart provides the funder with a graphic representation of the business's chain of command. The funder needs to understand the scale of the organization available to accomplish its mission.

• **Key employee résumés.** It's useful to provide the funder with résumés or at least short biographical sketches of all members of the management team and even some key staff members. Understanding the qualifications of the staff and the depth of bench strength is reassuring to funders when planning to expand the business.

A résumé defines and quantifies the background, education, and experience of each individual involved with managing the business and accomplishing its mission. This information is much easier to interpret if each one is prepared in a standard format with the same layout and style.

Another concern for all small business funders will be about executive management depth and succession. These questions can be easily addressed with more detailed information about the experience and training of the senior management staff.

Legal Entity Documents

Funders need copies of the legal registration documents under which the business is organized. State governments register corporations, limited partnerships, and limited liability companies through the office of the secretary of state.

There are four primary organizational structures for a commercial business, which include sole proprietorship (which is to say the business has no legal registration), partnership, corporation, and limited liability company. (See Chapter 2 for a detailed discussion of each.)

If the business owner is operating as a sole proprietorship, this status means that a distinct legal entity has *not* been created to distinguish the individual owner from the business enterprise. Therefore, the business generally does not require any administrative or legal filing, except perhaps a trade name registration if the business operates under a protected trade name different from its owner's.

A business owner may choose to conduct business without the protection of a legal entity for many reasons. However, unless the enterprise is very small and the minimal expense of organizing such an entity is disproportionate to the revenue stream, *everyone* should shelter personal assets from business activities with a corporation or LLC.

We live in a very litigious place to operate a business, and in recent years we have seen the evolution of many commercial liability claims that created severe financial consequences for unintended events. Business owners should be liable for their errors and negligence but should also be smart enough to build a firewall between their personal finances and their business activities.

Business owners who do take advantage of forming a legally recognized business entity provide a way to distinguish between who is liable and what is available to settle claims. Registration with the state is required for corporations, limited partnerships, and limited liability companies, whereas general partnerships form among persons and/or other organizations by creating a partnership agreement.

Funders will require a review of the organization's documents to understand how it's formed, who is involved, what it's authorized to do, and whether there are terms or conditions that would add risk or restriction to any funding consideration. The documentation required for each type of organization is defined below:

If the business is organized as a partnership, the following documentation is required:

- **Certificate of partnership.** The document used to register a limited partnership with the state for recognition as a legal entity is known as the certificate of partnership. In most states the certificate is filed with the secretary of state and is used to disclose the partnership's organization, ownership, registered address, and registered agent.
- **Partnership agreement.** The funder will need to review the business partnership agreement. The funder must understand the exact nature of the partnership, the identity of ownership and of the general partner, and the definition of the beneficial relationship among the partners. Additionally, the agreement must specify the partners' authority to borrow money, sell more partnership interests, or enter into another partnership/entity agreement as per the contemplated funding arrangement.

If the business is organized as a corporation, the following documentation is required:

- **Articles of incorporation.** The document used to register a corporation with the state to be recognized as a legal entity is known as the articles of incorporation. In most states the articles are filed with the secretary of state and are used to disclose the corporation's organization, officers, registered address, and registered agent. Also included in the articles will be a reference to the entity's authorized capital.
- **Bylaws.** The funder will need to review the bylaws, the document that defines the corporation's governing rules, management structure, and various authorities granted to the entity. In particular, the bylaws will spell out the corporate authority to borrow money or sell shares to other investors.

Bylaws usually indemnify the officers and directors from liability from acts of the corporation and define how the board of directors is elected.

If the business is organized as a limited liability company (LLC), the following documentation is required:

- **Articles of organization.** The document used to register an LLC with the state to be recognized as a legal entity is known as the articles of organization. In most states the articles are filed with the secretary of state and are used to disclose the LLC's organization, organizer, registered address, and registered agent. The articles will also include a reference to the authorized capital of the entity.

  An LLC is the most flexible of the various legal organizations, and its organizers can choose to adopt attributes that appear in either partnerships or corporations. For example, they can establish their governing authority as either a managing member or create a board of directors. They can sell ownership interest as fractional interests, units, or even shares. This flexibility permits them to customize the organization to best meet their planned course of business, particularly if raising equity capital is contemplated.

- **LLC operating agreement.** The funder will need to review the LLC operating agreement. This agreement will help the funder understand the terms under which the LLC was organized, identify the ownership and governing structures, and define the beneficial relationship among the members. Additionally the agreement must specify the LLC's authority to borrow money, sell more member interests, or enter into another LLC/entity agreement as per the contemplated funding arrangement.

For any registered organization, two additional documents will be part of a lender's loan-closing process. Depending on the legal organization, the owner will be required to execute either:

Corporate Resolution
Certificate as to Partnership, *or*
Certificate as to Limited Liability Company

The funder will require the business owners to execute one of these documents that provides an attestation of the legal authority of the entity to enter the financing transaction. This document must be signed by the appropriate officer (secretary, managing partner, or managing member) and confirms that the entity has authorized its representatives to enter into a particular financing agreement.

The other due diligence performed, the Certificate of Good Standing, will be obtained independently by the funder. This document is issued by the secretary of state and confirms that the business is duly recognized by the state as a legal entity, is in compliance with state registration regulations, and is authorized to conduct business in the state.

Business Financial Information

The core information of interest to the funder will be the business financial statements and related documents. Whether organized for 50 years or 15 minutes, the owner must provide or project the business's financial results with supporting detail and logical analysis. Depending on the scope of operations, number of years in existence, and history, the funder will require various financial information.

Business Financial Statements

The funder will require the submission of at least the past three years' business financial statements. This information provides the funder with evidence of success from the business's most recent financial performance and surveys the trends during the most recent periods. The funder will compare these annual results with the business's comparable industry results to evaluate how the company measures up with its peers.

Note: *Certification of Financials or Tax Returns.* Funders may sometimes require owners to certify the authenticity of the financial statements and tax returns submitted to support a commercial funding request. They may ask that the owner sign a statement of authenticity or maybe just add an original signature on the face of a copy of the documents.

The former is certainly easy, but the latter demands more attention. Adding a signature to an honest financial statement is no big deal, but certifying a copy of a business tax return is a little more complicated.

A business owner should not sign on the signature line of a copy of a tax return. Legally speaking the copy of the return could be interpreted as a new original by the IRS and potentially create a new tax liability claim. The owner should instead sign in the margin using a blue or red pen so that the signature is easy to find and obviously not copied.

Business Tax Returns

The funder will require complete copies of the company's income tax returns for the past three years.

There are many differences in financial reporting and tax reporting, since the tax code does not allow certain expenses to be used to lower taxable income and may offer a variety of depreciation options depending on current public policy. If there are significant differences in the two reports, it's helpful to prepare a summary of these differences and a brief explanation for the funder.

This advance work will provide more clarity for the owner as well and will answer and reduce any confusion that may be created, since the differences can sometimes be significant. Most businesses elect options to tax filing that will lower their income and accordingly their tax burden. But it's important to not let those results override the significance of the true operating results, which is usually a better indication of the company's actual performance.

Providing information about the obvious or subtle differences between the business owner's tax returns and financial statements will help the funder reconcile these differences and understand the owner's actual financial results.

Note: *IRS Form 4506.* To combat potential fraud many lenders now require businesses to submit IRS Form 4506, which authorizes the IRS to provide the lender with a transcript of the borrower's tax return from specific years. Lenders use these transcripts to verify that they match the information provided by the loan applicant.

Interim Financial Statement

The funder will require the financing proposal to include an interim financial statement no more than 60 days old. Updated financial information is particularly important during the last half of the company's fiscal year, when a majority of the current year will have elapsed since the previous year-end report.

Reconciliation of Net Worth

The business's financial statements should include a reconciliation of net worth, if needed. Often, there are financial statement adjustments made to the retained earnings or other equity accounts that render the net worth out of balance with previous reporting periods. These adjustments are not always obvious and can slow down the funder's analysis of the financial statements. The owner should prepare a reconciliation of any such changes ahead of time and provide a detailed explanation of all adjustments.

Such adjustments may be the addition or deletion of previous period revenues or expenses, owner distributions of capital, or even the issuance of additional capital stock. The net worth account is always a concern of funders, because it indicates the company's financial strength. It's watched closely by funders to ensure that the owner is not drawing that strength down recklessly. It is in the owner's best interest to be able to provide an explanation for any sudden changes to the business net worth account.

Receivable Aging

The funder will need an accounts receivable aging report as of the most recent interim or year-end financial statement. This gives the funder information to evaluate liquidity of the company's current position and working capital outlook over the next period. This report should balance and reconcile with the total accounts receivable stated on the appropriate financial statement.

Inventory Aging

If inventory represents a significant account on the company's balance sheet, the funder will need an inventory aging report as of the most recent interim or year-end financial statement. This report gives the funder information to evaluate the company's inventory assets (raw materials, work-in-process, or finished goods), which will provide the metrics to check progress on liquidity, sales strength, and even obsolescence. This report should balance and reconcile with the total inventory stated on the appropriate financial statement.

Payables Aging

The funder will need an accounts payable aging report as of the most recent interim or year-end financial statement. This gives the funder information to evaluate the payment demands and determine if the liquidity is sufficient to meet operation needs. This report should balance and reconcile with the total accounts payable stated on the appropriate financial statement.

Business Liability Schedule

The funder will need a schedule of the business liabilities as of the most recent interim or year-end financial statement. This gives the funder a breakdown of the long-term debt often compiled on the financial statement into a single number. This information should be on a worksheet that includes the lender's name, date of origin, interest rate, original loan amount, present loan balance, maturity date, collateral, and payment amount or amount due at maturity. The total sum of this report should balance and be reconciled to the short-term and long-term debt stated on the appropriate financial statement.

Profit/Loss Projections

The owner needs to prepare at least a two-year projection of business profit/loss for operations. This information helps make the owner's case to the funder about how the funding will be employed and demonstrates the owner's reasoning as to how the business will produce revenues, manage expenses, and create profits that will fund the loan repayment installments or dividend payments as scheduled.

The projection model should include a detailed description of revenues, cost of goods, and all overhead expenses expected to support the business operation. The owner should ensure that overconfidence doesn't get the best of competence. This projection model is not the place to make up numbers or fill the blanks with pie-in-the-sky guesses.

The model should use only logical estimates based on the expectation of the likely results. Anything more and the owner will be ripe for failure. There will be certain assumptions made, and they should be described in accompanying footnotes so that all parties are clear as to the estimations. A detailed explanation of how to use a profit/loss projection model is described in Chapter 10.

Business Cash Flow Projections

Concurrent with developing a profit/loss projection model, the owner should prepare a detailed cash flow projection model. This model breaks down the annual profit/loss pro forma into monthly periods. By using a starting cash balance and adjusting the revenue timing to represent the actual business cash cycle, the owner can predict how well the business will weather sales growth during the year on a cash-on-cash basis. Such attention to detail is very important to success.

The funder will also develop this information for its own analysis of the business's repayment capacity but probably can't accurately predict the cash cycles if the business sells on open account or has receivables. The funder may be too optimistic or pessimistic about the ability of the business to meet its obligations. The numbers are very important in this portion of the analysis.

Unlike the profit/loss projections, the cash flow model forecasts cash collections against cash outflows. This information dissects and quantifies how and when the business produces cash to meet its operating costs and obligations. The more exact the input information, the better the model will be as a tool to guide expectations, plans, and financing. And if the expectations get disrupted, a good model can help the business maneuver and recover faster.

The real value of a working cash flow model is that it reflects the actual schedule of when revenues are going to convert to cash and when expenses actually have to be paid. This level of detail is absolutely essential to responsibly manage a business intending to grow.

For example, an annual profit/loss model will show that property taxes must be paid for a certain dollar amount, but the cash flow statement will reflect that the actual payment is due in September. That detail is significantly different than just assuming that the business can accrue the expense for 12 months and pay it or that it is paying out only 1/12 per month. The business may accrue the expense monthly, but after 9 months of accrual it has to pay the entire sum for the year. How does that affect the working capital of the business to prepay 3 months' accrual of a major expense?

Likewise some expenses require payment in advance, such as single premium insurance policies. Planning for these large expenditures from the company's working capital is important to ensuring the business always has sufficient funding to operate while covering all its costs as they are scheduled.

The business owner will have the burden of convincing the funder that the business operation can produce sufficient positive cash flow consistent with the estimated profit/loss projections and meet all its obligations subject to the timing of expenses and revenue collections. A detailed explanation of how to use a cash flow projection model is detailed in Chapter 10.

Schedule of Lease Agreements

At the risk of providing information that a bank never asks for, business owners should offer a schedule of all lease obligations to all funders, even if not requested. The funder deserves to have a copy of any and all lease agreements that the business is obligated to fulfill. Whether it's the space occupied as the principal place of business or the copier down the hall, the funder needs to understand all obligations, including those that do not appear on the company's balance sheet.

Replacing the copier, relocating the business, or just upgrading the CEO's vehicle represent financial events that could marginally impact the company's financial results in any period and therefore affect the business's ability to meet other obligations.

The owner should expect that such information may result in the funder's requiring that the business owner modify the lease terms, negotiate extensions, or maneuver in other ways to answer some of the situations created by less important obligations earlier than required. While inconvenient, hopefully the funder will recognize that the owner placed everything on the table about the financial condition of the business.

This information provides the funder with details from which to assess the company's money cash needs and, as important, its ability to meet its obligations. This analysis is an important part of the funder's process to evaluate the proposed funding.

Financial Report Analysis

For their own benefit, all business owners should draft an annual summary of the financial results of their business. Memorializing a fresh explanation of what happened and why (good, bad, or otherwise) provides a good record to ensure that there is an accurate context to draw from when planning future business strategy.

The funder may be a little surprised to get a detailed narrative of the business financial reports describing the results of each reporting period, but such a document means the owner controls the analysis. Offering a context for the financial statements allows the owner to influence the funder's interpretation of the financial results and ensures a complete understanding of the business's operations.

Attention should be on information that provides an explanation of any negative results or that highlights positive results. If appropriate, the owner might even consider preparation of a restatement of the financial results with adjustments that reflect any extraordinary events that diluted results.

Business Marketing Information

The funder should be provided with descriptive information about the owner's operation to understand what the business contributes to the economy and how the owner generates revenue from that contribution. In this category the owner defines the business service or product, distinguishes its service or product from competitors, describes how the business finds clients by marketing, and provides a detailed plan as to how the business will maintain or expand future revenues.

Marketing information should be garnered through management's consideration and response to questions such as the ones in this chapter about the resources and capabilities of the business compared to external market conditions, trends, and opportunities within the industry.

Providing the funder with some details about the business's big idea and how to accomplish it requires more than just a fountain of optimism. Funders will look behind the owner's glossy words for substance: marketing research, demographic support, and industry trends.

Management needs to provide a clear answer to the following basic questions to successfully maneuver through the funding opportunity with a business savvy that will culminate in success and profitability.

- What is needed?
- Who needs it?
- What satisfies that need?
- How much will they pay to satisfy it?

The above are the major questions a business owner should address to construct a blueprint of how the business has identified or will identify what to sell to whom, where, why, and for how much. To maximize the potential of a product or service, there are no really bad ideas, only those with less potential.

A marketing plan is like a business plan within a business plan. It has many components:

- Defining company and products or services
- Identifying potential client wants and needs
- Positioning products or services to meet client wants and needs
- Communicating with client about products or services
- Measuring response of client to message

It is important for owners to catalog all of the ideas that don't fit today, because it's possible that some of these ideas will work tomorrow. Successful marketing requires that a business sell to a constantly changing, evolving marketplace. Complacency can mean the end to a business due to new competition, new ideas, and new clients constantly altering the landscape.

Business Profile

The owner must be able to succinctly describe the business identity consistent with the market in which it seeks to sell. An owner must ask: Is my restaurant establishment a fine-dining enterprise or a hamburger haven? Am I selling used cars or previously owned vehicles? Am I a professional search executive or a headhunter?

Business owners are largely who they decide to be. It's not complicated for them to invent who they are based on how they position themselves and to communicate that identity in the market. In today's world one can achieve status with fancy stationery, a premium address, and an innovative title at a fraction of the cost of the less imaginative business motif of yesteryear.

Does image sell? To many buyers and sellers it does. So realistically, it's safe to assume that there is a market for almost anything to be sold by almost anyone. Sellers decide to whom they want to sell, and buyers decide from whom they want to buy.

In order for business owners to understand to whom they want to sell, though, it's important for them to understand who they themselves are. The less definition they have of their own operation, the less information they have with which to control or pursue the market in which they want to operate within.

A fundamental determinant of the funder's interest in the business loan request begins with an evaluation of the industry in which the business operates. Every industry has some inherent characteristics that create some risk to a prospective funder. Many funders actually avoid loans to various industries if these inherent risks are determined to be beyond the degree of certainty that the funder is willing to accept.

Before seeking financing, small businesses should understand how they are viewed as an industry from the funder's perspective. For example, small business funders may feel more confident financing a local convenience store that sells gasoline than financing an oil and gas exploration company. While both are essentially operating in the same industry, the credit risk associated with each business is radically different. Obviously two different kinds of funders are needed to deal with the characteristics unique to each business.

Characterizing the business in a more favorable rank within its own industry helps the owner elevate the funder's perception and magnifies the transaction appeal. For example, instead of limiting a company's description to being a stadium hamburger stand, the owner should broaden the depiction to define the business as an entertainment and food-service provider.

A funder's personal bias against some industries could subconsciously interfere with its enthusiasm for a transaction. But characterizing a business as a food service rather than as a restaurant also effectively communicates the operational maneuverability of a business that owns a grill and a kitchen sink and that can feed hungry patrons in different ways.

As a food service provider, the owner has the flexibility to modify the strategy and products of the business to respond to unforeseen economic changes. The owner can swap hamburgers for chicken sandwiches if need be to respond to changing consumer preferences.

Knowing how funders perceive an industry can help prepare an owner for the search for capital. Where is the business within its industry's life cycle? How will the business exploit its position and opportunity? This preparation helps the owner define the risks that the funder will have to consider. The owner should address the obvious business risks to the funder with ideas already in the marketing plan.

Funders will be wary of a business trying to serve too many specialized markets from a limited operating base. For example, a grocery store with an in-house hair salon and sushi bar represents a unique business plan probably destined to fail. Such an operation would be hard to market effectively and would likely suffer from insufficient revenues. A focused business plan is easier for owners to master and funders to understand.

Funders will never understand who business owners are if the owners don't understand themselves first.

Business Product or Service

What products or services are produced by the business? What distinguishes them from others? Why should anyone care? A widget is a widget, right? Just what is the big idea?

The owner should define exactly what and how products or services are provided by the business according to the characteristics that make them different. It's easy to understand a company that sells radios, but it takes a few more details to relate to a company that manufactures digitized, variable overdrive power systems.

It's crucial to explain in simple terms exactly what the business does:

- Does it manufacture, retail, resell, liquidate, remodel, recover, research, distribute, or remanufacture the products?
- If it's in the information industry, does the business research information, analyze information, communicate information, or use information to provide advice or create solutions?
- If it's in the lunch business, does the business plan lunch, cook lunch, deliver lunch, serve lunch, clean up after lunch, or find other people who do these things?

The funder should be able to completely understand what specific niche the owner serves and what particular market the business tries to sell to. And the owner should attempt to distinguish the business's unique characteristics and enable the funder to understand why the business is discernibly different from its market competitors.

Most businesses are formed with the owner seeking to take advantage of a particular market opportunity. Situations arise, demographics evolve, and markets develop and dissipate. Ideas are a dime a dozen, but most can be successful if exploited at the right time. The secret is finding the right time.

The right time is not necessarily universal. The right time in Peoria may be after the idea crashes in Poughkeepsie. Understanding why a big idea is a big idea sometimes requires recognition of the timing.

Some big ideas may be unique and created entirely out of the imagination of the entrepreneur. Consider the Pet Rock and Beanie Babies. Sometimes big ideas are just a matter of identifying a particular demographic group and finding a way to exploit some unrealized demand.

Other ideas are obvious and captured by the person getting there first. When a new exit is developed on a busy interstate highway there is always a new list of potential business opportunities created, such as motels, restaurants, convenience stores, auto repair stores, and other enterprises to cater to travelers accessing the highway. The big idea may just be getting there first.

Not all big ideas are good ones and not all good ideas are practical. Sometimes people get a concept that captures their fancy before they have honestly considered the pitfalls. They may find all sorts of justifications to prop up their concept and the planning stage jumps ahead of the evaluation process.

The further that idea rolls along, the more difficult it gets for common sense to step in and slow it down. Sometimes the funder's rejection is required to stop it cold. Worse, sometimes the funder will be suckered into a bad idea too, and the business falls flat on its face.

There are thousands of good ideas that are just not practical. One concept I recall from late the 1990s was an Internet-based company that could dispatch local drivers to deliver anything to a home if the item was ordered locally online. The business model called for merchants to pay a little and the beneficiary to pay a little. It didn't work, and I suspect the only overlooked flaw was figuring out how much revenue would be gained from delivering a $17 bag of groceries five miles? Not much.

It sure sounded like a great idea, but obviously it was not really a practical idea. It failed.

Business owners must think their big idea through carefully. They should write it down and read it every day for a few weeks to make sure it sounds just as good on day 30 as it did on day 1. They should ask 10 people they trust about it. They should even ask a couple of folks they don't trust!

It is important for owners to develop a critical path of all the possibilities for their big idea. They should write down all of the operational junctions and detail how the business responds. They should prepare for every possible response and develop strategies for all results. This exercise will prepare them to make a decision, and the preparation will enable the funder to be more confident about the idea.

If the big idea can't attract the investment of a funder, it probably isn't an idea that is going to succeed.

Business Operations

How does the business operate? How are the goods obtained or produced? Who actually performs the services? The funder will need a detailed explanation as to exactly how the business will conduct its various tasks to produce.

Beyond defining the products or services of the business, the owner must explain how the business uses, sells, manufactures, or provides them. In addition, the owner should explain the logical sequence of events that occurs in the normal course of the business's operation.

The purpose of all this is to educate the funder about what the business does so that the funder can be more responsive to what the owner wants to do. Providing a functional understanding of the actual flow of activities helps the funder recognize the simplicity (or complexity) of the operation. Doing so empowers the owner to explain the financing proposal to a more educated ear.

How many details are too many? That question could be answered several ways. Depending on the transaction request, the funder, and the particular person fielding the request, the owner may be criticized no matter how much preparation was done. To be safe, the owner should make sure to explain the operation with clarity but not to an exhaustive degree of detail as an instruction manual might contain.

For example, the funder needs to understand that while it takes the business 20 minutes to prepare, fry, and glaze 10 dozen doughnuts, the owner can sell 15 dozen doughnuts in 10 minutes. With this perspective the funder will appreciate why the owner wants to acquire a larger capacity to produce more doughnuts.

It is important for the owner to identify the major cost components of the business, the necessity of real property, equipment, or data in the business. It helps the funder understand the nuts and bolts of the business in a brief, descriptive narration. An owner should keep the explanation simple and try to convey the main point through an example befitting the operation.

Customer Profile

Who will buy the products or services of the business? Two very important management challenges are knowing who the business's customers are and knowing who else they can be. These identities are crucial to determining the product or service design and its pricing, location, performance capacity, and strategic plan.

Sharing this information with the funder supports the owner's funding request because it assures the funder that the owner understands the market and has a way of exploiting it.

Knowing the buyer means that the owner understands who is using the product or service, which empowers the owner to recruit others who should be using it. Once the demographics are identified, the owner can focus efforts on targeting communication to attract and retain more business.

Who will buy is often a matter of determining either who needs, who wants, who has the resources, or who is susceptible. It takes a thoughtful evaluation of all the possibilities to fully develop the identity of those potential markets. Sometimes there will be prospective buyers from more than one projected category.

For example, Who needs a Pet Rock? Who is susceptible to buying a Pet Rock? An owner should think about those possibilities. The second question will probably get many more responses than the first one.

Sorting out the answers to these kinds of self-imposed tests will bring clarity to the core idea of the business and its potential marketability. The truth that cannot be escaped is that without customers, the business will not succeed. Identifying potential customers will surely help a business get them. Relying on an open-ended appeal to the masses usually falls flat.

Competition Analysis

The funder will be interested in identifying other businesses that provide the same products or services as the business being considered for funding and those that are trying to attract the same customers. The owner should be prepared to discuss these competitors with an honest assessment of each one's strengths, weaknesses, vulnerabilities, and advantages.

The owner should be specific about the position of each competitor in the marketplace. In explaining where the competition stands in comparison to the business, the owner should describe the plan to maintain or increase market share. The funder needs to know the unique features of the market in which the business under consideration operates. Further, the owner should help the funder recognize the future opportunities that the owner sees in that same market.

What are the latest trends? What new products are coming? Are there any unique opportunities to expand or consolidate? How can the owner take advantage of personal strengths? What is the competition planning to do?

These kinds of questions are of interest to the funder in order to assess the risk of dealing with the business. Providing this information before it's asked for communicates to the funder that the owner is in complete control. Afterward, it is a good idea for the owner to ask the funder what trends it sees in the industry. Funders deal with more than one business in a given industry and may be a valuable source of information.

The funder may be privy to information that the owner does not have about the industry, the market, or even the competition. The owner should appreciate the fact that sometimes the funder will be more qualified to make a business decision about the deal than was realized. Maybe there will be information that the funder will not disclose that completely wrecks the deal's financing.

What may be a rumor to the owner about a competitor may at the same time be a transaction the funder is deeply involved in as a principal financier. Sometimes the owner's funding request is competing against information the owner doesn't have, which accentuates the need to be clear about establishing the business's relevancy as a participant in the market.

A halfhearted explanation of the business may convince the funder that it will not survive. To address this possibility it is important for the owner to demonstrate the value of the business in the market through knowledge, information, and plans for the future.

The owner should be sure the funder understands all relevant personal qualifications and is aware of all strides made to promote the business and develop more trade. The owner must define the market, discuss market share, demonstrate an understanding of the potential business in the market, and show efforts toward increasing revenues. Passivity could spell an end to an owner's efforts with the funder.

Marketing Campaign

A detailed description of the ways in which the business will market and advertise its goods or services should be included in the funding proposal. There is no absolute right or wrong way to raise awareness about the business, but explaining the activities and media through which the owner promotes the business provides more credibility for the operation.

The funder should receive copies of any digital ads, direct mail pieces, flyers, brochures, specialty products, or other tangible items that have been distributed to advertise the business. The owner can also produce a detailed report about a website and any social media, or other advertising like signage or general media channels.

Also important are the civic organizations, trade associations, community activities, contributions, sponsorships, youth sports leagues, fundraising events, and other involvements through which the owner has promoted the business.

The funder will be interested in the owner's prior marketing activities and quite possibly in future marketing plans. Any conceptual ideas or new plans in development should be shared with the funder along with the expected budget.

Any good marketing plan should have a backup. If the owner's big promotional ideas miss their target, lagging revenues will help the owner realize very quickly that something is wrong. The master plan should have several alternative tactics to switch to if the desired response is not forthcoming.

It's important for the owner to let the funder know there are other ideas on the shelf but not to dilute the impact of the best ideas by describing all of the reserve plans. The owner should put forward confidence in the marketing ideas and resist self-doubt too early by publishing the entire list of fallback plans.

The funder will be looking for the owner's plan to reach potential clients and attract them to the business. The owner should make sure to have done thorough research on the identity, location, needs, and buying habits of the market in order to respond to any questions concerning the plan.

If the plan does not get the desired response, the owner should not abandon it entirely. The owner decided on a particular strategy for a particular set of reasons. Failing to get 100 percent response to the goals set does not invalidate all of those reasons. Sometimes the best plans need adjustment rather than cancellation.

Often just making simple changes can refresh a very good marketing plan that isn't meeting its goals. Targeting a slightly different audience with advertising, adjusting the price points, bundling products or services to emphasize value— these are all modifications that can change the way the business is perceived and may make all the difference.

One key about disappointing results from marketing efforts: an owner should not be afraid or too stubborn to change. One day or one week of dismal results should not cause a 180-degree change in direction. However, failing to generate sufficient results for a sustained period should make the owner realize that the plan is not working. The owner can change the plan, making minor adjustments, and if that does not create the results needed, then make bigger changes.

Miscellaneous Business Information

Some business owners will have to produce information to address unique attributes that will affect the lender's approach to the financing request. In particular, a business owner seeking financing that requires collateral, funds, construction, or money to open a franchise business will have unique documentation requirements to fulfill the funder's due diligence for each situation.

Collateral Information

It should be helpful to the lender and accelerate consideration of the loan application if the owner provides information up front about the assets to be offered as collateral to secure the loan. This data helps the lender evaluate the loan proposal and assess collateral adequacy for the requested funding more quickly.

Generally, business owners will not have any appraisals or professional reports at the time of loan application, except maybe the ones obtained when the asset was acquired. While arguably any available information on the collateral enhances the lender's review, owners should carefully consider the potential consequences before providing copies of old appraisal reports.

Since the 2007 real estate bubble, residential and commercial real estate values have plummeted and, with few exceptions, have remained lower. Depending on the appraisal date it's very likely that the earlier value was higher and reflected factors that may no longer be considered viable in the market. By pushing an old appraisal value, owners may communicate that they are oblivious to or ignorant of the values in the market.

Older valuation reports tend to be outdated in other ways, such as the particular properties used in the comparable sales data making it a poor representation of how the owner wants the property viewed today. The old conclusion may unfairly establish an undesirable metric in the underwriter's thinking as to how the owner positions the property now.

Current market conditions, subsequent development, more recent comparable sales, and other factors will impact how the value of the property is seen today, as even government tax assessments are falling. The best plan may be for the owner to allow the lender to get an independent appraisal and let that be the starting point for discussion, lest the owner get off on the wrong foot by suggesting an inappropriate value.

It's not a good idea for owners to commission their own appraisal in advance of the financing proposal and expect that the lender will use it. It cannot and will not. Suspicion over lender behavior in managing the appraisal process has become so sensitive that regulators have created elaborate rules that call for engaging a third-party appraisal management company to select and negotiate appraisals on behalf of the bank. The bank doesn't even speak directly with the appraiser any longer.

If an appraisal is necessary for any one of many good reasons, the owner should go ahead, but not expect that it will carry any influence with a lender's evaluation of the property to secure a loan.

Once the lender obtains an appraisal report there still may be a significant difference between the lender's and owner's impression of how the valuation should affect the collateral's support of the financing. Lenders will discount the market value of their collateral to determine its adequacy to secure the requested loan. This discount is necessary for the lender to maintain a margin to hedge against value depreciation and to cover potential liquidation costs.

Sometimes lenders are too conservative when determining a prudent advance rate on these assets. The owner can try to address this challenge with more information to strengthen the lender's view of the property's actual value. For example, providing the lender with recent rent rolls of credit clients, a description of significant capital improvements made since the appraisal, or other factors may solidify the collateral's value in the eyes of the lender. But convincing the lender that more confidence in the value should be rewarded with better leverage is probably a stretch. The owner has hit a credit policy wall, and it will be nearly impossible to get around it.

In determining leverage, lenders will use the lower of cost or appraised value of an asset. So even if the owner acquires a property for a price significantly lower than an appraiser's opinion of the market value, the lender will still base its loan and credit decision on the actual sales price. The business owner will not get credit or leverage against phantom equity.

Unfortunately it's not rare for a lender to approve a loan proposal with terms that include the requirement to encumber certain assets as collateral that was never offered—and never will be. To go beyond a prudent collateral request and demand excessive protection, bankers fall somewhere between unrealistic business expectations and plain arrogance. Business owners should always have a clear view of what they will or will not agree to provide for collateral ahead of the bank's decision, and they should let the bank know quickly if the bank suggests otherwise.

Sometimes extra collateral is requested just because there are assets on the owner's balance sheet that would virtually eliminate any potential risk of failure to repay the loan. The owner should recognize that using such collateral might also foreclose on potential options and flexibility that could someday be needed.

The business owner should resist the lender's inclination to secure too much collateral, challenge the lender to justify the quantity of collateral requested, and question its method of determining the adequacy of that collateral.

The business owner should not be shy in refusing a lender's offer and should make a counteroffer to secure the loan on more reasonable terms. *Everything is negotiable*. Often qualified owners can find a hungrier lender down the street who is ready to do business.

Ultimately this exercise may not change the lender's requirements, but it may cause the lender to either 1) reconsider the leverage (how much advanced) of certain assets or 2) give the business owner a better interest rate to reflect lower risk on the deal.

Another reality owners should remember when negotiating collateral is the lender's Golden Rule: "Those with the gold make the rules." Owners should know exactly what the company's and individuals' limits are as to each asset owned before loan negotiations begin.

Construction Loans

If the owner is seeking construction financing, the lender will require that the owner provide the following documentation to underwrite and administer the loan. A complete description of construction lending is contained in Chapter 14, but information on the documentation needed for these loans follows:

- **AIA construction contract.** The lender generally expects the owner's construction contract with the general contractor to use the AIA (American Institute of Architects) contract. This document is the industry standard to define the expectations and requirements of a contractor. It should be submitted with all attachments, amendments, or addendum in order for the lender to evaluate with the building plans.

   Most lenders require the owner's contract to provide a provision for retainage, which permits the owner to hold back a percentage of all progress payments until the project is completed and accepted. The retainage averages between 5 and 10 percent and amounts to holding on to some of the general contractor's profit until the owner is assured that a certificate of occupancy, or CO, can be issued and the contractor has completed all of the contracted work.

- **Building permit.** The lender will require a copy of the building permit obtained from the appropriate subdivision. The permit reflects the appropriate approval to build according to specific conditions imposed by the issuer, as have been provided for in the architectural plans.

- **Complete set of sealed construction plans and specifications.** The lender will require a complete set of construction plans, or blueprints, and specifications, signed and sealed by a licensed architect. The word *specifications* generally refers to a narrative provided by the architect that defines the materials, components, and other project specifications designated by the architect to construct the building. These plans and specifications will be independently evaluated by the lender's engineering consultant for feasibility with local building codes and the project budget.

- **Construction performance bonds.** The lender may require the general contractor to provide some form of financial surety, or bond, in order to assure the lender that the project will be completed even if the contractor does not perform. The bond is issued by a third party on behalf of the general contractor to ensure that any incomplete funding caused by the contractor's failure will be paid to complete the project.
- **Cost breakdown.** The lender will require a schedule of values that defines the cost assigned to each building component by the contractor. This information is relevant to the lender, who will have it evaluated for feasibility and reasonableness, and will be used to limit loan advances on each particular project cost category.
- **Curb-cut permits.** The lender may require the owner to provide copies of any curb-cut permits that have been obtained from the local jurisdiction when applicable. Curb-cut permits are issued to designate where the new project will be permitted access to a public road. They are issued with exact specifications of the size of the opening, required sidewalks, curbs and drainage, and the ingress and egress features needed for access onto the road.
- **Foundation survey.** The lender will require that a revised boundary survey be drawn of the project site after the foundation is set. This survey assures all parties that the foundation has been correctly placed on the property in conformance with local zoning, easement restrictions, and property lines. This survey must be reviewed before significant progress continues on other portions of the building.
- **Proof of project insurance.** The lender will require an insurance declaration form confirming that the project is adequately insured and specifically covers construction-in-progress. The declaration must name the lender as the "mortgagor" and "additionally insured" and provide for written notice to the lender prior to cancellation.
- **Proof of contractor's insurance.** The lender will require the general contractor to provide an insurance declaration form confirming that it has adequate liability coverage, workers compensation, and builder's risk insurance. The declaration must name the lender as the additionally insured and provide for written notice to the lender prior to cancellation.

- **Soil tests.** The lender may require the owner to provide copies of soil tests completed on the site to evaluate the percolation and compression. These tests are generally required to get the building permit.
- **Utility letters.** The lender may require copies of letters obtained from various utility companies confirming to the owner that these utilities have agreed to furnish their services to the subject property. These letters should be obtained from electricity, natural gas, telephone service, and water/sewer providers.
- **Zoning letter.** The lender will require a copy of a zoning letter from the appropriate subdivision confirming the zoning code of the subject property and defining the specific uses permitted on the property. This letter will generally be required to obtain a building permit.

Affiliated Business

An affiliated company is generally defined as any other business entity owned by any subject owner. If these cross-ownership interests are large enough (greater than 20 percent) or the affiliated companies are of a significant size relative to the owner's net worth, then they become fair game as part of the funder's underwriting, even though it is only looking to fund the subject business.

Said another way, the funder may feel the need to understand any and all business interests owned by any of the owners, partners, or shareholders and those will accordingly be reviewed along with the subject entity seeking funding.

The funder is justified in this kind of review, since it needs to fully understand the entire risk of funding not only the principal business but its owners, who may have other interests or obligations that create a conflict. The funder wants to ensure that no obscure, unexamined financial or legal relationship exists that could undermine the repayment of its funds or the perfection of its interests.

If affiliated businesses exist, expect that the funder will want to review the same depth of information that has been requested for the subject business (financial, etc.), because it needs to understand those entities just as thoroughly.

Franchise Business

Many small business owners choose to affiliate with a franchise business concept. Franchise businesses are those that have developed a specific concept, name, method, or image to conduct business and then leverage that through affiliated businesses that have been licensed to use the same. One of the strengths of this strategy is that franchisors usually are selling the business owner an operating plan that has been tested and proven successful with other business organizations.

There are many advantages to this strategy, such as the access to proprietary products; efficient, professionally developed operational plans; and a well-known business identity to sell. Name recognition in the public marketplace is easier to promote with the backing of a national organization.

All of these advantages come with a price, payable in the form of a sizable advance franchise fee and an ongoing royalty of sales or a contribution to national advertising costs based on a percentage of sales. However, businesses with a mature franchise organization generally do have a lower failure rate than nonfranchised businesses.

If the business owner is seeking to finance a franchised business concept, the funder will need the following information to evaluate the financing request:

- **Information on franchisor.** The funder will want to be familiar with the franchisor, particularly with less commonly known ones that may not yet have a profile in the territory. The funder should be provided with the marketing materials that provide sufficient information and that convinced the owner to select a particular franchise.

  The funder may also want independent references from others familiar with the franchisor's success in order to feel comfortable with the concept and value. It will probably also research the franchisor's operating history and financial resources on its own.

- **Franchise agreement.** The funder will require a complete copy of the proposed franchise agreement. The funder needs to know the exact terms of the agreement and how it impacts any proposed financing risk with the subject business.

  Learning more about the franchisor's operation and track record is pertinent, since the funder will evaluate the proposal from a worst-case scenario. For example, what would happen if the funder had to foreclose or takeover the franchised business?

  Does the agreement provide for the funder to assume the owner's rights under the agreement and use of the trade name? Can the funder assume other franchise rights in the franchise agreement such as proprietary equipment and business methods? Most important, would the funder face obstacles in transferring the franchise to a third party? Funders are in the finance business and will always sell the business rather than operate a going concern.

  The answers to these questions would directly affect the funder's interpretation of the transaction risk and how to value the franchise as a source of repayment.

- **Franchise Disclosure Document (FDD).** The Federal Trade Commission requires franchisors to disclose their operating statement and financial history, in addition to information about the franchise success and management. This report is intended to protect prospective buyers from being misled by fraudulent or incomplete information from unscrupulous franchise sales representatives. A copy of this report should be provided to the funder for review.

7

OWNER DETAILS

Lenders will require personal information about all persons who own an interest in the business and about those who may be prepared to guarantee the loan (in this chapter, both referred to as the "owner." The personal information is needed for the lender to assess these people's eligibility as participants in the business as per the lender's credit policy and to evaluate their contributions to the business and credit.

The information covers a broad range of facts relevant to borrowing ability as well as a confirmation of identity and background. Certain disclosures could result in further consultation by the lender concerning specific events or records. The information required includes:

- **Full owner name(s).** As simple as it may sound, the lender needs to know the exact *legal* name of each owner. "Bucky" may work on the golf course, but the lender wants to know if the owner's actual name is "Theodore," or something else. That being said, if the owner is also widely known by an unrelated nickname, the disclosure of that name is also pertinent.

  For an owner who has legally changed her name, a copy of the official document that mandated the change should be provided as well, so that the lender has the opportunity to satisfy due diligence for both names. Failure to disclose the existence of a name change may give the lender the impression that the owner has something to hide.

- **Current/previous address(es).** This basic information is required by the lender for its records for future contact, if necessary, and as identification confirmation when the lender requests credit reports or other reference information.

- **Date of birth.** While federal law prohibits a person's age from being used as a qualification (or disqualification) for obtaining a loan, the owner's date of birth is still important to the lender. This data is used to confirm identification when the lender requests a credit report or other reference information.

- **Social security number.** This information is required to confirm identification when the lender requests a credit bureau report or other reference information. It also might be required for any bank lender to comply with the reporting responsibilities it has with the Internal Revenue Service or other governmental regulatory agencies. The rise in identity theft, tax fraud, money laundering, and other financial crimes has led to a number of monitoring activities by various parties.

- **Credit authorization.** The lender may ask each owner for a written authorization to obtain a credit report on each owner, shareholder, or partner who will be guaranteeing the requested loan. The credit report discloses the past credit history of the owner along with other information affecting qualifications.

  This information is needed for the lender to determine whether the owner has satisfactorily managed earlier credit relationships or whether unresolved issues or problems exist that bring into question the likelihood of being repaid. The credit report will also reveal if there are any matters of public record regarding the owner, such as civil judgments, tax liens, bankruptcies, or debts under collection.

  Of note, the owner granting authorization for the lender to obtain a credit report generally signs a broad statement that authorizes additional information to be secured as well. Namely the lender is granted the right to contact past and present employers, creditors, and other parties whose experience may be relevant to the lender's assessment of credit risk. If owners want to limit that kind of authority they should be specific in whatever they sign.

  Owners should be aware that while they are protected from third parties gathering or using independent credit reports, business entities are not. The lender can obtain a business credit report (such as a Dun & Bradstreet Report) on the business at any time for any purpose. These business statements are generally much less accurate than owner statements, but the information is not considered private.

- **Place of birth.** Owners should expect any government-guaranteed lender to request the owner's place of birth. Whether it's additional evidence of identification, citizenship, or for a background check is unknown, but it is required information from the lender so the lender will ask.

- **Citizenship.** Due to the growing number of immigrants in the United States, most lenders have become much more conscientious about requiring owners to declare their country of citizenship. If the owner is not a U.S. citizen, proof of alien status may be required, and if the owner has not attained permanent resident alien status, it may be harder to obtain credit.

  The lender must confirm that the person will not be required to leave the country prior to the repayment maturity of the financing. Additionally, lack of permanent resident alien status will raise the question of whether or not the owner would be flight risk in event of default, depending on the nature of business and loan.

  Foreign citizens must have at least a permanent resident alien status to qualify for any government loan guarantee assistance such as SBA, USDA, or Ex-Im financing.

- **Military service.** Owners should expect a government-guaranteed lender to request information about military service. Whether it's for statistical records, special handling, or checking against military record problems is unknown, but it is required information from the lender, so the lender will ask.

- **Affiliated interests.** An affiliated company is generally defined as any other business entity owned by any subject owner. If these cross-ownership interests are large enough (greater than 20 percent) or the affiliated companies are of a significant size relative to the owner's net worth, then they become fair game as part of the underwriting for the lender who is looking only at the subject business for funding.

  Said another way, the lender may feel the need to understand any and all business interests owned by any of the business owners, partners, or shareholders, and, accordingly, they will be reviewed along with the subject entity seeking funding.

  For most government-guaranteed lending programs, the affiliate information will be germane for another reason—it will be used to collectively determine whether the owner meets eligibility limitations as to the size of the interests of the business.

Personal Financial Information

The lender will require complete financial disclosure of all the owners who have an interest in the business. This information is pertinent to fairly evaluating the proposed loan and the financial capacity to back it. For government-guaranteed loans, this information helps the lender confirm that all owners are eligible for financing assistance by not having exceeded financial resource limitations collectively or individually.

The financial information of all owners informs the lender about how well they have managed their affairs and, as important, what kind of resources they bring to the table for the prospective financing transaction. While no guarantee, the financial well-being of the owners will strongly influence the prospects for success in the pursuit of financing. The lender will require the following information.

Personal Financial Statements

The lender will require personal financial statements from all business owners and from any other party who may have been proposed to personally guarantee the loan. The personal financial statements provide the lender with an accurate summary of each owner's assets, liabilities, income, and other pertinent financial information.

Most lenders use standard personal financial statement forms. See Figure 7.1 for a copy of a form developed by Charles Green & Co. Even when not borrowing money, it's a good idea for all owners to prepare updated financial statements annually. This information is useful for their own financial planning purposes, such as making sure they have sufficient insurance coverage, their wills are up to date, and their estate planning has not changed.

Whether the owners prepare their own financial statements or have an accountant prepare them, they may be asked to submit this information on the lender's form. Most lenders will accept the form as long as it is attached to the signed form representing that the information is accurate.

All owners should also be aware that the lender will expect that this representation be no more than 60 days old. Submitting a financial statement that is 60 or more days old is useless, particularly if wealth is heavily represented by the value of the business, publicly traded securities, or other volatile-valued assets. The lender wants to have the most recent representation of the situation under consideration.

Sometimes owners submit inaccurate financial information, which hurts their chances of being approved for financing. Certainly some of these erroneous submissions are made out of genuine confusion or the lack of understanding as to how to define the requested financial information.

But other owners intentionally try to inflate the appearance of their financial wherewithal by offering information that they believe will convince the lender that they are a better qualified applicant than is the case. Even more disturbing is that

FIGURE 7.1 Personal Financial Statement

PERSONAL FINANCIAL STATEMENT
CONFIDENTIAL

NAME: _____

ADDRESS: _____

EFFECTIVE DATE _____

CITY, STATE, ZIP: _____

TELEPHONE: (H) _____   (B) _____

E-MAIL ADDRESS: _____

BUSINESS / EMPLOYER: _____

Section 1.	ASSETS & LIABILITIES

This Personal Financial Statement is provided to the bank ("Bank") to whom it is delivered for the purpose of inducing Bank to extend or continue to extend credit to undersigned Applicant ("Applicant"). The Applicant represents and warrants that the information provided is a complete and correct statement of the financial condition of Applicant as of the date of this document. Applicant agrees to promptly notify Bank of any material changes in the information provided that is detrimental to Applicant's ability to repay all amounts that are or may become due to Bank. In absence of such notice, Bank will continue to rely on this Personal Financial Statement as a complete and correct statement of the financial condition of Applicant.

ASSETS	(Omit Cents)	LIABILITIES	(Omit Cents)
CASH ON HAND & BANK ACCOUNTS .... $		ACCTS PAYABLE & OTHER LIABILITIES...... $	
SAVINGS ACCOUNTS .... $		CREDIT CARDS, LINES OF CREDIT,	
IRA, 401-k, & RETIREMENT ACCOUNTS .. $		NOTES PAYABLE & INSTALLMENT LOANS ... $	
ACCOUNTS & NOTES RECEIVABLE ...... $		(Describe in Section 2)	
LIFE INS. CASH SURRENDER VALUE ..... $		TAXES PAYABLE from prior years .... $	
(Describe in Section 4)		(Describe in Section 3)	
MARKETABLE SECURITIES .... $		LOANS ON LIFE INSURANCE POLICIES ...... $	
(Describe in Section 5)		(Describe in Section 4)	
CLOSELY-HELD SECURITIES .... $		MORTGAGES ON REAL ESTATE .... $	
(Describe in Section 6)		(Describe in Section 5)	
REAL ESTATE .... $			
(Describe in Section 7)			
AUTOMOBILES & VEHICLES (Section 8).. $		TOTAL LIABILITIES .... $	
OTHER ASSETS & PERSONAL PROP.... $			
(Describe in Section 9)		NET WORTH .... $	
TOTAL ASSETS $		TOTAL LIABILITIES & NET WORTH $	

INCOME		PERSONAL INFORMATION	
SALARY.. .... $		A. SPECIFY TOTAL CONTINGENT LIABILITIES	
INVESTMENT INCOME .... $		B. SPECIFY CURRENT BUSINESS / OCCUPATION	
REAL ESTATE INCOME .... $		C. MARITAL STATUS?	
OTHER INCOME (Describe below)* .... $		D. NUMBER OF DEPENDENTS?	
TOTAL INCOME $		E. PRESENTLY A DEFENDANT IN A LAWSUIT(S)?	
Description of Other Income Sources (Amounts)*:		F. HAVE YOU EVER DECLARED BANKRUPTCY?	
		G. DO YOU HAVE A WILL?	

SECTION 2. NOTES PAYABLE, INSTALLMENT LOANS, CREDIT CARD AND OTHER DEBTS

Note Holder	Original Amount	Monthly P+I or Interest Payment	Collateral or Endorsement?	Maturity	Current Balance
Total Monthly Payments			Total RLOC & Loan Accounts		

(continued on next page)

FIGURE 7.1 Personal Financial Statement *(continued)*

SECTION 3.		TAXES PAYABLE FROM PRIOR YEARS			
Taxing Authority		Payment Due	Payment Terms	Liens?	Total Obligation
			Total Taxes Due from Prior Years		

SECTION 4.		LIFE INSURANCE CASH SURRENDER VALUE			
Insurer		Beneficiary	Face Value	Cash Value	Policy Loans
	Total Policy Values				

SECTION 5.			MARKETABLE SECURITIES		
Investment or Account	# Shares/Units	Value Share/Unit	Market Value	Margin Debt	Net of Margin
			Total Portfolio Value		

SECTION 6.			CLOSELY-HELD SECURITIES		
Investment	# Shares/Units	Value Share/Unit	Source of Valuation	Shares Pledged?	Current Value

SECTION 7.	REAL ESTATE OWNED		
	Property 1	Property 2	Property 3
Property Description / Address			
Property Title In Name of:			
Date Property Acquired			
Acquisition Cost of Property			
Present Market Value			
First Mortgage Balance			
Second Mortgage Balance			
Net Property Equity			

SECTION 8.	AUTOMOBILES & OTHER VEHICLES			
Automobile & Vehicle Description	Acquisition Cost	Source of Valuation	Asset Pledged?	Current Value
			Total Auto & Vehicles	

SECTION 9.	OTHER ASSETS & PERSONAL PROPERTY			
Other Assets & Personal Property	Acquisition Cost	Source of Valuation	Asset Pledged?	Current Value
			Other Assets & Personal Prop.	

The undersigned Applicant authorizes Bank to make whatever credit inquiries deemed necessary in connection with this financial statement. And further, authorizes any third person, consumer reporting agency, or other reference provided by Applicant to furnish to Bank any information it has or obtains in response to such inquiry. Applicant certifies that information presented herein to be complete and factual and acknowledges that knowingly making false statements to a federally insured Bank is a federal crime punishable a by fine of up to $1 million, imprisonment, or both, pursuant to 18 USC Section 1014.

_____   _____
　　　　　　　Signature　　　　　　　　　　　　　　　　　Signature

_____   _____
Social Security Number   Date of Birth   Social Security Number   Date of Birth

some owners will try to understate their financial positions in an attempt to shelter certain assets from the lender's view.

These efforts are easily recognized by an experienced lender. It is good to keep in mind that lenders will quickly lose confidence in erroneous financial statements and probably decline a request without explanation. There are too many good deals for them to consider without wasting time with some shell game with obviously fraudulent information.

It is also important for owners to remember that misrepresenting *anything* in an application for a loan from a federally insured financial institution is a federal crime carrying severe punishment if convicted. While it's unlikely that owners would be prosecuted if the loan were turned down, think about what might happen if lenders believed these misrepresentations and it's later discovered that they were misled. That's when the quality of life of the owners starts sinking.

To prepare a personal financial statement that meets the lender's information requests and fully discloses a true financial position, there are some guidelines each owner should follow that will ensure compliance and provide an accurate picture of the information that represents all personal wealth.

Each owner should start by establishing a report date and describe the various asset and liability accounts at their approximate value, as best known on that date. Tying the statement date to the nearest month-end when statements for the various asset and liability accounts may have been received is a good reference point. The owner should round all financial entries up or down to the nearest $100 for simplicity.

The personal financial statement is not an audit, so each entry will not be verified to balance to the penny. Nevertheless, the owner should be assured that the lender can spot exaggerations and will raise questions about any entries that seem out of context or unrealistic. Credit reports are also used to compare any reported personal liabilities to the debt disclosed of the financial statement. They should match closely.

Here is a line-by-line description of all of the categories on a typical personal financial statement and an explanation of what information is being requested. Failing to include any asset in this declaration means that the owner will probably diminish her financial status by not including all of the value in her net worth. Failing to include any liability in this declaration may get the owner accused of trying to inflate her net worth by hiding debt. Each owner must take care to include everything relevant to describing a picture of true financial status.

Assets. Assets are tangible or intangible property that represent where owners have stored their wealth. By measuring either cash, cash equivalents, or other property that owners have accumulated, lenders can get a sense of their past income.

1. **Cash on hand and bank accounts** refer to cash that may be on hand, if significant ($1,000 or more), plus monies kept in demand deposits accounts (checking accounts).

2. **Savings accounts** refer to monies kept in restricted accounts, certificates of deposit, or other accounts that can be readily converted to cash at some point in the near future.

3. **IRA, 401(k), and other retirement accounts** refer to pretax savings and investments that are subject to penalties for withdrawal before age 62.

4. **Accounts and notes receivable** refer to funds owed to the owner, which should be converted to cash upon payment at a scheduled point in the future.

5. **Life insurance cash surrender value** refers to a portion of a whole or universal life insurance policy that can be withdrawn upon demand.

   Note: This figure *does not* refer to the face value of insurance coverage and is not applicable to term insurance policies. The financial statement provides space on the second page for more details about all life insurance policies where details can be added to better inform the lender about the nature of these assets and their value.

6. **Marketable securities** refer to investment-grade securities owned that are traded on a stock exchange and easily convertible to cash due to the existence of a readily available market for trading them. They are highly liquid, with constantly fluctuating values. The financial statement provides space on the second page for more details about these securities to better inform the lender about the nature of these assets and their value.

   Note: All liquid asset accounts (including any cash accounts or other assets that can be readily converted to cash) should be listed according to the most recent balance the owner can confirm with documentation. If the transaction depends on a contribution of cash from the owner as part of the deal settlement, the lender will usually require balance verification of these funds before closing.

7. **Closely held securities** refer to ownership interests in a business enterprise that does not have a readily available market to sell them to. This category is probably where the ownership value of the subject business would be listed. These assets should be valued according to a reasonable assessment of the market value of the company or, more conservatively, the company's book value. If market value is used, the owner should be prepared to justify these figures with some data.

   Any value should be prorated to reflect the owner's share of ownership. The financial statement provides space on the second page for more details about closely held securities where details can be added to better inform the reader about the nature of these assets and their value.

8. **Real estate** refers to ownership in any type of property and should be valued at the likely price it could be sold in a reasonable time. The financial statement provides space on the second page for more details about individual properties, including the address, titled ownership, purchase date, purchase price, current market value, and current mortgage balance. This additional information is necessary to provide context about the valuation of the property assets, which often comprise a majority of an owner's net worth.

9. **Automobiles and other vehicles** refer to the cars, trucks, boats, motorcycles, or other vehicles that are owned by the owner. The financial statement provides space on the second page for more details about these vehicles where details can be added to better inform the lender about the nature of these assets and their value.

10. **Other assets and personal property** refer to personal property assets (such as furniture, art, silverware, furs, jewelry, antiques, silver, and other household effects) or other nonliquid assets that don't belong in the previous categories but are not related to the subject business (such as equipment, livestock, patents, copyrights, etc.). The lender will not want to use these assets as collateral, but inclusion of these asset values is a relevant disclosure of the owner's wealth accumulation.

Categories 1–10 should be totaled to calculate the total assets.

Liabilities. Liabilities enumerate the owner's obligations to pay a debt in the future. Whether it's a mortgage loan used to purchase real property or credit card balances used on a business trip, the sum of liabilities will offset the total value of an owner's total assets.

11. **Accounts payable** refers to liabilities that include credit accounts from local sources, open accounts with vendors, sums owed to miscellaneous parties, or other liabilities not classified in any other category.

12. **Credit cards and revolving line of credit account** refer to liabilities that include any Visa, MasterCard, American Express, Discover, and other revolving consumer credit accounts not secured by real property.

13. **Note payable and installment loan** refer to liabilities that include any car loans, financing leases, personal notes, student loans, or other loans paid on scheduled installments.

14. **Taxes payable** refers to liabilities to a local, state, or federal tax authority.
15. **Loans on life insurance policies** refers to liabilities that have been drawn from a whole or universal life or similar insurance policy account.
16. **Mortgage on real estate** refers to a liability that encumbers the owner's real property including equity lines of credit.

Categories 11–16 should be totaled to calculate the total liabilities.
Net Worth is the total assets minus total liabilities.

Other Statement Details. After detailing the owner's assets and liabilities and calculating the net worth, other details will be requested by the lender to provide context to the financial information.

17. The owner will be requested to estimate total annual income and identify its primary source, such as salaries, real estate, income, investment income, interest, or other sources. These various sources should be detailed separately on an annualized basis.
18. The personal financial statement form includes questions requiring disclosure of other information. These questions may range from contingent liabilities, occupation, marital status, number of dependents, whether the owner has a will and, if so, the name of the executor.
19. The owner must be sure to sign and date the financial statement at the bottom of the second page. It's worthwhile for the owner to read the fine print contained on the statement, since signing it will indicate acknowledgment of, agreement to, and compliance with all that it says.

Personal Tax Returns

The lender will require owners to provide complete copies of their personal income tax returns for the past three years.

- **IRS Form 4506.** To combat potential fraud, many lenders now require businesses to execute IRS form 4506, which authorizes the IRS to provide the lender with a transcript of the borrower's tax return from specific years. Lenders use these transcripts to verify that it matches the information provided directly from the loan applicant.
- **Certification of Tax Returns.** Lenders may sometimes require owners to certify the authenticity of the tax returns submitted to support a commercial funding request. They may ask that the owner sign a statement of

authenticity or maybe just add an original signature on the face of a copy of the documents.

The former is certainly easy, but the latter demands more attention. Adding a signature to an honest financial statement is no big deal, but certifying a copy of a personal tax return is a little more complicated. An owner should not sign on the signature line of a copy of the tax return. Legally speaking, the copy of the return could be interpreted as a new original by the IRS and could potentially create a new tax liability claim. Instead, the owner should sign in the margin using a blue or red pen so that the signature is easy to find and obviously not copied.

Derogatory Personal Information

Every owner involved with the subject of financing must be prepared to respond to the direct questions concerning any derogatory events that may be part of his personal history. Preparing to face these issues in advance will enable the owner to answer more thoughtfully before being made to feel defensive and may assure the lender that he is transparent and taking responsibility for the situation.

If there are particular derogatory circumstances that will likely affect the lender's financing decision, these circumstances should be presented to the lender at an early stage of the application process. With increasing frequency, many owners have extraordinary conditions that require special handling by the lender on a case-by-case basis.

During the past several years, thousands of owners and businesses with great character and impeccable credit have encountered conditions beyond their control that have tarnished otherwise perfect financial histories. A lethargic economy, soaring divorce rates, and escalating traumatic health-care costs are constantly evolving attributes that have affected millions of people.

These circumstances can vary, ranging from the indiscretions of youth to family catastrophes. Often these circumstances have nothing to do with the owner's previous business performance, moral recognition of an obligation to repay debts, or prospects for succeeding in the future. However, some events take on a life of their own, and the owners will have to deal with the record of what happened.

With the 2008 financial crisis barely passed, the number of Americans who have or continue to face serious financial challenges is larger than in any other time in our history except during the Great Depression. And in today's more seasoned economy there should be more latitude to deal with industrious businesspeople.

Full disclosure about difficulties and the absence of recklessness can render a derogatory situation into something akin to forgivable, but the path to that point begins with complete honesty, direct responses to tough questions, and full disclosure without evasion.

Any response from the owner along the way that appears to be intentionally misleading or withholding anything from view will damage the owner's credibility. The more serious matters are a matter of public record anyway.

An owner should advise the lender if she or any other individual owner or partner:

- Has ever been involved in personal bankruptcy or insolvency proceedings (even if it preceded the 11-year credit reporting period)
- Has ever been an executive officer of a business involved in bankruptcy or insolvency proceedings
- Is currently under indictment, on parole, or probation
- Is currently involved in any pending lawsuits
- Is not current or paid up-to-date on all tax obligations (local, state, and federal)
- Has ever been charged with or arrested for any criminal offense other than a minor motor vehicle violation
- Has ever been convicted, placed on pretrial diversion, or placed on any form of probation, including adjudication withheld pending probation, for any criminal offense other than a minor motor vehicle violation

It's better to be forthcoming with this kind of information before being asked, even if the lender has not discovered it yet. Typically these kinds of facts will emerge sometime in the process anyway, and failure to introduce them could appear to be an effort to hide something.

The effect of this kind of history is entirely subjective based on the event, the owner's involvement and response, its cause, and the lender's interpretation of the facts. Obviously a prior conviction for embezzlement will be treated more seriously than a citation for exceeding hunting limits. Honesty is the best policy.

It's important for the owner to be meticulously forthright with the lender in discussing these situations. Was the owner at fault? Was the owner a victim? Can the owner rehabilitate this situation?

The lender must evaluate if, based on the facts presented, the owner presents a greater risk due to this event and should therefore be disqualified from financing. This question might automatically be answered in the affirmative unless the owner convinces the lender to consider these previous problems in a context that may mitigate obvious concerns.

The following suggestions are intended to assist owners in overcoming derogatory situations under which their personal record was tarnished through events that may or may not have been beyond their control. Hopefully, these events need not forever prevent owners from advancing to their next opportunity in life.

This discussion is not intended to instruct anyone on how to develop excuses to mask a record of failure, deceit, or fraud. By following these important steps in explaining the particular situation, owners can develop thorough documentation to support their required explanation in a transparent, honest manner.

The following topics represent some of the most common events that lead to derogatory credit. Owners should evaluate the ones relevant to their situation and develop an explanation, taking into account the suggestions offered.

Bankruptcy

Bankruptcy is a provision of federal law for an individual or a business to resolve the difficult financial situation of being insolvent or overleveraged with more liabilities than assets. From a business perspective, bankruptcy can be a radical strategy to manage the devastating impact of a severe business or economic disruption. Though susceptible to abuse, bankruptcy can be the debtor's best logical decision in many circumstances.

The decision to seek bankruptcy protection should not be made lightly and will definitely carry a steep price. Many businesses have filed for protection prematurely on poor or no advice without recognition of the consequences. Once the decision to file is made, the debtor will have to live with it for many years.

Often bankers will have a knee-jerk negative reaction against any party that has previously sought protection under bankruptcy, which probably reflects an institutional bias. They react to bankruptcy as the ultimate violation of business morality. Their predisposition is both unfortunate and unfair.

Legitimate bankruptcy cases do not involve morals—they are about money. Bankruptcy is usually not about an unwillingness to repay money but rather the inability to do so. Out of lack of understanding or perhaps an intolerant attitude, sometimes lenders' attitudes represent a challenge to obtaining financing once bankruptcy is part of a borrower's past.

Bankruptcy cases are under the jurisdiction of federal courts to protect owners or companies from creditors when their existing or potential liabilities exceed their assets. This protection is intended to prevent any particular creditor from unfairly collecting a debt at the expense of other creditors. It also protects debtors' legal rights while giving them safe haven to reorganize or liquidate assets in an orderly manner to repay their obligations. Bankruptcy can provide debtors a second chance without undue interference from creditors.

There are three classes of bankruptcy:

- **Chapter 7.** This class of bankruptcy is for liquidation of the debtor's estate to settle claims against it. A trustee is appointed by the court to supervise the sale of assets, and the proceeds are distributed according to the court-mandated priority of claims. Debtors can generally retain their essential property, such as personal residence, vehicle, etc., if they can continue paying the outstanding obligations they owe.
- **Chapter 11.** This class of bankruptcy is generally for the reorganization of a business, although owners can qualify for this chapter. In Chapter 11 debtors are permitted to retain most of their assets but have to restructure their financial affairs in a court-approved plan that reflects their ability to pay their debts back from future earnings from the continuing business operation.
- **Chapter 13.** This class of bankruptcy is for owners to restructure or renegotiate the repayment terms of all liabilities with creditors according to the priority established by the court. Regular payments are usually made through a court-appointed trustee until all debts are satisfied.

There are countless circumstances, reasonable and otherwise, that lead parties to seek protection in bankruptcy court. Many parties are forced to choose this strategy due to events beyond their control. In some cases, borrowers will have the chance to overcome the stigma of bankruptcy and start over.

One of the most widely studied U.S. corporate bankruptcy cases involved a publicly owned manufacturing company known as Johns-Manville Corporation. This company was formed in 1858 as an early asbestos manufacturer of roofing materials.[1]

Asbestos was used for decades in roofing, insulation, and other building products but was later determined to be a carcinogen, exposure to which is a cause of mesothelioma, a form of cancer. Johns-Manville was targeted with a flood of lawsuits from thousands of persons who had contracted the disease from exposure to asbestos materials. Johns-Manville was faced with a catastrophic liability that would have continued to grow until it consumed the company.

In 1982 the company filed a preemptive bankruptcy case that enabled it to develop a trust that could provide for payment of these undefined future liabilities while continuing to operate as business that would earn out the settlement claims. This action ensured its ability to survive and pay all eventual claims, which were filed for victims of its products. The trust still exists today.

---

1. http://en.wikipedia.org/wiki/Johns-Manville

This strategy was a bold move that changed how bankruptcy is viewed. Using bankruptcy as an offensive strategy permitted the company to settle its liabilities, which would have never been accomplished without court protection. And it meant the company would survive and pay later claimants, whose claims could not be quantified at the time of filing. Today Johns-Manville continues to produce over $2 billion in annual revenues and is owned by Berkshire Hathaway, the investment holding company controlled by Warren Buffett.

Obviously, bankruptcy is susceptible to being abused by those who file, but it must be stressed that bankruptcy can also be a legitimate, strategic tool available to make better a bad situation that threatens owners and businesses. Some lenders bristle at the notion of negotiating with borrowers who have had a bankruptcy case in their past, but each case must be evaluated according to its own particular circumstances.

The lender should not assume that a borrower who has been involved in a bankruptcy case has a character flaw. There are plenty of cases where overzealous or unreasonable creditors have forced bankruptcies rather than seeking more prudent and viable remedies to deal with problem situations. And lenders should recognize that another lender's inflexibility can sometimes only make bad situations worse and leave borrowers cornered with very limited options that unjustly penalize them over a longer term.

Lenders must consider the circumstances surrounding any borrowers who have been involved in a bankruptcy case and give them an opportunity to explain their case. Sometimes a better test of character is watching how the borrower manages to reemerge and start a new business again after bankruptcy.

Borrowers involved in a prior bankruptcy may actually become a lower risk for lenders. These borrowers have a wealth of experience in dealing with difficult situations, better preparing them for the economic risks associated with operating a small business. Surviving these tough circumstances adds to the borrower's management and financial education.

If a company has been involved in a bankruptcy case, the lender will usually discover this fact very early in the application process. It's better for the owner to disclose the facts before the lender reads the information in a credit report.

Credit reports include information about prior connections with any bankruptcy. In addition to personal bankruptcy cases the credit report records any business in which the borrower was on record as an owner, an executive officer, or a partner. Even if the owner had no control over the events leading to a business bankruptcy, he must be prepared to explain the circumstances of the case.

Because the proceedings of a bankruptcy case are a matter of public record, the lender will be able to obtain a copy of the entire case file to verify everything—the dates, creditors, debts, and final disposition of the case. In other words, a less-than-honest account of the bankruptcy case could permanently destroy the owner's credibility with the lender.

In addition to telling the bankruptcy story, the owner should provide a written explanation and accompanying documentation for the lender's study and review. Because the lender's representative will have to relay this information up through a hierarchal chain of credit authority, it's better for the owner to transcribe a detailed account as the basis for the lender's report without relying on the credit decision to be made with secondhand information.

The owner should document the circumstances thoroughly with a time line and substantiate any difficulties that led to seeking bankruptcy protection. If the owner was truly a victim of circumstances, the facts should be documented and supported with affidavits from other parties, accident reports, medical records, pictures, newspaper articles, and any other information available for corroboration.

The owner should prepare a detailed summary of how the case was resolved and remember to discuss what happened after the case was dismissed. This brief needs to be supported with documents verifying the owner's personal involvement in the situation, court filings, financial reports, and trustee's report. How have the owner's affairs changed since the bankruptcy? What has the owner accomplished toward putting things right?

If the bankruptcy experience was due to imprudent management rather than tragic circumstances, this truth is equally important. Depending on how much time has elapsed, how much money was lost by the creditors, and how the owner has managed in the postpetition period, the lender may still consider the loan application.

Litigation

Living in the most litigious society in the world can give a new meaning to the word liability. Because over 75 percent of the world's lawyers are in the United States, American citizens have higher odds of being sued over a dispute. This exposure is increased for small business owners. Sometimes they must spend considerable sums and suffer financial damage when the only wrong they committed was to be accused.

When the owner's financial statement is scarred with the extraordinary costs of defending a suit or settling one to limit defense costs, the owner needs to provide a detailed explanation to the lender to set the record straight. When the owner puts the matter in context, the lender has a chance to appreciate the impact of the litigation on the company's finances. This explanation helps the owner move the application process beyond the legal situation so that the positive aspects of the funding proposal can be considered.

The lender should receive copies of the lawsuit and the owner's response. In justifying the business's side of the dispute, the owner should be prepared to provide copies of invoices, receipts, and other documentation to show how the business was affected by the suit. If the owner's attorney wrote a detailed opinion of the owner's situation, the lender should be given access to a copy.

At least the lender will understand the owner's situation after this disclosure and not fear the risk of unknown parameters. Nevertheless, even if sympathetic, the lender retains the responsibility of underwriting the proposal in the best interest of the lender and will have to take the outcome of the lawsuit into account, regardless of whether or not the owner was at fault.

Most lenders will not proceed with a loan request if there is a material lawsuit pending at the time of the application. Routine matters that occur in the normal course of business and do not threaten the owner's financial condition should not interfere with the funding application. However, if there are any unresolved substantial matters against the company, the lender will probably wait until final judgment has been rendered before proceeding.

Judgment against the business could significantly change its financial condition. If the owner were forced into a large settlement or if the other party was given a lien on the business's assets, the lender could suddenly have a problem loan. The collateral assets securing the loan could possibly have more claims outstanding than value.

If the situation has already cleared the judicial process and the owner has lost the judgment, the lender will be interested in how the owner handles the matter. The owner must honor the judgment, and the lender will be watching to see how the owner reacts, since it may be indicative of the owner's character and fortitude to move on.

Divorce

Divorce can be disastrous for an owner. Because the process can be emotionally strenuous for all the owners involved, months of underperformance in business responsibilities may result. In addition the financial stability can be disrupted if one spouse is forced to buy out the business ownership interests from the other.

If the owner has recently completed a divorce, it's important to provide an explanation to the lender about any impact the divorce had on the business or on the owner's personal financial condition. The owner should document this explanation with copies of bank records, of financial statements, and of the final divorce settlement. Disclosing personal (that is, emotional rather than financial) aspects of the divorce should be avoided, as they are not only irrelevant but also potentially distracting and therefore detrimental to the funding application.

Because of the stressful issues in divorce cases, the vengeful actions of one party may create liabilities for the other party. Alternatively, one party may refuse to pay legitimately allocated liabilities that are in the names of both parties. Divorce can become a disaster to the owner's credit history and to the future ability to borrow money.

The owner needs to carefully document these circumstances in order to demonstrate vulnerability in such situations. Divorce is probably the most abused excuse used by people with bad credit. To earn credibility, the owner has to show how the negative credit performance was created through the irresponsible actions of the former spouse.

The best defense the owner can put forward is to make payments toward or pay off any unpaid accounts whether individually or jointly held, regardless of who was supposed to pay them according to the divorce decree. It is important for the owner to try to protect a good credit history when possible and pursue the other party later for recovery of these sums. To limit future exposure, the owner should immediately close the joint credit accounts when the divorce process first begins and notify creditors that he will not be responsible for future liabilities created on any account by his spouse. While the owner can't escape liability on joint balances, a notice can prevent a creditor from holding the owner liable for subsequent charges.

After discovering negative credit report information as a result of the divorce the owner should contact the three major credit bureaus, Experian, Transunion, and Equifax and provide a short, concise statement detailing the situation. The credit bureaus are obligated to include this explanation in all future reports.

If the divorce is not yet finalized, the owner should consider waiting until it is before seeking business funding. While the owner is resolving the complicated and emotional issues of divorce, anxiety will be compounded by the pressures of business finance. The owner will benefit by focusing on the business at hand—one major negotiation at a time.

Bad Decisions

To err is human, but some mistakes are more costly than others. In a challenging economy and a digital age, strategic decisions must be made and remade on a routine basis. Because owners are constantly making decisions with long-term implications they will sometimes make costly mistakes.

In a rapidly evolving world small business owners often perform as the chief executive officer, chief financial officer, chief operating officer, advertising agent, transportation specialist, tax expert, and computer programmer; then they go home to be a compassionate parent and a loving and supportive spouse. These roles are defined and regularly redefined by a constant stream of ideas from reality TV, sitcoms, talk show hosts, YouTube, movies, talk radio, social networking, blogs, and billions of e-mails. So how can anyone make mistakes? Maybe the real question is how can anyone really know the best decision with the world changing so much day to day?

It's an age overrun with ideas and communication. Today's eighth wonder of the world is tomorrow's dinosaur. More decisions are demanded than ever before, but humans are still limited to one brain.

When discussing errors with the lender, the owner's candor is factored into an assessment of the actions taken to overcome the mistake. If the owner qualifies under the other criteria necessary to obtain financing, previous errors should not preclude it.

Bad Health

Consider what would happen to the economic status of an owner who becomes ill for an extended period. There are many possible consequences, and most of them include serious financial damage. Should that mean that the owner can never qualify for business funding? What if the owner had a spotless track record before the illness?

It hardly seems fair that after battling to survive personally, the owner should also have to battle for the survival of the business. Once the owner recovers, there remains the hard work of helping the business to recover.

The answer is for the owner to provide written proof to communicate and confirm the medical circumstances to the lender, who wants to know how the illness affected the owner and the owner's participation in the business.

The owner can hope for compassion for these situations but should still expect to bear the burden of proof. Rather than telling the lender of all of the gory medical details related to treatment and procedures, the owner should just give a generic description of this personal information.

After informing the lender of any health situations, the owner should turn the conversation's focus to the financial details of the business. The lender will ask: How much time did you have to spend away from the business? Who replaced you and at what cost (both salary and lost revenue or productivity)? Is the illness behind you and the financial damage contained? If the owner provides satisfactory answers to these questions, the parties can begin evaluating whether a new loan can be part of resuming normal business activities in the future.

Bad Credit

Compounding several of the problems mentioned earlier is the trickle-down effect each problem has on the owner's personal credit history. If the owner's cash flow is interrupted for any reason and cash reserves are exhausted, payments to creditors will slow accordingly. This problem must eventually be dealt with, since slow credit payments are one of the most troublesome problems in the eyes of the lender.

It's important to manage personal credit closely to keep one's payment history clean and avoid perpetuating negative entries into a credit record. Lenders focus on a number of aspects in the credit report, including the total amount of credit outstanding, payment history, and any public records that indicate the unsatisfactory conduct of personal affairs.

Nowadays, to assess a prospective borrower's creditworthiness, most lenders rely on a credit score, which is a proprietary index determined by a number of demographic factors and quantified behavioral statistics, including:

- Length and continuity of current and previous employment
- Length of residency and whether the borrower owns or rents
- Amount of total indebtedness
- Ratio of outstanding credit to total available credit
- Evidence of any legal judgments, tax liens, foreclosures, or bankruptcy
- Payment history on existing and previous debt over the last seven years
- Evidence of unsatisfied collection effort on private debts
- Number of inquiries from prospective lenders

As recently as 2009, the national average credit score was around 700, with about 58 percent of the population having scores of 700 or higher. Statistically it has been asserted that an owner with a score of 599 or less has a 51 percent probability of a serious default (60 or more days) on a mortgage loan.

Understanding how to manage this process cannot change a previous poor credit record, nor is there a magical way to repair bad credit. It is wise to be wary of people promising to repair credit and improve a credit score overnight. The debtor can do for a fee whatever these people can do. All they can do is root out the errors and mistakes on a report and possibly improve its accuracy. And even attempting to do that for someone else may be illegal in some states.

Modifying current and future performance can improve a business owner's situation and end the poor performance reflected in the recent credit report. Owners should begin by using the following strategies:

- Pay off as much credit as possible by using savings, having a yard sale, taking back recently purchased merchandise, liquidating assets, withdrawing money from the business, collecting outstanding debts, or drawing down the cash surrender value of a life insurance policy.
- Cash should be obtained (without borrowing more) to pay off these accounts as fast as possible. Rather than reducing all the accounts, the ones with the lowest balances should be paid off first. It's better to have 5 past-due accounts than 10.
- After the small debts are cleared, the owner should prioritize by paying off debt with higher payments or higher interest rates first. Paying off these accounts first gives the owner more flexibility in the future.
- Payments should be managed so as not to ever go beyond 30 days past due if possible, even if it means hand-delivering the payment. Payments less than 30 days late are not reported to the credit bureau.
- If cash shortage is temporary, the owner should arrange to limit the number of creditors who will receive late payments. Rather than making one $500 payment on time and being late on four payments of $125, it's better to pay the four accounts on time and be late only on the one $500 payment.
- The credit bureau does not receive reports of late payments from such liabilities as public utilities, telephone companies, cable operators, insurance policy loans, and private note holders. Slowing payments to those accounts will not affect a public credit record and may help keep it clean. Getting too far behind on utility bills, however, risks service disconnection requiring a deposit be paid to restore service.

If the business owner has bad credit the lender should be told why. Sometimes bad credit is not the result of poor management or lack of responsibility but rather of circumstances that affect the business owner's ability to meet business responsibilities consistently. To earn the lender's confidence, the owner must prove that those circumstances have improved to the degree that they will not interfere with the owner's ability to repay the requested financing.

Make the Case

Lenders will discover all of the derogatory information early during their due diligence process, so it's better for the owner to introduce the topic and provide a full explanation up front. Voluntary revelation removes any lender suspicion that the owner may have attempted to hide information and provides a transparent forum in which to illuminate the lender's understanding of any such history.

Notwithstanding the owner's willingness and preparation to come clean, it's strategically worthwhile to first get the lender interested in the deal. Introduction of any derogatory information too early may end the chances of getting fair consideration for the corpus of the deal. Once the lender has enough data to be genuinely interested in the deal, then, and only then, should the owner introduce any derogatory issues that need explanation and get them out of the way. At the right time, the lender will move the dialog about how funding needs can be met in light of the owner's former situation.

The owner should support the explanation of derogatory information by preparing the following documentation as needed:

- **Detailed explanation of derogatory event.** Provide a concise, well-written explanation of the derogatory event providing a logical sequence of all pertinent details. It shouldn't be so long as to be tedious or beyond relevance, but it shouldn't be so short that the lender doesn't get the full story.
- **Chronological chart.** It can help support the explanation to have a chronological chart showing when relevant, specific events occurred. The chart should be easy to read, short on wordy references, and 100 percent consistent with the written explanation.
- **Supporting documents.** Provide any pertinent documentation generated by other parties that support the explanation—copies of checks, charge invoices, paid notes, court filings, police reports, insurance records, and whatever else is relevant. These items should be indexed and available for review. Never hand over original documents.

While a substantive explanation is intended to overcome the lender's concern about the owner's derogatory experience, the owner should elaborate as necessary and move the discussion back to the main topic: getting money for the venture. If the lender can't get around the owner's former problem, the owner should move on to the next lender and not beg.

8

TOO LITTLE VS. TOO MUCH MONEY

One of the most critical decisions to make in the process of chasing business capital is determining how much to ask for. If the business owner can't justify the amount of the financing or articulate a clear path to return it, the deal is going to be declined.

Without preparation, the business may find that it has spent considerable time, effort, and money getting financing that is either too small to cover the identified needs of the business or too large to comfortably repay. A thoughtful effort to create a reliable budget for the financing is imperative.

Homing in on the right amount to finance requires attention to details and consideration of some of the contingencies that face the enterprise. The company must dissect all the components of the original funding purpose and quantify all direct and indirect costs involved.

Underestimating how much external financing is needed threatens to over-extend the internal financing resources, since the business will be committed to a particular strategy and will have no choice but to move forward. If the external funds don't go as far as expected, the business will have to utilize internal resources that probably were planned for use as operating capital.

Such underfunding can mean that other important costs do not get met, and the business falls behind with inadequate resources. This situation can lead to many bad consequences while the business scrambles to keep operations going. Failure can follow quickly.

The ugliest part of inadequate funding is that the lenders sometimes share the blame. In the rush to book a deal they may either cajole the business owner into reducing the loan size for the lender's protection or the lender may not adequately evaluate the owner's budget to determine whether the loan is adequate for the outlined plans.

Overestimating can be as detrimental as underestimating. Extra unused funds may create a false sense of liquidity that can lead to imprudent or reckless spending. Plus, the company is saddled with inflated debt service on funds that ultimately are not creating wealth for the enterprise.

Business owners often inflate, or sandbag, the details of how much money they need to convince the lender to extend a larger loan than may really be necessary. The extra cash is intended to either provide a cash reserve for themselves or cover costs that may not be eligible for financing. Often business owners are trying to just lower their equity contribution by raising the size of the loan and repaying their own funds back after the deal closes.

The risk of this strategy is that the extra money also inflates the cash repayment requirements. Will the extra money result in higher sales or profits? Most likely not, but higher payments narrow the margin between profits and payments, meaning the owner will have less cash to reinvest in the business or to distribute.

The added risk to the business owner means that the transaction is a higher risk to the lender. Higher risks often pay off for both parties, but the other possibility is that the business does not succeed due to higher costs and less cash. These conditions can snowball into a very difficult operating environment that ultimately does not survive.

The lesson here is to be focused on how much money is really needed by the business when assembling a proposal for external financing. The business owner should examine and reexamine the proposal budget to ensure that the results are as realistic as possible. Inaccurate financing, whether too little or too much, can wreck a good business plan and lead to business failure.

How Much Capital Should the Business Seek?

When presenting a financing proposal the information will represent many weeks, maybe months of consideration to provide a plan of action for the business that needs money to work. The business owner should provide a detailed assessment of the capital needs and show how the money helps the business generate profits that repay the loan.

But how does the owner know how much to ask for?

The owner must know the playing field. Before presenting a proposal to any lender the owner should have an understanding of exactly how that lender leverages certain financing situations, particularly those similar to the one at hand.

Commercial banks, for example, operate in a common business environment, but there are many factors that affect their lending policies and how they approach particular loan opportunities. How much a bank will extend on a real estate loan will be influenced by the bank's age, capitalization, location, and regulatory condition. Further, the bank management's experience in real estate lending, its real estate portfolio size, and its portfolio mix will also affect the leverage, pricing, and risk appetite with which it will review the owner's proposal.

These circumstances mean that before the business is even finished preparing its proposal, the owner must be out talking to a number of potential sources to sound out how each will react to the general loan scenario. The owner must consider these talks to be the same as doing research or gathering intelligence.

Discussions at this stage of the search should be more about the bank than about the business. Important details of how the lender approaches the loan the owner seeks will help the owner finalize the proposal and establish more realistic expectations. The owner should not allow the conversations to get drawn into the business yet, but rather should find out what the lender can do.

Important intelligence to gather about a lending institution's approach includes:

- How much leverage will the lender give for the owner's business purpose, or what percentage of the total money needed will the lender advance?
- What loan-to-value limitations does the lender set for the particular use of funds?
- How does the lender determine what interest rate to charge for a loan in the discussed category?
- What kind of closing costs are typical for a loan in the specific category?
- Will the lender include those closing costs in the loan calculation?
- How would the lender secure such a loan?

Important intelligence about an investor's approach to gather includes:

- What stage of business funding is the investor attracted to and what is the size limit of the investor's investments?
- What size returns is the investor looking for and in what time frame is the ideal investment redeemed?
- What is the investor's due diligence process and what kind of agreement is the lender looking for in the investment transaction?

Investing the time to determine this kind of information from many funders will help the owner understand which funder is best suited to meet the needs of the business. By seeking this information from a number of sources the owner will understand not only the funder but also the entire market.

This kind of information can greatly assist the owner with the final financing proposal. Leverage, pricing, and closing costs are major components of any plan and the more specific, accurate information the owner has up front the better prepared the owner is to present a realistic proposal.

So, armed with this information, how much financing should the owner seek? As much as is needed, of course, up to the funder's leverage limits and approach to financing the costs. Less than the funder's maximum leverage is desirable for many reasons discussed below, but it is important for the owner at least to understand what the lender's maximum loan would be and not ask for more.

The research done on the available lenders should equip the owner with the ability to determine approximately how much money the lender would advance if its many criteria were met. There will be differences, sometimes huge differences, in how different lenders approach a loan such as the one the owner suggests.

These differences are created from many influences that may not even be important to the owner. But ultimately the determination of how much the owner requests should be decided by reasons unrelated to "how much will they give me?"

How much the owner requests should be a calculation of total funding needs less the owner's financing contribution. If this calculation results in a shortfall greater than the maximum lender's leverage, the owner will know the money can't be obtained.

How Much Capital Should the Business Expect?

A funny thing may happen when the owner attempts to assess the financing market in the area in which the business operates. A particular lender says that it will advance up to 90 percent leverage on a particular loan type. The owner spends a month developing a plan based on that information and when presented to the banker, it's rejected. Why? Because the owner wasn't told all the conditions that needed to be met to get the higher leverage.

As in advertising, there are always conditions under which certain offers are available. It's defining those conditions where the owner really learns about the availability of financing. Consider automotive sale ads that describe a brand-new car as available for only $199 per month. It sounds very affordable.

The fine print of the ad then describes why: to get the payment down to $199, the buyer must make an extraordinarily large down payment (better known as equity) and agree to a financing term that will probably last longer than the car.

The same is true with some commercial lenders. They will promise the moon to get an owner in the door and then try to influence the owner to accept their deal. Their deal is a nice way to describe the amount of money they feel comfortable advancing the owner without fearing that the owner won't be able to repay it.

Similar to the earlier advice about not letting the business's needs be determined by how much a lender will lend, the owner should also not let expectations be set by how much the lender says it will lend, until a commitment letter is on the table. If the lender promises the owner 80 percent loan-to-value (LTV), the owner should try to limit the request to 75 percent LTV.

The point is that it is important for the owner to exercise good judgment rather than to allow a third party to make these decisions based on what's in that party's best interests. Setting expectations is an important component to business planning.

The owner should expect to get what she wants by setting expectations on realistic terms. The owner should not look for the maximum leverage, but rather try to strengthen the funding proposal by lowering external funding needs.

If the owner does the homework she'll understand what kind of money is available to the business in her market. The owner should allow this information to temper the funding request and lower her needs rather than set targets that aim to leverage the business to the hilt.

Financing the Business Should Consider

If the owner can be honest and competent with regard to business, he will determine how much financing, internal and external, is needed for the business plan. Hopefully, good instincts and sound judgment will ground that determination with a reasonable balance between the new venture risk and the risk of exposing financial security.

Selling this concept and good business sense to a lender may be an easy task or a tough sell. Depending on how aggressive the owner is or how conservative the lender is, a deal may be negotiated seriously based on the respective needs or requirements of the parties.

The owner should not accept any financing offer that does not completely meet the needs of the business. And the needs of the business should be decided by the owner and not by someone else. In particular, the owner should not let someone else who does not have a personal stake in the business or the financing decide what is best for the business. Or worse, the owner should not let people who stand to make money only if the owner follows their advice to decide. The owner must decide what meets the needs of the business.

Many loans can go bad before they are made. Some lenders try to squeeze their exposure lower by convincing the business owner to accept a smaller sum. Some business owners decide they can make things work even when faced with inadequate financing. Owners and lenders get wrapped up in making the deal rather than focusing on what the financing is supposed to accomplish.

Business owners sign the financing contract and become responsible, often personally, to repay or return the money. Promissory notes and investor agreements don't restrict repayment to only those parties whose ideas succeed; everyone is expected to return the funding on time and at the price as agreed. Therefore the owner should unilaterally take responsibility for the decision of whether to accept the financing offer.

If the financing offer is inadequate the owner needs to go back to the drawing board and come up with a new plan. Changing plans and directions at the negotiating table just to adapt to a particular financing offer means that someone else's needs have become the priority. If the lender's needs can't be met within the confines of financing that meets the owner's needs, the deal should be scrapped. It's not worth the risk to the owner to just make a deal.

It's normal for there to be a certain amount of negotiating involved in any deal, but the owner should shy away from transactions that greatly reduce the amount of money requested. Unless those funds are immediately replaced by an alternative source or are available from internal reserves, the owner should stick to what was asked for.

The owner should not alter the business plan at the negotiating table. If the owner can't get the money at that time, retreat and reevaluation of funding alternatives and their affect on the business are in order. There may be other sources or different ways to approach the situation. Most likely there is a competing lender that will have a different answer or at least a different approach.

Which Comes First—the Plan or Capital?

How does the owner start over if the proposal is rejected? Hopefully, with the same vigor and energy with which the owner began the financing process. But, on the second round, the owner should try to work smarter rather than harder.

If the business proposal gets rejected, part of the explanation may be that the credit policy of the lender will not permit the proposed deal. Or maybe the structure of the deal is too highly leveraged for that lender or for the market. Only the research will tell.

So the owner has to modify ambitions and determine whether it is possible to generate the resources for the enterprise in another way. Where to start? At the very beginning, of course.

Before altering anything, the owner should proofread the proposal to ensure it's accurate in terms of what needs to be done, how much it will cost, and how it will be paid for. Sometimes simple mathematical errors creep in during the process of assembling massive amounts of data.

Is each cost number correct? Do the pro formas make sense? Is the financing proposal realistic? Why was it declined? To get financing on some terms the owner will have to start over and rethink the strategy to fit the market for financing, if possible.

But modifying does not mean retreating entirely. Maybe the idea is right but the owner's style is to move too big, too fast, or too soon. Maybe the plan needs to be scaled back to a slower pace rather than rewritten. Maybe the logic is fine but needs some time to percolate so that everyone can be comfortable with the scope of the projected growth.

The owner should move slowly to modify the proposal and make sure that all changes are consistent with long-term plans. Scaling back costs usually means scaling back income potential. Projections will have to be overhauled to adjust to a different size enterprise.

The owner must examine and reexamine planned expansion, making sure the reasoning is sound, and review assumptions as to how various data gets translated into supporting the plans for the business. The owner has to question everything again and take nothing for granted.

It is important for the owner to remember that financing must come from internal sources as well as external sources. Plans must strike a balance between the new venture risks and the heavy external debt reliance risk. The owner should limit or scale back plans to a level where internal funds can pay for at least 20 percent of the costs.

If the final numbers of the revisions don't work, then the owner should wait. Maybe today is not the right day to get funding approved. Maybe the owner's ideas are beyond what is affordable. Maybe the owner has to find another way to attract financing, like finding a partner or working as an employee of someone else. The owner should take care not to try to force the idea into a situation where there are inadequate funds.

The owner should ask: Is my proposal consistent with the market for financing? Did I do enough research? Or did I ignore the research results? The owner is limited to what is available, so the deal has to conform to what external sources are there. If it won't, the owner must wait.

Part 3

Financial Reporting for Rookies

9

FINANCIAL INFORMATION
MAKES OR BREAKS THE DEAL

Too many small businesses pay accountants and bookkeepers thousands of dollars annually for preparation of financial statements and tax returns without reading a single report they prepare. Incredible as it sounds, many business owners probably wouldn't even have these financials prepared except that they are required to file tax returns, and, if they want to borrow money, the bank requires financial statements.

These facts are even more disappointing when considering that business owners "just don't know what they don't know." Embracing the financial metrics of a business is getting to the real starting line of success.

Every lender will require and analyze the balance sheet, income statement, and statement of cash flows for a business. By tracking the financial results, ratios, and trends, a lender can quickly assess the strength of a company and will even compare it to other companies in the same industry.

By determining the positive (or negative) trends of these results, a funder weighs the risk of providing money to a business. After all, the funder is primarily interested in the owner's ability to produce future profits to either repay the loan to a lender or build the value of the company in order for an investor to sell her interests.

The funder's analysis and decisions are generated from information found in the financial statements and tax returns that the business owner is already paying a lot of money to produce. Shouldn't the owner understand what all the fuss is about and maybe even understand it *before* making it a part of the funding proposal?

This chapter explores the fundamental construction of the financial statements, defines the various parts of the statements, and connects the statements as they integrate a variety of information that illuminates the DNA of the business.

No one should be more concerned about the financial reports of a business than its owner. By gaining command of this information, the business owner has a powerful tool to improve the management of the business and plan for its success.

A 60-Minute Lesson in Accounting

Accounting is the documentation of the financial history of a business. Every transaction—that is, every penny of income and expense, every asset acquired and owned, every liability incurred or accrued, and the sum of the contributed or earned owner's equity is recorded according to generally accepted accounting principles (GAAP) and constitutes the financial statements.

The financial statement itself does not describe success or failure—those are the interpretations of the business owner or funder reading it. The financial statement does reflect the results of business operations, defined as a profit or loss, and the relative financial strength of the enterprise based on the accumulation of assets in excess of liabilities, defined as equity or net worth.

Business accounting uses a number of different statements and levels of analysis. The information the business owner needs to present and to what degree the lender requires that the information be independently verified are dependent on the relative size of the business and how much money the owner is seeking from other parties.

A financial statement has two primary components, the balance sheet and the income statement, which are explained below in detail with all their classifications and categories.

Balance Sheet

The business statement of condition is universally referred to as the balance sheet because of its basic construction: three main classifications of financial accounts (assets, liabilities, and owner's equity) are quantified there. The relationship of these three classes must be equal (or balanced) as follows: Assets must equal the sum of liabilities and equity. These three classifications and their subcategories are defined below.

Assets. Assets are the tangible or intangible properties of the business. They might include real property, equipment, patents, rights to cash, and any other assets that are categorized and totaled at their fair value.

- **Current assets.** Some of these business assets will be cash or other assets that will be converted into cash within the next 12 months. They are known as current assets. This asset category includes cash, accounts receivable, inventory, and short-term notes. These assets are recorded at their net realizable value.
- **Fixed assets.** Some assets have been acquired to facilitate the business operation's efforts to generate revenues. These assets generally are used by the business over a long term and are known as fixed assets. This asset category includes land, buildings, leasehold improvements, equipment, furniture, and vehicles. These assets are recorded at their cost but adjusted annually to reflect their declining value (depreciation or amortization).
- **Other assets.** Some assets may or may not be used in the business for revenue generation. They may be tangible (insurance cash surrender value, or CSV, security deposits, etc.) or intangible (trademarks, copyrights, or goodwill) and are known as other assets.

Liabilities. Liabilities are obligations of or monies owed by the business, contracts to pay, and estimates of future debts in committed transactions.

- **Current liabilities.** Some debts or obligations required to be paid within the next 12 months are called current liabilities. This category includes accounts payable (repetitive expenses such as utilities, couriers, and other service invoices) and the portion of mortgage or note installments due in the next 12 months.
- **Long-term liabilities.** Some debts or obligations that are due after 12 months are called long-term liabilities. This category includes the portion of loans, leases, notes, or other obligations that are scheduled for payment after the next 12 months.
- **Other liabilities.** Some obligations, such as deferred liabilities that represent an obligation of the business but are not definitively scheduled as a current or long-term liability, are classified as other liabilities.

Equity. The sum of monies invested by the owners in the business along with the increase (decrease) in earnings over time is defined as the business equity or net worth.

Note: In this text and in many other sources, the terms *equity*, *owner's equity*, and *net worth* refer to the excess value of business assets minus business liabilities. These three phrases are interchangeable and equivalent and all represent the same number.

- **Owner's equity.** These funds may be represented on the financial statement in several different ways, depending on the legal organization of the enterprise and the order of preference of the investors in the business. For partnerships, equity may be listed as interests. For corporations equity will be listed as shares, either common or preferred, depending on the preference rights granted by the business to shareholders. LLCs might list equity either way.
- **Retained earnings.** The other contributor to equity is the ongoing, undistributed retained earnings of the business. Whether cumulative (prior periods) or current (profit/loss since the end of the last fiscal year), this equity category reflects growth when the business holds on to its profits.
- **Treasury stock.** Sometimes the business will buy back or retire ownership shares or interests held by owners, and the sums paid for these shares or interests will be referred to as treasury stock.

The basic construction of the balance sheet is that assets minus liabilities equals the equity of the business. A positive equity reflects that the business has more assets than liabilities and therefore a better outlook. A negative equity reflects that the business has more obligations than assets, which technically is bankruptcy.

A representation of how these components relate to each other to produce a balance sheet is found in Figure 9.1.

For each entry made to each balance sheet general ledger account recording the business activities, whether asset, liability, or equity, there must be a debit and credit for every entry. Simplified, it means that each receipt, payment, addition or subtraction to any assets, liabilities, or equity accounts requires two entries—an offsetting debit and credit. There must be a counter-entry to an asset account for each entry made to a liability or equity account.

For example, paying an invoice lowers the company's liabilities (credit) but also lowers its cash (debit). Making a profit at the end of the year adds a sum to retained earnings but must be represented in the assets as a corresponding higher balance in cash, receivables, or even inventory. Accordingly, the corresponding balance sheet relationships must always be in sync.

There are common metrics used to analyze a company's balance sheet that are described later in this chapter. These ratios can help the business owner or funder better measure and track how much cash the business has or expects to collect to cover its obligations (its liquidity) and how high the business's obligations are compared to its equity (its leverage). Tracking these statistics will be useful when predicting the ability of the business to pay its bills and to repay borrowed funds used to finance the business.

FIGURE 9.1 Balance Sheet Component Relationships

	ASSETS		LIABILITIES		OWNER'S EQUITY
	Current Assets		Current Liabilities		Equity Contributions
plus +	Fixed Assets		Long-term Liabilities	plus +	Retained Earnings
plus +	Other Assets	plus +	Other Liabilities	minus -	Treasury Stock
equals =	**TOTAL ASSETS**	equals =	**TOTAL LIABILITIES**	equals =	**OWNER'S EQUITY**

BALANCE SHEET

TOTAL ASSETS

equals =

TOTAL LIABILITIES

plus +   OWNER'S EQUITY

Other Balance Sheet Relationships

	Total Assets		Total Assets		Total Liabilities
minus -	Total Liabilities	minus -	Owner's Equity	plus +	Owner's Equity
equals =	**Owner's Equity**	equals =	**Total Liabilities**	equals =	**Total Assets**

Income Statement

The summation of business operations is known as the operating statement, more commonly known as the income statement. This financial statement component reflects the sum of operating revenues, less the direct costs and indirect expenses associated with producing revenues, and finally tabulates the net profit (loss), which is the sum of what revenue is left after all the costs and expenses are recognized.

Note: There are two interim and one final calculation of operating results to segment where operations are producing profits: gross margin, EBITDA, and net profit. These interim calculations provide management with better insight as to where revenues are being spent to create income along the path to profitability.

There are several key account subcategories contained in the income statement:

- **Revenues.** The total sum of monies paid to the business for goods or services produced in the normal course of operations. This account will also include any discounts granted and any nonrelated revenues generated from investments or extraordinary activities.
- **Cost of goods sold (COGS).** The sum of all direct costs spent to produce goods or services that are sold to customers. The COGS are limited to those that are directly tied to the business output, including raw materials, labor, and other such expenses necessary for production.

- **Gross profit.** Revenues minus COGS is commonly referred to as the gross profit, or operating profit. This figure is a litmus test of profitability to determine if a business is earning money on its core business operations before the indirect expenses or overhead is considered.
- **Expenses or overhead.** The sum of all indirect expenses incurred by the business is described as overhead, or operating expenses. These costs may include such expenses as rent, accounting, legal, insurance, property taxes, utilities, and any other expense except those costs used directly to deliver goods and services.
- **EBITDA.** This is an acronym for the calculation of "earnings before interest, taxes, depreciation, and amortization" and describes the operational profit (or loss) before the costs of external financing, taxes, or its noncash asset depreciation or depletion expenses are taken into account. This calculation goes further to determine how the business performs based on revenues minus direct and indirect costs.
- **Net profit.** The net sum of total revenues minus COGS, overhead, financing costs, depreciation, amortization, and income taxes is described as the net profit. This figure is the ultimate result of the business operation.

A representation of how these components relate to each other to produce an income statement sheet is found in Figure 9.2.

Timing

The annual financial statement is prepared at the end of the company's 12-month operating period. Most businesses use December 31 as their year-end date to coincide with the calendar year, but any date of the year can be used. Sometimes, companies may choose to use the month they began business as the beginning of their fiscal calendar or will round forward (or back) to the nearest quarter end. Common fiscal years end on March 31, June 30, or September 30.

The annual financial statement describes operations from the first date of the fiscal year through the next 12 months until their end date. For example, if December 31 is selected as the year-end date, a financial statement on that date reflects operations from January 1 through December 31.

It's a good idea for business owners to prepare financial statements at least on a quarterly basis to monitor ongoing financial progress. Better-managed businesses will track their financial statements on a monthly basis. A timely financial statement is ultimately the strongest tool used to measure the success of a business. Understanding the components used to construct it and monitoring its content is essential for any entrepreneur intending to sustain growth and optimize success.

FIGURE 9.2 Income Statement Component Relationships

	Total Revenues
minus -	Cost of Goods Sold
equals =	**GROSS MARGIN**

	Gross Margin
minus -	Operating Expenses (Overhead)
equals =	**EBITDA**

	EBITDA
minus -	Interest costs
minus -	Income Taxes
minus -	Depreciation
minus -	Amortization
equals =	**NET PROFIT**

There are three levels of financial reporting:

Compilation. This financial report has the lowest level of independent review, since the accountant tabulates only the internally generated report of receipts and payments with limited responsibility to disclose more than the obvious. This financial data is less formal and compiled into a statement based only on classifications defined by the business.

The accountant will correct any blatant errors but will typically depend on the business owner's representations as to the accuracy and integrity of the report. The owner provides all of the information, which the accountant reports in a standard format.

Review. A review level financial report is prepared by the accountant who compiles the company's financial information and verifies its accuracy consistent with internal accounting policies and a complete record of company performance.

The independent accountant accepts a greater responsibility for the accuracy of this financial report by issuing a review opinion. This report is more expensive than a compilation, but the work product is viewed as much more reliable by the third parties who will request this information, such as investors or lenders.

Audit. The audited financial report requires the highest degree of accuracy and integrity of the three levels and is issued solely by certified public accountants, or CPAs. In an audit, the accountant prepares the financial statement after independently verifying that company records agree with outside customers and suppliers—in other words the accountant tests various revenue and expense categories to be assured that the business actually recorded the sales and paid the various costs represented in its financial records.

The accountant also tests the valuation of asset and liability accounts annually. The accountant confers with outside legal counsel to affirm that there are no material threats to the business. The accountant verifies that all accounting policies and procedures exist and are strictly followed by the company.

The audit report must contain the CPA's opinion regarding the quality of the internal controls and whether the report fairly represents the financial condition of the business according to GAAP. The report may be issued on a qualified (with conditions) or unqualified (without conditions) basis.

There are no legal or tax code requirements as to when a business should use one level of financial accounting report or another. This decision will be made by the business owner according to the need for accountability and verification of the business's internal financial controls and results, or as required by third parties when the business is engaged in an effort to raise business capital.

That being said, there is a definite need for greater independent review of financial reporting as a business gets larger. One owner cannot ensure the integrity of all employees to manage the business's money accurately or honestly, and it's the independent accountants who provide protection as the business grows larger.

Additionally, at some point when the owner plans to exit the business, depending on the size of the operation, third-party acquirers will require independently verified financial accounting to assure them of the valuation of the company ahead of acquisition.

Any business reaching the million-dollar revenue threshold would be wise to move up to the review level of financial reporting to get the benefit of independent verification of financial controls, to have reliable information for third parties, and to acquire a more accurate management tool with which to drive growth and monitor progress.

A compiled financial statement may be fine for a smaller, closely held company that is operated directly by its owner, no matter how large the company's sales are. Such a statement would suffice when there are no other shareholders, the owner does not plan to borrow money, and has a hands-on knowledge of the revenues and expenses of the business.

It is important for the business owner to recognize that the financial statement is probably the most important part of any financing proposal and greatly influence the lender's decision. Therefore the quality and independence of the statement are germane to the company's ability to raise external financing.

Any business with over $500,000 in revenues should utilize an in-house book-keeper or accountant to track its financial transactions and draft operating financial statements. A capable, experienced person in this role is essential, since this information is the basis for all accounting work performed for the annual financial statement and tax reporting. This function can be outsourced for a timely, cost-effective reporting stream as well.

Once external financing is obtained, lenders will require the owner to submit annual financial reports. With money in hand, the pressure for good, reliable data increases once the owner is being held accountable for the results. And such information should be available within 90 days after the end of the fiscal year.

Understanding the basic information contained in this section is as important as getting a business license. For the owner's own protection and for the opportunity to grow the business, it is necessary for the owner to learn about financial reports, what they reveal, and, as important, what they tell everyone else who receives them. Having reams of financial data without understanding it not only depletes the owner of an important management tool, but it can lead the owner to be discredited when pursuing valid opportunities for external financing.

Essential Financial Statement Literacy

Understanding the importance of maintaining sound financial reporting is only half of the battle required to fulfill the information needs imposed by external financiers. The stream of information they want will be broad, constant, and with a critical eye toward timing and accuracy.

Owners are expected to provide a continual flow of information showing the financial results of operations along with detailed reports that back up the more important fiscal representations. As borrowing needs increase, so too will the amount of data required to provide lenders with an in-depth, up-to-the-minute picture of the financial health of the business.

When the lender imposes financial covenants on the funding agreement, such covenants are intended to serve as a guardrail within which the business is expected to perform. The metrics to monitor these covenants will be reviewed on a regular basis, maybe monthly. If the lender is advancing funds against the company's current assets, the lender may review the account reports daily, since the current assets convert to cash on a regular cycle.

It is incumbent on the business owner to understand exactly what financial reporting is being requested before agreeing to provide it. If the owner is not prepared to generate and sustain the flow of data from the date of funding, she is also probably not ready to get the money. Starting out without the ability to report financial results in a timely manner means the owner would be constantly playing catch-up, which is expensive and stressful. Lenders are serious about information requirements and will become concerned if their requirements are not met on a timely basis.

It is not enough for business owners to understand what constitutes a financial statement; they must also be aware of what financial information lenders may request, how the lenders will use it, and what they, the owners, need to know *before* providing it. What follows is a more detailed description of these things.

Annual Financial Statements

As explained earlier the financial statement is an annual report card of the financial results of the business, reflecting the accumulation of assets, liabilities, and equity and of the profit/loss from operations. The owner will be expected to provide at least three trailing years' worth of statements (if available) at the initiation of a financing proposal.

The lender will examine the statements to evaluate the financial performance during each period and will compare them to understand how the results are trending. Trends will define longer-term success (or lack of it) as the business matures and management can influence revenue and profitability growth.

The lender will compare many year-to-year metrics and dissect the results to review a number of factors. The lender wants to understand the company's earnings growth, cash flow, liquidity, leverage, and performance, all of which helps the lender assess the risk of investing in the business. The owner's understanding of these same performance indicators helps in the search for funding, but more important, it helps the owner better manage the business.

Interim Financial Statement

The lender will usually require the financing package to include an interim financial statement that is not more than 60 days old. Updated financial information is very important to all parties but is even more urgent during the last half of the fiscal year, after more time has elapsed since the previous year-end report. Since business trends evolve constantly, without updated financial information, the previous year-end results may be irrelevant as an indicator of the strength of business operations.

If the business is a smaller one or is a business seeking lower funding amounts, internally prepared interim financials are generally accepted without being reviewed by an independent accountant. That said, the interim report should still be consistent with the recent year-end report and not introduce confusing information. The equity in particular should be consistent with the balance at the fiscal year-end so that the lender can follow exactly what happened from the last report to the new one.

Without the assistance of an accountant, the business may or may not accrue the ongoing depreciation or amortization expenses, or it may not be accounting accurately for the actual interest expenses being paid. The owner should be aware that the lender will discover these kinds of errors and may ask that they be corrected in the interim results before replying to the request for funding.

Reconciliation of Net Worth

A particular area of interest on the balance is the equity, or net worth section. Lenders initially want to know what the owners have contributed to the business in terms of start-up capital and then how well that sum has grown through the addition of earnings.

In a perfect scenario, the equity contributed by the original owners and investors is sufficient to get the business through the start-up phase and into profitability. At that point the net income produced each period is accounted for as retained earnings, unless dividends or capital distributions are made.

Dividends are periodic financial payments made to investors as a return on their investment, comparable to interest paid to a lender. Capital distributions are stock retirement or redemption, indicating that the business is lowering its equity by extraordinary payments to owners.

Lenders want see equity grow particularly by the retention of profits. Lenders don't like to see equity get lower, particularly with operating losses or by paying distributions or buying out owners. Beyond the addition of the current profit or loss to last period's ending equity, *whatever* causes the equity balance to change requires an explanation.

The business owner should provide the lender with a reconciliation of net worth, if needed, when submitting the financial statements. Sometimes this number will be changed by late adjustments made to the previous fiscal period's accounts that are not reflected in the final financial report. This is not a problem. The owner just needs to explain it to the lender rather than leaving it to the lender to figure out.

Providing a detailed explanation or schedule of these adjustments in the financial statement helps the lender acquire confidence in the financial reports and avoids the distractions of a protracted examination to define the adjustments.

Statement of Cash Flows

Formerly known as the statement of changes in financial conditions, this report summarizes how the changes in the balance sheet accounts and income affect cash and cash equivalents and breaks down the sources from operating, investing, and financing activities. As an analytical tool, this report is useful to determine the short-term viability of a company and its ability to meet its obligations.

Lenders weigh this report heavily because it breaks down the sources and uses of cash in the business without masking the origin of the cash or its use. Owners cannot hide behind greater borrowing or other concerns, such as rising inventories or overreliance on churning receivables. This report probably requires more study in order to comprehend it fully, but it is a good tool for lenders to use to see a given period's operation from a purely cash perspective.

Footnotes

All reviewed or audited financial statements will contain footnotes at the end. These notes are a narrative that provides the lender with a concise explanation of what happened, how the company performed, and other details to help interpret the numbers. This additional activity disclosure is deemed necessary to provide full disclosure of the company's condition.

Accountants may have to make some estimates or judgment calls to explain certain components of the financial report or account valuations. The footnotes provide the forum to fully explain these circumstances as well as describe conditions outside the financials that impact the company and its financial outcomes.

Financial Statement Analysis

In the age of spin control, it's beneficial for the owner to try to influence the interpretation of financial reports. This influence might positively affect the lender's reaction to real or apparent marginal trends in the business's financial results.

Preparation of a detailed narrative telling the facts behind the numbers will be helpful to explaining the conditions that led to the operating results, particularly when they contain less than positive results. When provided up front, such an analysis offers the owner the chance to answer many questions before they are asked.

Behind every number is an explanation of the result. Absent an explanation, the lender may interpret the data incorrectly. If the owner can guide that interpretation with pertinent information, it may make a difference in how the proposal advances.

In certain circumstances the owner may even prepare a comparative restatement of financial results if certain events or conditions unfairly skewer them. The restatement could highlight the results with and without particular adjustments in order to demonstrate the full impact of the noted information.

For example, imagine that a tax law change unexpectedly alters how the business may depreciate certain assets against taxable income. Such a change would affect the level of earning on the business's tax return in the form of higher depreciation expenses that lowered profits. While the change lowers the tax bill, it might cause the funder to think that profits are lower. An explanation of this situation is needed to provide insight into what transpired.

The asset would still be financed over a particular period and could still be in service to the business long after it was fully depreciated. Demonstrating the impact of this change by restating results (without the subject tax change) would give the lender a better perspective as to why, although profits may have been less than expected, the change did not result in a problem for the company.

Even without negative results or unexpected surprises a business owner should make a habit of narrating financial reports to demonstrate command of the information and ensure that the lender recognizes the accomplishments of the business.

Receivable Aging

For businesses that provide considerable open credit to their customers or accounts receivable, lenders will require accounts receivable aging reports. It's a good idea for owners to provide these reports for each previous year-end report submitted with the proposal.

The total of the aging should be equal to the balance sheet entry for receivables in that period and be segregated by the various categories of aging, i.e., 30 days, 60 days, 90 days, etc. The lenders will measure to determine how long the average account takes to pay and how much money is tied up in accounts and in past-due accounts.

Aging reports provide a summary of the company's accounts that quantifies the expectation of future cash collections and speaks to the quality of the accounts by their aging. Lenders watch the level of slower paying accounts, a concentration of volume in single accounts, and how many accounts ultimately do not get paid as indicative of the company's account policies, diligence to collect them, and quality of company sales.

The company should have a definitive policy about open accounts and be sure that the reports conform to the policy. For example, the company may stop advancing sales credit to clients who have unpaid invoices after 60 days. In this way, the owner presses the clients for some discipline and does not allow them to make the business their bank. If that is company policy, the owner should make sure that there are not any 120-day-old unpaid client invoices concurrently listed with unpaid 30-day invoices.

The presence of stagnant accounts or accumulation of bad debt will negatively impact the business by lowering cash collections for monies owed for operating investments. Alternatively, a higher number of accounts paying as agreed indicates that the business has liquidity with cash available to fund operations.

Inventory Aging

For businesses that utilize a significant volume of finished goods or raw material inventory to support operations, lenders will require inventory aging reports. It's a good idea for owners to provide these reports for each previous year-end report submitted with the proposal.

A good-performing business will manage all its inventory components so as to maximize the turn of those assets by converting to cash as efficiently as possible. Inventory might be classified in three distinguishable categories: raw materials, work-in-process, and finished goods. The inventory for a shirt manufacturing operation might include:

- **Raw materials,** such as bolts of cloth, boxes of buttons, and spools of thread
- **Work-in-process,** such as several stacks of cloth that have been cut into patterns or half-completed shirts with one sleeve attached and no buttons
- **Finished goods,** such as a completely sewn shirt, folded and packaged in a plastic wrap, ready for shipment

These assets must be managed to ensure that the company weighs the need for inventory on one hand with the availability and need for cash on the other. For example, the company should know how many raw material units it needs on hand to meet the work-in-process (WIP) cycle to convert to finished goods in sufficient quantity to meet monthly sales demands.

If that number is 5,000 units, the company should ensure it does not buy too many units in advance and tie up its cash too far in advance of conversion, lest it put financial pressure on working capital.

Aging reports provide a summary of the company's inventory that quantifies the expectation of future cash conversion for the business and speaks to the quality of the inventory by its age and how fast it converts or turns into cash. Lenders watch for the level of slower moving goods, WIP, and raw materials that move through the full conversion cycle and get sold as finished goods.

The presence of stagnant goods or accumulation of unrealized WIP will negatively impact the business by slowing cash conversion and possibly causing the business to write down operating investments in unsold goods. Alternatively, a higher turnover volume of goods indicates that the business has liquidity with cash available to fund more operations.

If inventory is a major component of the company's assets, the lender will be interested in how the business values its inventory, particularly which valuation method is used to account for it. Two predominant methods are available with which a company can record its inventory values:

- **First in, first out (FIFO).** This inventory valuation method records inventory based on the unit cost when it's acquired. That means that the units are expensed when they are sold based on the original price paid per unit.

  This valuation method is the more aggressive of the two methods, because it permits the business to retain presumably higher-valued units on the books while expensing the typically lower cost units. This method results in a higher inventory valuation and possibly lower COGS in the period.
- **Last in, first out (LIFO).** This inventory valuation method records inventory based on the highest cost unit. That means that the units are expensed when sold based on the latest market price paid without regard to the actual price paid for the particular unit.

  LIFO is the more conservative of the two methods because it requires the business to expense the higher-price units earlier as they are depleted, which results in a lower inventory valuation and higher COGS.

  While LIFO generally lowers period profits, it also lowers corporate taxes. Using the higher cost values from inventory over the course of years will tend to result in an inventory valuation that could be significantly lower than the actual market value of the goods.

Payable Aging

If the business depends on trade financing to augment its working capital, the lender will be curious about the company's aging report. This information provides insight into how much the operation depends on borrowed money to support sales and how well it's paying its bills. It's a good idea for the owner to provide these reports for each previous year-end report submitted with the proposal.

Whether and when the business pays suppliers, creditors, and taxes is indicative of its liquidity. Should payments begin to slow, the lender will take a hard look for causes of inadequate working capital.

Sometimes the business may get into occasional disputes over invoices or mistaken payment transfers. Generally these situations are one-offs and rarely show up more than one or two months. The lender will expect the owner to be in compliance with terms of trade creditors though, since they are a cheap source of financing.

Business Tax Returns

While the business will always be evaluated on its financial statements, lenders will also require copies of income tax returns. Three years' worth of returns are generally requested, and the returns should include all schedules.

There are some differences between tax reporting and financial reporting requirements that may result in differences in the business's results as reported on each respective report. Business owners often embrace expenses that can legally reduce their taxable profits where possible. Some of these expenses may not be fully deductible from the taxable income, meaning the taxable income may be higher than that reported on the financial statement.

At the same time, financial statements reflect the company's actual financial results, cash in and cash out. These statements are typically used by lenders and investors to evaluate financing transaction proposals.

When the differences between the two reports are significant, it's helpful if the owner provides a reconciliation of the reports to clarify the effects on the business. This information helps inform the lender about the different presentations and avoids confusion.

Understanding Other Financial Metrics

Lenders use a number of ratios to analyze the financial statement and determine the relative strengths and weaknesses of the business. These various calculations measure the liquidity (cash on hand compared to cash required), leverage (ratio of equity financing to debt financing), operating performance (profitability), and coverage (funding available to service future debt obligations) of the business. Lenders may compare the results to a composite of other businesses of similar size in the same industry.

Depending on the owner's financial acumen and effort, the owner can calculate and track these ratios on the company's financial results to get a better understanding from a different perspective of how the operation is performing.

This insight will help the owner know what to expect from the lender's evaluation of the financing proposal. More important, familiarity with these metrics will make the owner increasingly sensitive to the minutiae in the financial performance of the company, leading to the owner's becoming a better manager.

Tracking these ratios year-over-year helps the owner compare relative progress (or lack of it) by looking at ratios rather than at raw numbers and their relationship to changes in financial performance. Inclusion of such analysis in any proposal would certainly be a good demonstration that the owner has an interest in and command of the financial side of the business, which may benefit the proposal if the numbers are positive.

The most common financial ratios used to evaluate small companies are discussed below with an explanation of how they are calculated and what information they provide. A summary of these basic financial ratios is found in Figure 9.3.

Ratios are neither right nor wrong; they are simply figures that measure the borrower's financial performance period to period and relative to the performance of other borrowers in the same industry. Many bankers use the Risk Management Association (RMA) Annual Statement Studies as a guideline for industry norms when making a comparative analysis of financial ratios.

These RMA reports gather voluntary submissions of financial statements from thousands of businesses in every industry, as defined by the North American Industrial Classification System (NAICS). These financial statements are compiled and averaged to determine the median and mean of operating standards for every industry each year. These results are published by NAICS category in order to provide information about the relative financial condition and performance of each industrial sector.

The Annual Statement Studies offer business owners a comparative analysis of how their business measures up to its industry peers. Nonmembers can purchase the studies from RMA at: www.rmahq.org/RMA/RMAUniverse/ProductsandServices/RMABookstore/Downloads/StatementStudiesSIC/.

Liquidity Ratios

Liquidity ratios refer to measurements of the company's current assets to meet its current liabilities when due. Evaluating these components of the balance sheet will help the owner understand the adequacy of working capital at the current level of sales and predict how the business will fare with changes in revenues.

Current Ratio. The current ratio is a rough measurement of a company's ability to pay its current liabilities with its current assets. The word *current* refers to company assets that either are in cash or will be converted to cash within 12 months or are

FIGURE 9.3 Summary of Basic Financial Ratios

Liquidity Ratios

Current Ratio
$$\frac{\text{Current Assets}}{\text{Current Liabilities}}$$

Quick Ratio
$$\frac{\text{Cash \& Equivalents}}{\text{Current Liabilities}}$$

Sales/Receivables
$$\frac{\text{Sales (net)}}{\text{Accounts Receivable}}$$

Day's Recievable
$$\frac{365}{\text{Sales/Recievable Ratio}}$$

COGS/Inventory
$$\frac{\text{Costs of Goods Sold}}{\text{Inventory}}$$

Day's Inventory
$$\frac{365}{\text{COGS/Inventory}}$$

COGS/Payables
$$\frac{\text{Costs of Goods Sold}}{\text{Accounts Payable}}$$

Leverage Ratios

Fixed/Worth
$$\frac{\text{Fixed Assets (net)}}{\text{Tangible Net Worth}}$$

Debt/Worth
$$\frac{\text{Total Liabilities}}{\text{Tangible Net Worth}}$$

Operating Ratios

%Profits/Assets
$$\frac{\text{\% Profits before Taxes}}{\text{Total Assets}} \times 100$$

%Profits/Net Worth
$$\frac{\text{\% Profits before Taxes}}{\text{Tangible Net Worth}} \times 100$$

Sales/Assets
$$\frac{\text{Sales (net)}}{\text{Total Assets}}$$

company liabilities that must be paid within 12 months. The ratio measures the relative strength or weakness of the business's working capital, which is the quotient of dividing the current assets by the current liabilities.

With a 1.0x ratio the business has exactly the amount cash it needs to cover its liabilities. A higher ratio means the business has excess cash available to meet its liabilities over the next 12 months. The composition and quality of current assets are critically important to understanding the liquidity of a business.

This ratio is calculated as follows:

$$\frac{\text{TOTAL CURRENT ASSETS}}{\text{TOTAL CURRENT LIABILITIES}}$$

Ideally the business should be aiming for a minimum current ratio of 1.25x.

Quick Ratio (Acid Test). Referred to as the acid test, the quick ratio provides a more strenuous test of liquidity based on existing cash assets and cash equivalents that will quickly be converted to cash in the current period. For most businesses this definition means that accounts receivable can be used in this calculation but inventory cannot.

If the resulting ratio is significantly lower than the current ratio, it probably means that the business is relying heavily on the conversion of inventory to liquidate current liabilities rather than on converting previous sales to cash.
This ratio is calculated as follows:

$$\frac{\text{CASH} + \text{RECEIVABLES} + \text{EQUIVALENTS}}{\text{TOTAL CURRENT LIABILITIES}}$$

Ideally the company's quick ratio should never be below 1.0x.

Sales/Receivables Ratio. The sales/receivables ratio measures the number of times the accounts receivable are converted to cash, or turn over, during the year. If a company's ratio equals 12, that means the receivables are completely paid 12 times a year or are fully paid about every 30 days.

A higher ratio is desirable because it means that there is a shorter time span between the sale and cash collection. If a company's ratio is smaller than the rest of its industry, then it's underperforming. Perhaps the quality of the company's receivables or its credit and collection policies may need to be reviewed.

Reviewing this ratio over a period of several months and determining an average figure is a more effective way to track this ratio with greater confidence.
This ratio is calculated as follows:

$$\frac{\text{SALES (net)}}{\text{ACCOUNT RECEIVABLES}}$$

Depending on the industry norms and company's mix of cash and credit sales, the business generally should aim for a minimum 12x ratio, which would indicate that the business was completing collections of its receivables every 30 days. This calculation should be completed using the net sales figure, which is the final sales total after subtracting discounts, return, or adjustments from the gross sales total.

This ratio may not be a good analytical tool for companies with seasonal sales fluctuations or those with a high proportion of cash sales to total sales. It also only measures receivables to net sales at one point during the course of the fiscal year. Calculating this ratio monthly and tracking its average over time is the best way to use this ratio.

Day's Receivable Ratio. The day's receivable ratio defines the average number of days required to collect an account. Higher ratios (45 or more days) are indicative that the company's clients are dragging out payments and present more of a risk of becoming past due (depending on terms offered) or in default.

This ratio may point to the quality of the company's credit policies and procedures, its ability to influence clients with terms, or the quality of its client accounts.

This ratio is calculated as follows:

$$\frac{365}{\textbf{SALES/RECEIVABLE RATIO}}$$

Depending on the industry norms and the mix between cash and credit sales, generally the business should aim for an average 30-day turnover of receivables.

COGS/Inventory Ratio. The COGS/inventory ratio measures the number of times the inventory converts to sales or turns over during the year. If a company's ratio equals 12, that means the inventory sold 12 times a year or about every 30 days.

A higher ratio is desirable and indicates that the inventory components are being converted to cash more often, which usually means the company has better liquidity and good distribution. If a company's ratio is smaller than the rest of its industry, then the company's inventory may not be selling, may be obsolete, or may be overstocked.

This ratio is calculated as follows:

$$\frac{\textbf{COST OF GOODS SOLD}}{\textbf{INVENTORY}}$$

Depending on the industry norms, the products sold, and the manufacturing cycle, generally the business should aim for an average 12x ratio, indicating that the complete turnover of inventory every 30 days.

This ratio may not be a good analytical tool for companies with seasonal sales fluctuations. It also only measures inventory to cost of sales at one point during the fiscal year. Calculating this ratio monthly and tracking its average over the course of time is the best way to use this ratio.

Day's Inventory Ratio. The day's inventory ratio expresses the COGS/inventory ratio in the average number of days required to turn the inventory on hand. This ratio may be indicative of the adequacy of sales, quality of inventory management, or the quality of the inventory.

This ratio is calculated as follows:

$$\frac{365}{\text{COGS/INVENTORY RATIO}}$$

Depending on the industry norms, the products sold, and the manufacturing cycle, generally the business should aim for an average 30-day turnover of inventory.

COGS/Payables Ratio. The COGS/payables ratio measures the number of times the company's trade payables are completely paid off or turned over during the year. The larger this ratio, the shorter the time between the company's purchase of goods and subsequent payment of invoices.

If the company's ratio is lower than the industry average it may reflect a liquidity problem causing the company to pay its bills slowly. Lower ratios also may be caused by generous sales terms provided by suppliers or temporarily over disputed invoices.

This ratio is calculated as follows:

$$\frac{\text{COGS}}{\text{TRADE PAYABLES}}$$

Depending on the industry norms, credit terms, and the mix between cash and credit purchases, generally the business should aim for a minimum 12x ratio, indicating that the complete payment of invoices occurs every 30 days.

This ratio may not be a good analytical tool for companies with seasonal sales fluctuations. It also only measures one day's payables to cost of sales. Calculating this ratio monthly and tracking its average over the course of time is the best way to use this ratio.

Leverage Ratios

Leverage ratios provide a measurement of the financial protection that the value of a company's assets provide as a guarantee of repayment of the obligations owed to its creditors. Higher-leveraged firms reflect a heavier reliance on external financing. Evaluating these components of the balance sheet will help the owner understand the vulnerability of the company to a downturn or its chances of future access to external financing.

Fixed/Worth Ratio. The fixed/worth ratio compares the size of a business's investment in net fixed assets (land, buildings, and equipment after adjusting for depreciation or depletion) relative to its tangible net worth (excluding any intangible assets such as trademarks, patents, goodwill, etc.). By measuring the portion of equity that is employed in fixed investments, the business owner can evaluate the relative adequacy of its investment in fixed assets that support revenue production vs. its current assets that reflect operations.

Therefore, a higher ratio indicates more investment in fixed assets, and a lower ratio indicates more concentration of equity in current assets.

This ratio is calculated as follows:

$$\frac{\text{FIXED ASSETS (net)}}{\text{TANGIBLE NET WORTH}}$$

Debt/Worth Ratio. The debt/worth ratio compares the size of a business's tangible capital financing (internal) to its debt financing (external). By determining the relative investment that the owner provides in relation to the company's debt, the ratio defines the degree of risk that the lender assumes to extend credit. A larger ratio reflects more risk to the external funding source.

This ratio is calculated as follows:

$$\frac{\text{TOTAL LIABILITIES}}{\text{TANGIBLE NET WORTH}}$$

Although lender restrictions will vary, expect that they will begin to get concerned as the debt/worth ratio climbs past 4x.

Operating Ratios

Operating ratios measure the business owner's performance through the use of the company's assets and equity for the production of revenues and profits.

Percent of Profits Before Taxes/Total Assets Ratio. The percentage of profits before taxes/total assets ratio measures the pretax financial profit (as a percentage of sales) against total assets, which reflects the efficiency with which the business owner is employing the company's assets to produce business profits.

This ratio is calculated as follows:

$$\frac{\text{\% of NET PROFITS BEFORE TAXES}}{\text{TOTAL ASSETS}}$$

$$\times 100$$

This ratio may not be a good analytical tool for mature companies with heavily depreciated assets, large amounts of intangible assets, or unusual fluctuations of revenue or expenses. It also only measures one period's profit to total assets. Calculating this ratio monthly and tracking its average over the course of time is the best way to use this ratio.

Percent of Profit Before Taxes/Tangible Net Worth Ratio. The percentage of profits before taxes/tangible net worth ratio measures the pretax financial profit (as a percentage of sales) against tangible net worth, which reflects the efficiency with which the business owner is employing the company's capital to produce business profits.

This ratio is calculated as follows:

$$\frac{\text{\% of NET PROFITS BEFORE TAXES}}{\text{TANGIBLE NET WORTH*}}$$

$$\times 100$$

This ratio may not be a good analytical tool for mature companies with heavily depreciated assets, large amounts of intangible assets, or unusual fluctuations of revenue or expenses. It also only measures one period's profit to tangible net worth. Calculating this ratio monthly and tracking its average over the course of time is the best way to use this ratio.

Sales/Total Assets Ratio. The sales/total assets ratio measures the company's revenues against its total assets, which reflects the efficiency with which the business owner is employing the company's assets to produce revenues.

This ratio is calculated as follows:

$$\frac{\text{SALES (net)}}{\text{TOTAL ASSETS}}$$

This ratio may not be a good analytical tool for companies with heavily depreciated assets or labor-intensive operations. It only measures one period's sales to total assets. Calculating this ratio monthly and tracking its average over the course of time is the best way to use this ratio.

A problem with many of these ratios is that they may be skewed by business circumstances that distort the results. It's always a good idea for the business owner to determine the root cause of any numbers that do not compare favorably with industry standards or past business trends.

The owner should be mindful of (and remind the lender) that there are no good or bad ratios; they are always relative. Even if the financial performance of the business is very impressive, the company may not compare well with the RMA results because of extraordinary local reasons that cannot be reflected in the study. These studies alone should not determine whether the funding proposal is approved or rejected.

The ratios are useful for understanding how the company is faring in a number of measurements. Comparing the business's results to the average ratios of peer companies is useful but not definitive.

10

PROJECTING REASONABLE OPERATING RESULTS

External financing is predicated on a simple expectation: funders want to get all of their money back with a premium paid for its use. From the time the business owner submits a financing proposal, the funder will evaluate the owner's ability to repay or return the financing with funds generated by the business or exit event.

The owner's capability to either create cash flow or enterprise value is integral to obtaining financing.

The funder will expect the owner to provide a realistic explanation about how the proceeds of the financing will be invested to generate revenues for the business. Further, the owner should identify the costs the business incurs to produce these revenues and project the resulting profits from which the financing will be repaid.

The integrity and reasonableness of these projections are often the most important factors in getting financing. In constructing financial projections, the business owner must be honest not only with the funder but also with himself; representing unrealistic figures is unethical and self-defeating.

The funder is usually not an expert in the owner's field and may not recognize exaggerated revenue projections or inadequate expense estimates. Failing to be prudent and to exercise good judgment can place the company and the owner's personal financial stability at risk if the money obtained cannot be returned as scheduled.

Financial projections take into account the estimated operating results of the business for a defined period in the future. Most funders require that operating results be projected for a minimum of two years. It's useful to project the first 12 months on a month-to-month basis in order to illustrate the immediate effects of the new funding on the current business cash cycle. Projecting financial results beyond 24 months is difficult due to multiple factors and economic cycles that the owner can't anticipate or predict.

In developing the operating projections the owner should use a model that emulates the business profit/loss statement (referred to as a pro forma) and insert estimated values accordingly. The starting date of the projections should coincide with the date of the next fiscal year or just beyond a reasonable estimate of the funding date.

Written details of significant revenue sources, cost of goods sold (COGS), and major expenses are necessary to explain and substantiate estimates. Rather than overloading this worksheet with rows of itemized minutiae, the projection model will be easier to read if the owner streamlines it by combining the many small detailed accounts into larger revenue and expense categories.

For example, the many different expenses of hiring, compensating, motivating, and providing benefits to and paying taxes for employees should be projected as salaries rather than detailed into several line items. This larger, general category would include all salary-related expenses, such as payroll taxes, unemployment insurance premiums, employee benefits, employee insurance costs, payroll processing costs, and other direct expenses attributable to the employment costs of the business.

The owner can detail specific accounts of the salaries expense category in schedules that can be readily produced if requested. Meanwhile these details won't distract from the main information. This exercise helps the owner organize information better and keeps the funder focused on the big picture.

Providing the funder with line-by-line calculations of the expected revenues or expenses could create many unnecessary, extraneous questions as well as confuse the funder as to exactly what the owner's exact revenue or costs are. The owner does not want the funder to micromanage the business or to lose sight of the overall projected results.

Producing this projection model will assist the owner in planning and subject the proposal to a financial litmus test. The most important guideline is to be realistic. The owner needs to have a reality-based confidence in the expected revenues the business can generate and the expected costs necessary to produce that revenue.

A simple profit/loss projection model is shown in Figure 10.1. It's easy to use this model to estimate operating results by showing the specific revenues minus the expenses. A spreadsheet model in a program like Excel can perform automatic calculations, and the projection becomes a powerful management tool for the business.

Figure 10.1 provides a simple example of a company's projection of future income and profits. The fictional business is a successful medical practice, Acme

FIGURE 10.1 Income Statement Pro Forma

Acme Medical Partners, Inc.			August 15, 2012		
	Year Ending 6/30/13			**Year Ending 6/30/14**	
INCOME					
Total Revenues	$ 2,560,000		$ 2,636,800		
Costs of Goods Sold	$ 623,450	24%	$ 642,154	24%	
GROSS MARGIN	**$ 1,936,550**	76%	**$ 1,994,647**	76%	
EXPENSES					
Salaries and Labor expenses	$ 738,302	29%	$ 760,451	29%	
Owner's Salary	$ 350,000	14%	$ 360,500	14%	
Administrative expenses	$ 73,211	3%	$ 75,407	3%	
Advertising	$ 4,500	0%	$ 4,635	0%	
Auto / Truck	$ 36,000	1%	$ 37,080	1%	
Bank Charges	$ 2,579	0%	$ 2,656	0%	
Entertainment / Travel	$ 34,778	1%	$ 35,821	1%	
Equipment Rental / Maintenance	$ 1,000	0%	$ 1,030	0%	
Insurance	$ 137,500	5%	$ 141,625	5%	
Postage / Courier	$ 22,541	1%	$ 23,217	1%	
Professional Fees	$ 32,000	1%	$ 32,960	1%	
Rent / Occupancy	$ -	0%	$ -	0%	
Taxes—Other	$ 2,400	0%	$ 2,472	0%	
Telephone / Internet	$ 10,344	0%	$ 10,654	0%	
Miscellaneous	$ 7,792	0%	$ 8,026	0%	
	$ -	0%	$ -	0%	
	$ -	0%	$ -	0%	
TOTAL EXPENSES	$ 1,452,947	57%	$ 1,496,535	57%	
EBITDA	**$ 483,603**	19%	**$ 498,111**	19%	
Interest	$ 63,750	2%	$ 63,000	2%	
Depreciation	$ 89,450	3%	$ 89,450	3%	
Amortization	$ 11,300	0%	$ 11,300	0%	
Income Taxes	$ 60,000	2%	$ 62,000	2%	
NET PROFIT	**$ 259,103**	10%	**$ 272,361**	10%	

Medical Partners, that has decided to buy the building it occupies from a retiring investor. The illustration shows what it might provide its banker to demonstrate that it has sufficient profits to repay the requested loan. In Year 2, it simply increases the revenues 3 percent and adjusts the COGS and expenses to a commensurate level as a percentage of sales.

Relevant Expense Categories

The expense categories that follow are representative of the many kinds of expenses that are incurred by most businesses. Combining many related expense categories under broader descriptions makes the financial statement easier for third parties to read, but the consolidation of expense categories should also reflect cost allocation. All major expense categories should be represented. The business owner's projection model should mirror the exact revenue/expense categories included on the business financial statement. Here are some of the most common categories:

Revenues

- **Sales/income.** Monies expected to be received by the business in payment for products sold or services provided to its customers. This category will also include discounts to revenues and miscellaneous sources of income.
- **Cost of goods sold (COGS).** Expenses that represent a direct cost associated with producing or acquiring the products or services sold by the business. (If there is uncertainty about which expenses to include here, an accountant should be consulted.)
- **Gross margin.** The result of subtracting the COGS from the sales/income (also referred to as the gross profit).

Expenses

- **Salaries and labor expenses.** Labor costs (except the direct labor costs included in COGS), FICA tax payments, unemployment taxes, benefit insurance, other employee benefits, and all other costs incurred by the business to acquire indirect labor.
- **Owner's salary.** The typical entry to define the labor expense of the company's owner and management. Funders are often interested in how well owners plan to reward themselves.
- **Administrative.** Costs associated with managing the operation, such as office supplies, petty cash, refreshments, light equipment maintenance, copier supplies, and other expenses associated with the administrative functions of the business.
- **Advertising.** Costs of marketing and advertising the business, such as brochures, advertising, web ads, media commercials, corporate gifts, direct mail, telemarketing, and other promotion efforts.

- **Auto/truck.** Costs of maintaining vehicles for the business use, such as forklifts, delivery trucks, etc., or reimbursements for use of employee's vehicles for business purposes. This expense should not include auto allowances paid to any employees as part of their compensation.
- **Bank charges.** Costs of any banking service charges or fees (except interest on loans); also an optional place to expense merchant fees charged on credit card transactions.

  Note: If merchant fees occur on a majority of revenue sales, that cost should be reflected as a "discount" in the revenue section of the pro forma.
- **Entertainment/travel.** Costs of entertaining prospective clients and business travel, such as sales calls, service calls, or trade conferences or other general purposes.
- **Equipment rental/maintenance.** Costs of purchasing light equipment assets that are acquired with the entire expense recognized in the same year or equipment leasing costs. Equipment maintenance and repair expenses should be included in this sum.
- **Insurance.** Expenses for general liability, property, casualty, auto, workers' compensation, and any other insurance expenses of the business (except employee benefit insurance).
- **Postage/courier.** Costs of postage, postage equipment, courier fees (UPS, FedEx, etc.), and other special handling costs (such as certified mail).
- **Professional fees.** Costs of any professional services anticipated for the business, such as legal, accounting, tax, information technology, management consulting, etc.
- **Rent/occupancy.** Costs of occupancy including rent, CAM (common area maintenance) charges, utilities, real estate taxes, repairs, facility maintenance, and any other expenses associated with the business premises.
- **Taxes—Other.** Costs included in administrative fees to a government subdivision, licenses, property taxes, or other non-income-related taxation on business.
- **Telephone/Internet.** Costs of the basic telephone service, long distance, answering services, communication equipment rental, Internet service, DSL, cable, WiFi, and any other expenses related to providing telephone, wireless, or Internet for business communications.
- **Miscellaneous.** Various costs that are not well defined in the other categories and represent small or temporary expenses that might not justify a separate entry.
- **Total operating expenses.** Total sum of projected expenses.

Profit

- **Operating profit or EBITDA.** The gross margin minus the total operating expenses equals the operating profit or earnings before interest, taxes, depreciation, and amortization, also referred to as EBITDA.
- **Interest.** Interest costs expected to be incurred for all debt balances during the period. The actual interest rate and loan amortization schedule for all balances should be used to calculate the proposed financing according to the terms requested.
- **Depreciation/amortization.** Noncash expenses based on the useful life of capital assets or prescribed amortization period. (These expenses affect the profitability of the business but not the cash flow.)
- **Income taxes.** Federal and state income taxes, based on expected profits. Funders may not be interested in income tax projections due to many variables that make reliable estimates difficult to calculate. Still, it's a better idea to project them to have a realistic expectation about what kind of net earnings can be retained.
- **Net profit.** The operating profit minus interest and taxes equals the net profit.

Be Realistic

Owners will always be required to provide financial projections of the company's operating performance for at least two years. These estimates are intended to give the funder confidence that the owner can service debt with cash flow from operations or is building enterprise value from the business's operations.

The funder's confidence (or lack of confidence) will be based in part on the owner's ability to forecast these results, the level of detail the owner uses to develop the estimates, and whether the projections are credible.

These projections are more difficult to estimate for start-up businesses or for businesses intending to use the proceeds for major changes in their operations. It's incumbent on the owner to be as accurate as possible when developing projections, since these numbers will be very important to ultimate financing approval.

The owner must be realistic, honest, and smart and must not create fictitious numbers to justify receiving money without the confidence that the business will meet expectations. If real projections won't work, the owner must rethink the business plan and find alternatives. Above all, the owner should not suggest numbers that the company can't produce.

Revenue Projections Must Reflect Reality

How will the owner increase revenues? One of the most important things the owner can provide to funders is the marketing plan, which describes how the business will increase revenues. If the financing is to provide additional assets or capital to grow the business, the owner needs to back up the proposal with a plan detailing exactly how such increases will be accomplished.

The financial projections provide a numerical measure of expected revenue growth, but the marketing plan must define the impetus for those predictions. In other words, the owner has to describe what actions will be taken to make revenues increase.

For example, if the owner wants the loan to buy equipment to enable the business to increase production by 50 units per hour, the projections will have to show how much of this new production capacity will actually be sold, each, daily. The marketing plan will have to describe how the business will communicate to its customers that it has more doughnuts to sell.

Such details lend credibility to the financial projections and illuminate the owner's rationality for wanting to expand. Dissecting the correlation between the marketing efforts and financial results communicates that the owner understands the balance among all the various operational components of the business.

Suggestions for developing a marketing plan are described in Chapter 6. The financing proposal will be much more credible if the owner ties in the financial projections to the details discussed in the marketing plan.

What Will It Cost to Operate the Business?

Sometimes predicting revenues is easy compared to the task of estimating the total costs of supporting sales. As important as projecting sales, the owner must be able to clearly visualize all of the expenses required to acquire, create, manufacture, convert, or resell the business's products or services. Unexpected or unmanaged costs can quickly turn the venture into a disaster.

With minimal effort, it's easy enough estimate the obvious costs associated with any operation, such as rent, utilities, and wages. However, it's the unexpected or overlooked costs, such as employment taxes, common area maintenance charges, and insurance that will often wreck the most well-crafted plans.

Considering this planning risk it should be obvious why most financiers are skeptical of start-up ventures. The lack of experience in recognizing all of the costs involved can render a business plan moot. It's hard to know what you don't know.

The business owner must have hard data to understand what the costs will be to create the business planned. Such information might come from a number of sources, such as accountants, suppliers, and contractors. But to really get concrete answers, the owner should consider reaching out to a noncompeting owner in the same business who can offer advice about what to expect.

Care must be taken to balance the major costs and minor expenses. Focus will naturally be on the major costs that are ahead for the business. But the owner must also take into account all of the smaller expenses that will be added to operate the building and vehicles, which certainly compounds the burden of writing a business plan and figuring the costs.

Trying to tie down every penny can take weeks of time. Estimating too broadly can cause the business to fail. The owner must think not only about the major costs, but also about the inherent pricing risks that may accompany these costs. For example, understanding the cost of a fleet of vehicles will focus the business owner only on whether the business can service the related debt. Such an estimate might have been made assuming the fuel expense at $1.50 per gallon, but the business owner needs to also examine how the business could manage fuel at perhaps $4.00 per gallon, and how that affects the forecast.

The trade-off comes in making the larger expenses a priority without avoiding the necessity to understand the other costs required to operate the business. There are plenty of miscellaneous decisions the owner can postpone, but the decision to make a profit is not one of them.

If projections show that the business will significantly outpace the industry, the owner is probably missing something. Unless the owner has stumbled onto some revolutionary delivery system, everyone in the industry will face the same costs of doing business. They too are trying to deliver goods to the market as profitably as possible.

Even if the owner has a creative strategy to do things better, it is unwise to bet the farm on it. It's better for an owner to beat the budget by padding expenses rather than by believing that the job can be done for less.

It is necessary for the owner to pay close attention to the revenue stream after costs are determined. It may be that the profitability the owner was counting on does not exist. Maybe the game plan was to price goods more cheaply than the competition and thus make bigger profits. Coming to grips with the true costs to operate the business may mean the owner has to revisit pricing assumptions and sales projections.

Sorting Variable vs. Fixed Costs

When projecting the operational costs, the owner should define every expense as either a variable or a fixed cost. Another way to express these costs would be as direct or indirect. Variable costs are those costs that increase with each additional unit or measure sold. Fixed costs are those costs that are not affected by additional sales.

Variable costs are always classified in their entirety as COGS, since they represent the costs that are directly attributable to the production of the goods or services. While some expenses can change according to many factors, only those varying costs based on each incremental unit sales are to be defined as COGS.

Fixed costs are always associated with those remaining expenses labeled overhead. Overhead includes those expenses that are important to the business but that are not directly related to the cost of producing goods or services. Rent, utilities, postage, and bank charges are good examples of expenses that are usually not incrementally related to the production of revenues.

The financial model of a business should be constructed so as to automatically adjust these direct, variable costs as projected sales move up and down. By defining each category up front, the business owner can create a management tool that will prevent underestimating the costs as revenue volumes change.

COGS in particular will be compared to that of other businesses in the industry, since it's such a primary metric of the business. While there may be subtle differences based on factors such as location, quality, and technical advantages, the industry should have consistent costs of producing most goods.

Overhead might be comparable as well, but the fixed costs are influenced by other factors. Location affects rent, so an ice cream store in Manhattan will certainly face higher overhead than a similar store in Akron, Ohio. Likewise, security, taxes, and employee costs are generally going to be higher in high-density urban areas than in isolated rural areas.

The ideas and personal style of the owner also affect overhead with regard to how the business should be operated. Some owners may choose a grander promotional style, while others choose a fancier environment. Others may choose a very low-key operation with no frills. The most flamboyant owners will pay higher costs with the intent to attract higher-margin revenues.

Distinguishing the differences between variable and fixed costs can help project more accurate operating and cash-flow models. Owners should define each cost accordingly.

Reasonably Predicting Cash Flow

Income projections will provide the expected profits (or losses) of the business. The next step for the owner is to develop a cash-flow projection. Regardless of expected income, it's important for the owner to remember that there will never be all that money in one place at one time.

The business operates on a cash cycle that is dictated by the timing of when expenses must be incurred and when revenues are converted to cash. If a business is a concession stand at the local little league, it's easy to see how the owner can purchase sodas and snacks in the morning at Costco and sell them that afternoon for cash. Profits are earned on the same day and reinvested the next morning to buy more sodas and snacks.

But what if the business needs several days to acquire raw materials that must be paid for with cash, spends a week of payroll to convert them to finished products, and ships them to a buyer who gets 30 days to pay? Obviously, figuring out and managing the cash cycle is a little more complicated.

How much cash is needed to get the products shipped? When will the business actually get paid? And what about cash needed for overhead and debt service on all those loans needed to get the business started?

Basic Debt Service Ratio

In a very simple cash-flow model used by some lenders, noncash expenses (depreciation and amortization) and interest expenses are added to the company's annual net profit. This basic calculation provides a quick estimate of the total cash available during the year to service the projected debt payments. This calculation is as follows:

NET PROFIT

+ DEPRECIATION

+ AMORTIZATION

+ INTEREST EXPENSES

= GROSS CASH FLOW

With this calculation, the lender is primarily interested in determining whether the ratio of available cash is sufficient to pay the total debt payments required on the proposed loan.

The debt service coverage ratio (DSC) is calculated as follows:

$$\frac{\text{GROSS CASH FLOW}}{\text{TOTAL PRINCIPAL + INTEREST PAYMENTS}}$$

This ratio roughly measures a company's ability to meet its scheduled obligations and to service debt with its estimated cash flow, based on past or projected profit/loss cycles. By comparing gross cash flow to the total debt payments, the ratio estimates the capacity to take on new loans. If this ratio is less than 1.0x, cash flow is not covering the current payment burden.

Most lenders require a DSC ratio to be at least 1.25x, or higher, depending on their loan policy and other business factors. It's important to state the obvious: The lender's projection is intended for underwriting purposes, but that is no guarantee that the projection is accurate. Just because the lender says the owner can afford the payments doesn't necessarily indicate that the lender has a true understanding of the owner's cash cycles or that the owner will actually produce the cash to make the payments.

Uniform Credit Analysis

A more formidable evaluation of the ability to repay debt by lenders is to use RMA's Uniform Credit Analysis (UCA) model, which evaluates cash flow using the statement of cash flows approach. Recall that the statement of cash flows draws information from both the income statement and balance sheet to determine how a company funds operations.

The UCA model determines a company's year-to-year cash flow through a series of calculations used to distill the operations down to net cash flow, as reflected in Figure 10.2.

It's almost assured that the lender's estimation of a company's available cash to service debt is going to be lower—maybe much lower—using the UCA model rather than the basic evaluation described above. Plugging net cash from operations in the same debt service ratio calculation will likely reflect a lower ability to absorb additional debt. The good news is that such a calculation is probably a more accurate estimate of how well payments can be managed and therefore protects the bank and borrower more effectively.

$$\frac{\text{NET CASH FROM OPERATIONS}}{\text{TOTAL PRINCIPAL + INTEREST PAYMENTS}}$$

FIGURE 10.2 Uniform Credit Analysis

	REVENUES
Plus +	Changes in ACCOUNTS RECEIVABLE
Equals =	CASH SALES

	COST OF GOODS SOLD
Plus +	Changes in INVENTORY
Plus +	Changes in TRADE PAYABLES
Equals =	CASH PURCHASES

	CASH SALES
Minus -	CASH PURCHASES
Equals =	CASH GROSS PROFIT

	CASH GROSS PROFIT
Minus -	OPERATING EXPENSES
Plus +	Changes in BALANCE SHEET ITEMS *
Minus -	CASH TAX PAYMENTS
Equals =	**NET CASH FROM OPERATIONS**

* Balance Sheet items may include net changes in fixed and other
assets, and long-term debt and equity.

Shock Tests

Another question the bank must consider when projecting cash flow and the company's ability to repay its loan is what changing payments the business could face on a variable rate loan. The bank underwriter will simply shock test the cash-flow estimates against historic and projected results to see whether payments can be covered if the interest rate increases.

This test is just to compare the same level of available cash to payments calculated at 1 and 2 percent higher than the planned rate at loan funding. The inability to meet payments as easily at the higher rates will not necessarily change the lender's funding decision, but the lender needs to assess how bad the cash flow would be in a rising rate environment. It may lead to a subjective requirement to lower the loan or require more equity in a rising rate environment.

It's worthwhile repeating that if the lender's calculations are mistaken, the owner will still have to repay the loan. Therefore, the owner should also be making shock tests to ensure the ability to pay higher rates.

Global Cash Flow Evaluation

Now that you have a better idea of how a bank analyzes a business's ability to repay its debt burden, it's time to explain how the lender goes deeper to evaluate the global cash flow of the enterprise, which extends beyond the business to its owner. A small business concern is generally the largest asset belonging to the owner, and the financial health of both business and person are closely related. If one party needs resources, it usually looks immediately to the other.

To that point, when the business produces strong profits or cash flows, the owner generally sees that as personal profit or cash flow, sometimes without regard to the business entity or its obligations. Likewise, when the owner overindulges on expenses or debts, the owner is authorized to take a higher salary to cover these personal obligations.

A banker will look to quantify the personal debt obligations the owner has in tandem with the business obligations so as to assess how much external pressure (or competition) there is for the business cash flow to repay the bank debt.

For example, an owner with a $1,200 monthly mortgage payment and no auto or credit card debt presents a better risk profile than an owner with a $7,000 mortgage payment, two auto leases, student loans, credit card debt, and a second home with monthly association assessments to pay.

Figure 10.3 presents an example of how the basic cash-flow evaluation can be misleading unless the bank looks deeper into the obligations of the business owner.

The debt/income ratio is used to assure the lender that the owner's income is sufficient to meet all debt obligations, tax burdens, and other living expenses, such as food and incidentals. When the ratio is under the lender's limit, the lender is comfortable that the company's cash flow is fully available to service the company's obligations.

Note: The bank will not add any excess personal cash flow back to the company's cash flow, as reflected in the example. That illustration is included to show how the conservative owner's spending provided extra resources that could protect the company.

When the ratio exceeds the bank's expectations, the overage will be charged against the company's cash flow to account for the exposure the company will have to its owner's personal debt burdens. Any addition to the business debt burden calculation will lower the debt service ratio and raise the risk of the transaction.

This global-cash-flow evaluation is made in recognition that repayment of the bank loan is subject to how well the owner handles personal financial obligations outside of the business enterprise.

Better Management

A priority management tool the owner should incorporate into planning is a month-to-month cash-flow projection model that can track revenues and expenses in reasonably accurate relation to when they actually occur in the business.

FIGURE 10.3 Global Cash-Flow Comparison

	COMPANY A	COMPANY B
BASIC DEBT SERVICE ANALYSIS		
Net Cash from Operations	$ 300,000	$ 300,000
Debt Service on Loan	$ 170,000	$ 235,000
DEBT SERVICE RATIO	**1.76x**	**1.28x**

Company A appears to present a lower risk to the lender based on the company information presented, but continue looking at the "global" numbers, and analyze the impact of the owner's financial situation:

GLOBAL CASH-FLOW ANALYSIS		
Owner's Salary	$ 200,000	$ 200,000
Annual home mortgage payment	$ 88,900	$ 24,000
Annual credit card payments	$ 32,000	$ 1,000
Second home mortgage & condo fees	$ 4,500	$ -
Annual auto lease expenses	$ 36,000	$ 16,000
Total Annual Personal Expenses	$ 161,400	$ 41,000

Bankers evaluating the business and its owner's "global cash flow" will compare the owner's personal obligations to their personal income to determine a personal debt/income ratio, which is used extensively in mortgage lending. The lender will have a maximum ratio allowable, and any deficit will enter the company underwriting since it is assumed that the owner will draw on company resources to meet a personal cash shortfall. For reference, FHA guidelines limit debt / income ratio to 43% for all mortgage and other debt obligations.

	COMPANY A	COMPANY B
Over (Under) FHA Guideline	$ (75,000)	$ 45,000
GLOBAL DEBT SERVICE RATIO*	**1.22x**	**1.47x**

* Company debt service ratio adjusted to reflect debt/income ratio of business owner.

Regularly analyzing the cash cycle will reduce surprises, since it will provide a better acquaintance with the cash conversion cycle of the enterprise.

Using a month-to-month cash-flow pro forma will enable the owner to more exactly account for actual expectations of cash receipts and expense timing. The owner can include any variables to more accurately predict the business cash cycle. By keeping a detailed legend the owner can better recall and decipher the assumptions used in developing the pro forma.

Figure 10.4 shows an example of a good cash-flow projection model. This model can be modified easily to match a company's financial reporting simply by customizing the revenue and expense accounts to match the company's financial

FIGURE 10.4 Working Capital Projections

Date _____

	Month 1	Month 2	Month 3	Month 4	Month 5	Month 6	Month 7	Month 8	Month 9	Month 10	Month 11	Month 12
1. **CASH** (beginning)												
CASH RECEIPTS												
2. Sales Revenues												
3. Other Income												
4. Loan Proceeds												
5. Capital Contributions												
6. **Total Cash Receipts** (Total Lines 1-6)												
CASH PAYMENTS												
8. Costs of Goods Sold												
9. Gross Wages												
10. Owner's Salary												
11. Payroll Taxes & Benefits												
12. Accounting & Legal												
13. Advertising												
14. Auto / Truck												
15. Bank Charges and Discount												
16. Entertainment / Travel												
17. Equipment Rental												
18. Insurance												
19. Office Expense												
20. Rent												
21. Repair / Maintenance												
22. Supplies												
23. Taxes—Other												
24. Telephone / Utilities												
25. Miscellaneous												
26. Total Loan Payments												
27. Total Lease Payments												
28. **Total Cash Payments** (Total Lines 8-27)												
29. **CASH** (ending)												

(Line 6 – Line 28; enter here & top of next column)

statement. Other variables that have an effect on a business's cash flow, such as debt payments and quarterly tax payments, can also be taken into account.

Another benefit owners can get from a good cash-flow model is knowing how much sales growth the company can handle with its present working capital and the sales level where additional funding would be required. Without a clear idea of the business cash cycles, growth can be fatal. Since profits get absorbed with new demands for higher sales, the business can quickly get swamped without adequate cash.

Projecting a Transaction Onto the Balance Sheet

It's good to know before closing how a financing transaction will affect the company's balance sheet. A debt transaction will increase the company's leverage, which may make additional debt financing impossible for a while. The owner should run the numbers first.

If the business is a start-up operation, the balance sheet pro forma will be easy to assemble by simply accounting for all of the assets acquired, liabilities incurred, and equity contributed during the financing transaction. The starting balance sheet position may literally reflect only organizational costs and the owner's capital.

If the business is already in operation, the owner should use the most recent interim balance sheet as the starting point from which to illustrate estimated changes to the balance sheet.

Here's an example showing the changes to a company's balance sheet for the contemplated transaction. The planned debt financing for a successful medical practice, Acme Medical Partners, has decided to buy the building it occupies:

Building Price:	$1,000,000
Financing:	Bank loan arranged for $850,000 for 20 years
	Principal payments total $20,211 in first year (@ 7% interest)
	Seller note for $50,000 (subordinated) for 10 years
	Principal payments total $3,403 in first year (@ 8% interest)
	Closing costs will total 4% of the loan
	Down payment in cash
	Appraisal states property value at $50,000 and improvements at $950,000

This transaction would be accounted for on the balance sheet in Figure 10.5. Note that the left column is the beginning balance sheet, that the figures in the middle column represent the actual accounts affected by the transaction as listed above, and that the addition of these transaction balances will transform the

FIGURE 10.5 Balance Sheet Pro Forma

Acme Medical Partners, Inc.						August 15, 2012	
ASSETS		June 30, 2012 Beginning Balance [Pre-Transaction]		Transaction [Changes + (-)]		Ending Balance [Post-Transaction]	
Current Assets							
Cash	$	250,000	$	(140,000)	$	110,000	
Accounts Receivable	$	375,000	$	-	$	375,000	
Inventory	$	38,500	$	-	$	38,500	
Total Current Assets	$	663,500	$	(140,000)	$	523,500	
Fixed Assets							
Land	$	-	$	50,000	$	50,000	
RE Improvements	$	-	$	950,000	$	950,000	
Equipment	$	721,500	$	-	$	721,500	
Minus Depreciation	$	(229,234)	$	-	$	(229,234)	
Net Fixed Assets	$	492,266	$	1,000,000	$	1,492,266	
Other Assets							
Other Assets—Intangibles	$	12,485	$	-	$	12,485	
Transaction/Org. Costs	$	-	$	40,000	$	40,000	
Total Other Assets	$	12,485	$	40,000	$	52,485	
TOTAL ASSETS	$	1,168,251	$	900,000	$	2,068,251	
LIABILITIES							
Current Liabilities							
Accounts Payable	$	67,300	$	-	$	67,300	
Current Portion of Long-Term Debt	$	29,055	$	23,614	$	52,669	
Short-Term Notes Payable	$	75,000	$	-	$	75,000	
Taxes Payable	$	-	$	-	$	-	
Total Current Liabilities	$	171,355	$	23,614	$	194,969	
Long-Term Liabilities							
Long-Term Notes Payable	$	273,000	$	46,597	$	319,597	
Mortgages on Real Estate	$	-	$	829,789	$	829,789	
Other Long-Term Obligations	$	-	$	-	$	-	
Total Long-Term Liabilities	$	273,000	$	876,386	$	1,149,386	
TOTAL LIABILITIES	$	444,355	$	900,000	$	1,344,355	
OWNER'S EQUITY							
Capital Stock	$	50,000	$	-	$	50,000	
Additional Paid in Capital	$	250,000	$	-	$	250,000	
Retained Earnings	$	423,896	$	-	$	423,896	
Total Owner's Equity	$	723,896	$	-	$	723,896	
TOTAL LIABILITIES & EQUITY	$	1,168,251	$	900,000	$	2,068,251	

particular accounts post-transaction to a revised balance sheet shown in the right column.

This demonstration shows how a transaction affects the balance sheet and how essential it is for the owner to understand how the business will be impacted post-transaction.

Part 4

Best Sources for Start-Up Capital

11

THE FIRST DIME

After an exhaustive, comprehensive, and painstakingly accurate financing proposal has been written, the first people who should read it and consider its merits are the owners. That is, the owners should read it personally to consider how much financing they are willing to provide to the venture.

Seriously, the first place to start shopping the deal is at home. No one understands the business better than the owner does. No one is more committed to making the business succeed and getting the deal financed as proposed. No one wants it to happen more than the owner.

Depending on the kind of business it is, one overarching principle the owner should adopt is this: use personal resources to the fullest extent possible and lower reliance on other people's money. The owner should try to minimize rather than maximize the leverage and always start the funding search looking inward rather than outward.

For most people, suggesting that one examine personal resources probably conjures the vision of their checkbook. Actually, the idea of resources is intended to suggest that there is a much longer list of places to source financing for a business within one's sphere of influence, but doing so requires thinking in different terms.

The owner should not limit the search for funding only to places where cash is stored. A common mistake many owners make is limiting their view to cash. Virtually any thing or service can become currency when trying to accomplish a business goal.

After all, what is money? Money is an artificial asset that serves as a universal medium of exchange. It's supposed to enable us to value every good or service in common terms so that we can trade with anyone using a mutually accepted valuation representation: dollars, euros, etc.

Since the United States abandoned the gold standard, the value of the dollar is simply the trust we place in the good faith and credit of the U.S. government. But what if an owner doesn't have cash? What if most of the owner's accumulated assets are stored in other ways? Sometimes these other assets can be leveraged in exchange for or in lieu of cash and may be the answer for financing the business plan.

The key is for the owner to think beyond the account balance of dollars and cents and utilize a variety of resources in support of the goal. Two of the most important assets an owner possesses are critical thinking skills and imagination. If used well these assets may move the business financing quest further along than other assets might. The owner may be surprised at how far personal resources will go toward making the business plan a reality.

One other important point about using personal financing: it should be used sparingly. The owner should assume the role of a highly risk-averse banker and not be flippant with personal assets.

Bootstrapping—Starting with No Money

Zero. That is the ultimate sum with which to start a business. No financing needed, no share certificates, and no personal guarantees. How can an owner do it? Simple—sell something, collect the money, buy or build it, and then deliver it to the buyer. What is financing except the currency needed to fill a time gap between creation and delivery?

If owners rearrange the order of the business cycle, they eliminate the need for any other funding support whether from their resources or from the resources of others. Disruptive thinking and the audacity to ask might get a business further than the owner thought possible. Recent media stories have detailed how businesses achieved sales of over $500,000 in the second year after starting up with less than $150.

This self-reliant mindset has evolved into a movement. *Bootstrapping* means that the owner is actively working to minimize the cost involved to start a business with its inherent cash burn rate or even create the enterprise totally without funding. Many entrepreneurs have found success utilizing this concept to move business to an impressive scale relying on ideas rather than cash.

Bootstrapping is essentially a collection of ideas; there is no definitive list nor proprietary claims on what will work or not work. These ideas are not mutually exclusive and are highly dependent on circumstances. What works for one owner may not work for another. That's what makes it so entrepreneurial.

Here is a list of a few big ideas (strategies) and little details (tactics) that can help owners lower or defer the cash requirement in the business start-up or expansion. Some may seem more obvious than others, but all of them will catch someone by surprise. *Why didn't I think of that?*

- **Lower the scale of the business launch.** Start small with the available resources and don't be running around perpetually frustrated at not being able to raise the money for a huge business plan. Get into the revenue now.
- **Don't worry about image; worry about delivery.** You will have years to get things just the way you want them, but everything may fall short if you delay delivery until the image of the business is better. Get it going for now, and get it perfect down the road.
- **Frill is out; frugal is in.** Starting a business is not about lifestyle, it's about starting a successful enterprise. You will have to sacrifice and earn your way to the top. Fancy offices, expensive lunches, and business travel can wait. Sacrifice now to win at business.
- **If you can live without it, why are we having this conversation?** Don't waste time debating about what color to paint the walls. Time is as precious a commodity as any other asset, particularly cash. If you can live without it, then do.
- **Speak loudly, even though you have a small stick.** Your business may not be large yet, but that doesn't mean you can't put on airs to sound as if you are. Push for opportunities by making some noise and shamelessly promote your business to get to the top.
- **Project business from the bottom up.** Don't try to convince investors that you will capture 20 percent of the market; rather, convince them that you can open a new branch each quarter that will sell 1,000 units per month. Building revenues from the bottom up helps you illuminate how to do it rather than trying to meet a number you really can't measure.
- **Just say no to overhead.** Don't worry about the offices you occupy, the desk you sit at, or the phone you are talking into. Concern yourself with the functions that have to be accomplished and how, when, and what can be accomplished with the lowest cost.
- **Don't pay yourself.** The ultimate sacrifice entrepreneurs make is to work for free. It's not easy and may be counterintuitive to your entire career. Focus your capital on the business and it will pay rich dividends for years to come.
- **Don't pay others.** There is more free labor available than you might imagine. Rising college students and recent graduates are begging for experience. You can offer them the rich experience of riding along with your start-up, and

they'll contribute their time for free in exchange for the exposure and your mentorship. A word of caution is to be sure you don't recruit more help than you can offer meaningful work and sufficient supervision to.

- **Don't pay rent.** Before you sign a lease on office or commercial space, ask yourself if it's really necessary. If your home has the space, you can seat people around the dinner table to get things started. You don't need a store if you can sell and deliver directly to your customers through the Internet and UPS. You don't need manufacturing space if you can get started by outsourcing.

- **Profits are nice, but cash flow keeps you alive.** The desirability of profits by no means overstates that cash flow is the most important consideration during the first year of operations. Don't get hung up on the bottom line in the year everyone expects you to lose money anyway.

- **Get someone to pay you to develop it, and then sell it to everyone else.** Imagine that your development stage is spent on a consulting assignment solving a real client problem. Building your future product on a paid assignment and then applying the corpus solution to a broader market is a way to be paid to develop your business.

Obviously this list can go on endlessly because of the many different types of businesses, owners, and situations. But the most important idea is about the mindset: working the business plan as close to the ground as possible, at the lowest cost. Business owners should defer rewards until later, which may include not only delaying 401(k) contributions but entire paychecks.

Owners must embrace the ideals of bootstrapping and then try to be an exemplary entrepreneur by starting the business with pennies rather than with dollars that belong to someone else.

Get Started Using One's Own Money

Notwithstanding the broad examination business owners give to the entire array of assets, to begin the quest for financing, owners have to start with their own money. To be credible, an owner has to have money in order to borrow money. Cash, checking accounts, savings accounts, money market accounts, certificates of deposit, investment accounts, mutual funds, bonds, and even the cash surrender value of life insurance are the places that liquidity can be found. The owner must decide how much of it to use.

It is important for owners to recognize that the use of their own money has several implications. First, it's the best expression of confidence in the business and in its strategy. By putting out the first dollar, owners are demonstrating that they are paying more than lip service to faith in the enterprise.

Second, by putting their own money at risk, owners prove their commitment to the business. It's harder for owners to walk away from or become disinterested in a situation in which they have spent their own resources. A personal investment cements the notion of commitment to the venture with ideas, efforts, and capital.

It's easier for most people to ask someone else to put up the money rather than utilize their own. But it is important for owners to realize that a personal investment in cash will help keep them more tuned in to the risk of each decision, because they are personally vulnerable to losses. This participation level heightens focus on the business and leads to even greater success.

Cash represents stored value that owners probably worked hard for and sacrificed to accumulate. Lenders want these funds in the deal, since they are a little more personal than the equity from a rental house. Besides, if owners are borrowing cash from another source to create equity, they are increasing the risk of the deal for both themselves and for lenders. When cash resources are expected, lenders are referring to real liquidity.

How much cash should be used in the deal will depend on several factors:

- **How much debt can be leveraged for the deal?** Preliminary research should indicate how much the lender expects the investment to be and any loan-to-value limitations placed on the type of transaction at hand.
- **How much debt should be leveraged for the deal?** Management decisions based on market limitations, resource availability, and operating requirements will settle on an amount of debt to actually use. It is better to strengthen the transaction by lowering the debt rather than by using the maximum available.
- **How much cash is on hand?** The business owner should ensure that the business will have sufficient post-transaction liquidity for a broad range of potential operating results. While it's desirable to reduce external debt where possible, it's also necessary to provide for sufficient operating capital and not invest a disproportionately high sum in capital assets.
- **What other resources are available?** While use of some cash is essential, there are other financial resources from which to withdraw funds that are discussed later in this chapter. The composition of these resources will affect how much cash is actually accessible for investing in the business.

Prudent entrepreneurs will figure out how to launch their enterprise without using every dollar available to them. If owners have only enough cash to meet the minimum requirement, they really don't have enough.

Ever hear of contingencies? Sometimes things happen that increase costs, delay revenues, or cancel sales. Once owners initiate the business plan, they shouldn't subject it to teetering on the smallest disruption in financial projections. They must be prepared for unmet expectations by having some cash on hand. They should always hold back something for a rainy day.

Bartering

One frequently overlooked source of small business financing is known as bartering. Quite simply it's exchanging one's own goods or services for the goods or services of others without cash. In the process the need for cash is lowered by exchanging value-for-value without compromising profits. Bartering allows owners to avoid using cash while still creating a taxable sale for the business.

For example, if an owner sells professional time as a lawyer for $250 per hour and needs an accounting service that charges $100 per hour, the owner could exchange 1 hour of legal services for every 2.5 hours of accounting services. Or maybe the owner could exchange that hour of legal advice for $250 of meals at a local restaurant.

But how do owners find people to barter with? They probably have some vendors or suppliers that buy what they sell and sell what they buy. That kind of informal bartering is easy to negotiate directly. But what do owners do when they need something supplied by vendors that they do not know? And how can they possibly know who would be willing to exchange their goods or service for theirs?

Barter clubs have been growing in number to provide an exchange on which business people can trade goods or services for in-kind value, or trade dollars, that can be used to acquire other goods or services. While owners can't borrow trade credit, offering their goods or services in this platform is another marketing channel to accelerate sales for those other businesses that need them and accordingly earns the owners trade dollars to use for what they need from other businesses.

The trade clubs facilitate sales with the use of brokers that manage member trades by sourcing needed goods or services. The clubs are usually compensated with a small cash fee for their services connecting buyer and seller. At the end of the transaction, if the business has a good gross margin for whatever it sells, bartering should be a positive source of new revenues, getting what the business needs and conserving cash.

Owners should be aware that the barter clubs will track all sales and provide an IRS form 1099-B for the value of goods purchased. Bartering does not carry an extraordinary tax burden on purchases but is actually an equitable accounting for what is received as income for the goods exchanged. Thinking through the process, business owners traded a good or service that was expensed to the business as a direct or indirect cost. They will always deduct those costs from their taxable income.

The 1099-B merely quantifies the value of goods or services received in exchange for the costs expensed. If owners accumulate trade credit without using it, there is no declaration of income. The 1099-B is issued at the end of the year only if owners used the trade credit in that year.

Bartering is a smart way to boost sales to an unseen, unadvertised marketplace that owners likely never would have found otherwise and opens the opportunity for them to acquire many goods or services that they would have had to spend cash on with the value that they exchanged.

Crowdsourcing

A relatively new financing phenomenon is called crowdsourcing. Part benevolence, part microfinancing, this funding strategy operates through one of many websites developed to help raise funding for a variety of nonprofit and for-profit enterprises and causes. Some popular sites specialize in generating funding for such socially responsible challenges as the environment, education, arts, citizen journalism, and poverty.

Crowdsourcing is included in this chapter because it is sometimes offered as debt and sometimes as equity. Needless to say, it's untraditional and dependent on many factors to succeed. For-profit companies will probably be successful generating funds through this strategy only if they have a socially responsible product or service. Their ability to raise money will be dependent on their ability to get attention that incites enthusiasm for the enterprise.

Funding is offered in small increments and therefore takes hundreds or thousands of participating lenders or contributors to generate the money needed. The most prominent crowdsourcing site, Kickstarter (www.kickstarter.com), requires that the project reach its funding objective before the financing is actually accepted and distributed.

This source may be perfect for a very early stage enterprise that has some curb appeal, the mission to make some money while making the world a better place. Depending on the site, business, and pitch, the funds may be in the form of grants (equity) or loans (debt). The loans are expected to be repaid and many participating lenders actually roll their funds on into the next opportunity. Participants pay into the pool either with debit or credit cards or PayPal accounts.

Leverage Assets Thoughtfully

There are many strategies business owners can employ to plan the use of their personal resources, depending on the assets and conditions about when and how much funding they need. Accordingly the remainder of this chapter addresses a commonly used strategy utilized by some business owners: borrowing equity from other personal sources.

Borrowing a higher percentage of funding from multiple sources is nothing new. The idea was made popular in the 1980s among many self-appointed real estate gurus who sold a lot of books and seminars extolling the virtues of shameless leverage to buy real estate. These gurus and their shills convinced many budding entrepreneurs that they should borrow 110 percent of whatever funding was actually needed and use the extra 10 percent to pay themselves a bonus for being so stupid.

They didn't really concern themselves with the risk of what they were selling and as long as real property values continued to soar, there were enough "success" stories to continue selling a handsome volume of books and seminars. But then the savings and loan crisis hit, and the Resolution Trust Corporation took no prisoners. The domestic real estate market went into a tailspin, and all these books hit the Dumpster along with their ill-conceived notions that one should borrow as much as anyone would lend.

The whole cycle repeated itself in the first decade of 2000, as the capital markets overheated with inventory and had to lay off more leverage than the market really needed—much of it to unqualified borrowers. Real estate crashed again in 2008. The capacity to repeat this cycle will be a few years coming, but it will repeat itself.

Be that as it may, for some owners, a very few, there are conditions when it may make sense to leverage 100 percent of their business opportunity. Doing so substantially increases the loss risk but can make sense in some circumstances.

Increased leverage in any business increases the risk of failure, particularly when that added financing is secured with personal assets. The owner has greater exposure to losing the source of future income along with the net gains earned from previous efforts. Still, consider that if the owner's noncash assets are employed in a manner that can generate higher returns than their current use plus the interest cost to convert them to cash, the owner has a legitimate argument to increase his leverage to generate higher returns.

Owners should clearly understand all of the risk involved. Leveraging personal assets for the business gets more cash into the enterprise than it would be able to generate on its own. The payoff may be to accelerate the growth rate and earn more profits sooner. The downside is that the availability of more capital does not lower other business risk but raises the costs by the amount of the owners' pledged assets if things don't work out. Owners should proceed with a realistic assessment of their exposure to loss.

Leveraging other personal resources is possible when they are held in assets that can be borrowed against, usually by other lenders than those lending to the business. Home equity became a popular piggy bank for business owners for years, as real estate inflation became one of the safest bets to invest in. But the recent real estate bubble caused much of that value to evaporate, and millions of home owners are still underwater.

Maybe a business owner has accumulated a rich 401(k) plan or IRAs. These monies are pretax savings that have been put aside for retirement, when they will be taxed at a lower rate when withdrawn. These assets have always been off-limits to be subject to lender liens and unavailable to be used as collateral. But recent product innovations have led to the development of the idea of moving these monies from the investment in the equity stocks of a publicly traded company to the equity stock in the owner's company.

These kinds of options allow the owner to use the cash value of an owned asset to pursue growth in another asset (the business). The owner's assets may not be as obvious as in these examples, but it is important for the owner to recognize that cash value can be found in security accounts, a vacation home, a family trust, a lottery award, a boat, or even a fine piece of jewelry. All these assets can be used as collateral to get cash loans from lenders not concerned about business plans.

One of the key conditions to justifying this strategy is that the earning power of that asset should be higher in its present state than the cost of borrowing against it. If that's not the case, it is better for the owner to sell the asset for the cash instead of leveraging it. The earning power of some assets is only measurable by estimating their annual appreciation. And when considering leveraging assets, also it is important to ensure the borrowing cost is reasonable.

Something else owners should expect is that more conservative lenders will be interested in why they are borrowing money. They offer the best interest rates, and they will be interested in the plans for the money. While lenders probably won't object to their money being used for business purposes, they want to be sure it can be repaid from existing income resources. No lender wants to knowingly get into a loan where the likely source of repayment will be the liquidation of the collateral.

Leveraging personal assets is a strategy. It's not an option for most people, but it can be a really good decision for others. Regardless of how smart it may be, owners should never underestimate the risks and must proceed with caution: there is a chance to lose everything. Owners should consider what level of exposure they really can live with before they start employing this strategy.

Keep an Eye on the Future

Having given you some advice that may sound too risky, it's only fair to qualify it in the American tradition of a semilegal disclaimer: Using this information to expose your life's savings in order to borrow even more money may make you lose all your money faster. Do it with extreme caution.

Remember why you saved the money or bought the asset in the first place:

- If your dream has always been to accumulate the money in order to own your own business, go for it.
- If you have been sacrificing for years to save money for a comfortable retirement, you may want to slow down and think about the risks of such a decision.
- If the big corporation for which you have toiled hard for the past 25 years has told you to clear your desk in 30 minutes, stop. You need to wait a few months until all of your hard feelings have been cleared before committing a dime of your nest egg to a new venture.

Big financial decisions demand thoughtful consideration. When deciding to invest money in a new business venture or in expanding an existing operation, owners have a lot at stake. Accumulated savings, inheritances, and other significant assets represent earlier battles that someone fought and won. Equity means that owners have accumulated more than they have consumed.

And if owners have families, they must think about more people than just themselves. The financial security they have is providing protection for others. There is a fine line between expressing confidence in themselves and in their enterprise and putting their future at risk. While owners have to make their own decisions for their own reasons, they must take care to ensure that those decisions are made with adequate time, clarity, and reflection.

Owners must think of life beyond today. Regardless of their age, there will be other opportunities if they choose to sit out one particular deal or if the deal doesn't get done. Entrepreneurship does not die with one missed deal.

In our hypercaffeinated culture that virtually staples preapproved credit card applications to college diplomas, people often go into debt for things as trite as utility bills, magazine subscriptions, and breakfast. There is another way. Working hard, saving money, and employing some real long-term planning for the future are primary virtues that need reconsideration. You think you don't have time to wait? Give that question deliberate pause before proceeding.

Reflective time spent generating capital the old-fashioned way will add many things to a business venture: maturity, experience, seasoning, and equity. The future is a long road. By spending a few years getting there, owners will not erode their opportunities. They will just make them easier to attain.

It's difficult to read about another 22-year-old billionaire who launched that 1-in-10 million business out of her dormitory, took the company public, and today is set for life. We all want to do that. Or we want to win the Power Ball lottery, be the number one draft choice, or live on Fantasy Island. It won't happen for most of us.

It is important for owners to know the difference between fact and fiction, and to know who they are and what they do well. Our history is full of self-made people who didn't achieve everything by age 30 or even 40, but then enjoyed great successes after decades in the trenches. They looked to the future as a road and followed it where it led. You can too.

12

BETTER FUNDING SOURCES

Connecting goals with positive results may require business capital in one form or another. Later chapters will discuss how to position a business and find capital from a variety of funding sources, from a business owner's hometown bank to Wall Street. But sometimes, for one of many reasons, those sources are not going to be able or willing to provide the money needed. That's life.

Understanding that reality can help business owners avoid wasting time in a futile search for capital if their deal is outside funding limitations. Meanwhile, owners should try to create the capital they need in other places and in other ways. Often alternatives are hidden in plain view.

A not-so-subtle theme in this book has been to lower external financing wherever and whenever possible. So many owners waste lots of dollars in their business only because they are spending someone else's money without regard to the long-term cost of fulfilling the obligation to repay it.

This chapter discusses other sources where business owners may find capital, or sometimes just a capital idea—ideas on how to reduce the need for money. Lowering costs is the economic equivalent of generating funds to spend.

There are countless ways to generate or eliminate business funding. Entrepreneurs should examine these ideas first with the notion that these sources are ongoing methods to reduce or eliminate some external financing requirements during almost any point of the business cycle. Slowing or eliminating external financing might benefit the company's profitability, albeit on smaller growth tracks.

The following pages suggest a few ideas, although many of them may be impractical for a particular business. As important are the ideas that are not listed, those left up to the imagination and personal observation. Business owners should always try to cut waste, avoid unnecessary costs, find untapped revenue potential, and seek alternative ideas to spending capital.

Consider a Partner

Some businesses will learn too soon that the business is never going to be financed by an external source. Due to whatever business reason, business risk, or funder's common aversion, there are businesses that are not directly fundable by institutions or investors.

More often than not, it's smaller business owners who have a more difficult time accessing financing than larger businesses, particularly in the start-up stage. Some of these enterprises just cannot be financed, due to risk factors that fall outside of a prudent credit profile or because they are too small to be of interest to investors.

In these kinds of businesses getting a partner is a viable financing option. As opposed to an investor, a partner goes into business with the owner and splits everything with the owner. A partner will have a voice in every decision but will also have to do much of the work. Depending on negotiations, a partner may even get control of the business if he puts up most of the money.

Ideally business owners will find a partner with some business experience they don't have and who can contribute to the success of the enterprise in more ways than writing a check. As with any relationship, a partnership should not be rushed into but rather discussed and negotiated through a process intended to avoid any later problems. Similarities in work ethic, risk tolerance, business outlook, and exit ideas are important to assure that there are no conflicts waiting to crash the business.

Many entrepreneurs don't want a partner. Maybe there is some negative history in trying to work with someone else. The idea of a partner is just undesirable for some people. But owners should recognize that it's a good strategy that may enable them to launch or expand the business as opposed to not being able to do so. Partners dilute returns, but they also double resources. It may be better to get 50 percent of the return on something rather than 100 percent back on nothing.

Finding a partner takes time. The process of identifying prospective partners, learning of common interests, and discussing the possibilities of a business together is very much like courtship and marriage. Whether the parties have known each other for a long time or not is irrelevant—they must establish their relationship on trust, respect, and mutual recognition. Recruiting a partner is no time for speed-dating.

Owners should exercise caution and spend the time necessary to ensure compatibility, understand mutual strengths and weaknesses, and share common goals.

Otherwise a stormy marriage may ensue, which is painful for everyone and can wind up in the divorce of the business.

Owners should consider a partner as a potential financing source insofar as the partner brings cash to the business or doubles borrowing capacity. A partner also reduces some of the cost the business would be required to cover without any contributions to management or employment in the enterprise.

Clear the Closet—Liquidating Assets

Small businesses are not for pack rats. Many businesses accumulate stuff for short-term needs that have no long-term value for the company. As the business cycle unfolds, technology matures, and business plans are revised, owners find that assets that were important to the business yesterday are white elephants today.

Advice to owners: Get rid of them! Accumulating unneeded assets is a cost to the business. All assets cost something to acquire and if, with reasonable assurance, owners determine that a particular asset will no longer be valuable to the business, they should sell the asset. They should get the cash back out of it, whatever it is worth, and reemploy that money elsewhere in the business.

As simplistic as that may sound, the number of companies that rent storage space for years to shelter unusable computers, that pay property taxes on land they will never use, or that insure warehouses that are half empty is incredible.

Unused assets are sources of business capital. This capital has already been employed, but that utilization has matured. So many times a residual value can be realized with the investment of a few telephone calls.

Owners should liquidate assets that are not going to be used in the foreseeable future to generate revenues or profits for the business. They should explore several alternative channels for selling the assets and find where the best price can be obtained for the quickest turn. There is a market for just about anything.

Owners should consider the excess land or building space they have. Tying up money for unused property is very expensive. And if the owners have owned the land or building space for a long time, there may be some appreciation to realize that will pay a bonus. Carving off small tracts from a larger tract may be an opportunity to shed an unused asset, lower property taxes, and create cash. Some land unusable to the operation may be very suitable to someone else.

Selling these assets may or may not make sense, depending on the business's growth plans and the long-term viability of local property values. Alternatively, maybe space can be leased in order to employ the asset more beneficially.

Raw land sometimes attracts tenants that need to park trucks, store trailers, or even stockpile materials. Or if the property fronts a busy thoroughfare or highway, maybe there is an opportunity to lease some ground for a billboard or a golf driving range.

Liquidating the asset in this scenario means that the owners can produce some income from the asset in the short term while preserving ownership. Excess becomes largess.

With the explosive growth in storage warehouses and small office buildings, making excess warehouse or other commercial space available for another company's benefit could be a way to offset occupancy expense, even if the owners do not own the building.

Owners can't allow such a tenant to disrupt the business. However, they should consider whether there is an opportunity to generate extra cash from another party that could utilize the underused space. Often passive space is needed by businesses for a variety of reasons, and this need could be a source of revenue that is pure profit.

Have you been to a flea market lately? People literally sell trash because somebody is willing to buy it. There are folks who collect virtually everything, and there are artists who routinely make something from items discarded by others. Imagine those obsolete 15-year-old personal computers cleared out of a storage area and offered for sale at one of these bazaars. Or maybe disassembled and converted to jewelry, Christmas ornaments, or pop art. Getting rid of them can be profitable and giving them to someone just for the price of picking them up can double profit and clears closets.

If owners have a quantity of tools, materials, supplies, or raw materials, they can have a yard sale. Depending on what is being sold, the sale can be open to the public or by invitation only. Priced to move, people will buy things they will never use if it's a real bargain.

Or, owners can contact a commercial liquidator, maybe an auction company that specializes in selling off businesses or repossessed business assets, and inquire about adding their goods to the next sale or auction. Generally there is no cost unless the owners sell something.

Owners can also contact a used furniture dealer in the area and either sell furniture assets or place them with the dealer on consignment. The dealer may refer the owners to other dealers interested in other assets. Maybe there is an opportunity to barter obsolete goods with another business. Trading an old desk for some service or other good is very profitable.

Getting rid of clutter opens up space that can be employed in other ways to earn money. Owners may not even imagine such opportunities until they see the empty space made available by shedding all of the junk they have been hoarding.

Wringing the cash out of trash is a source of found money that may marginally lower the need for external financing to fund and grow the business. It may lower the cost of operating or even open up new possibilities for the business that the owners haven't stumbled upon yet.

Enhancing Sales, Sacrificing Profit Margins

Hopefully curiosity will get you to read this section, which may sound strange: lowering profits to produce cash. It can happen in some business situations.

Naturally, lowering prices will mean cutting profit margins. Why would owners do this? The obvious reason is to win business they were about to lose or to retain sales under threat from others. But how about just to pump up the sales volume by using price as a competitive edge?

The latter reason is the focus of this section—building sales through price reductions works in some business lines. Owners may lower profit margins but effectively increase profits due to the higher volume of revenues that they attract. The notion is not always advisable or needed, but owners should be aware of it as an alternative.

There are ways to employ this strategy selectively. If the pricing scheme is negotiated privately with each client and the terms are not transparent among them, owners can negotiate lower prices with only new or prospective clients to pick up new business.

In other words, owners should leave the present pricing matrix in place for existing clients but use lower prices to attract additional business that may presently be served elsewhere. Often the company will have certain fixed costs that are covered through breakeven sales. Additional business only increases variable costs, so the final profits grow with the extra volume even at lower prices.

Retail businesses that must post prices may not enjoy this luxury as selectively but can certainly determine whether price reductions work faster. Convenience stores generally price their gas sales daily, based on what their competition is doing. Many consumers track gas prices and make varying choices weekly based solely on price. These consumers can survey the differences from the comfort of their car.

Due to its competitive pricing, gasoline is a loss leader that is frequently priced with the intention to get people to drive up to a particular convenience store. The owner may not earn much profit on the gas but will make it up with the more profitable convenience sales inside the store or from other onsite revenues.

Using profit margin as a sales tool is sometimes a risky strategy because owners may learn that their competition is able to operate less expensively than they are. If owners start a bidding war by aggressively lowering prices and if competitors then match those lower prices, owners may learn that not only did they eliminate some profit opportunities but that the competition can go further.

Business owners should think through this strategy before trying it, but they should also count it among the options for building profits.

Borrow from Customers: Prepaid Sales

Imagine a situation where you were paid by every client ahead of performing a service or providing a product. How does that impact your financing needs? Obviously if your clients provide your working capital, you could operate more efficiently at a lower cost, maybe without the need of external financing. While this arrangement is normal for some businesses (think vending machines or movie theaters), it's absent in many businesses, such as manufacturing. If you can introduce such a payment pattern in your business—even if only partial payments—these funds can provide a valuable, inexpensive source of financing.

Some companies that create more expensive and unique products or services must invest significant working capital into production that is customized for the buyer. Since they only have one buyer for it, producing it without a majority of the costs being paid in advance would be a huge risk. Prepayment assures them that they will be paid and not get stuck with something they cannot sell to anyone else.

Prepayment means that this company will not be left unpaid with raw materials or specialized labor for their production. They must invest fixed costs necessary to have the expertise and infrastructure able to produce but, given their specialization, they don't spend on the variable costs without payment from the client.

Other companies sell commodity products or services that are very common without custom features or scarcity. Because of competition and readily available supply, requiring prepayment would probably damage sales. Imagine going to a grocery store for eggs, but the proprietor tells you to come back tomorrow and she will have some for you then if you pay today. You would most likely move on to the next store.

But there are ways a commodity supplier can generate prepaid sales. Think about Costco. It operates as a buying club, where members pay an annual fee to be able to purchase goods there—groceries, fresh produce, household goods, electronics, office supplies, and tools. At face value, why would anyone pay to go to a store that sells nothing unique but only commodities?

Costco offers price advantages. Its strategy combines the requirement of buying larger quantities from a smaller selection in a warehouse environment. All three characteristics lower its delivery costs, since it turns more inventory, stocks fewer goods, and spends less on real estate. Costco has lower labor costs, since many products are put out on pallets rather than being shelved; it concentrates on goods proven to sell high volumes; its warehouses are situated in larger, unimproved spaces on secondary streets.

If Costco's average price is 10 to15 percent below normal retail, customers get a tangible break and save money. The tradeoff is that customers must spend at least $500 before any actual savings are realized and must accept larger quantities. A case of soda is a more tolerable quantity than a gallon of mayonnaise.

The prepayment of the annual and ancillary fees is the real profit of the business and provides important cash flow and internal financing. The ability of many businesses to generate prepaid sales may not be traditional or apparent, but with some creativity can be a rewarding business model that preserves capital and lowers cost.

Borrow from Suppliers: Trade Credit

One frequently overlooked source of funds is from trade creditors—the companies that supply a business. While these sources may not exist for some industries, in others they thrive and represent a valuable source of inexpensive financing. At any given time there is about $1 trillion outstanding on open accounts, business to business. The average outstanding term to payment is 56 days.

Trade creditors offer business customers their goods or services on an open account to encourage sales. One example that almost everyone has access to are the utility companies. While you may have to put up a security deposit, utilities provide electricity, gas, and water on an open account. After getting the bill, you have 20 to 30 days to pay for your usage interest free.

Make no mistake—that is financing for a business. While most businesses probably have electric bills that total less than $5,000 per year, imagine a manufacturing company that may pay $300,000 per year for electricity. What if the company had to prepay it?

A $25,000 loan for 30 days at no interest becomes a little easier to visualize. If that cost were to have been required in advance, $25,000 would have been paid out of the business capital, lowering use in other places, or the company might have drawn it from a credit line with associated interest costs. Both sources represent significant costs to a company.

Trade credit enables the business to get a running start in its own cash cycle by gaining access to goods or services associated with the generation of revenues. This short-term credit is critical funding to give the business time to convert its production into cash with which it will pay its suppliers in turn.

Considering that some suppliers offer cash discounts for prepayment or very quick payment in 10 days, it's not always accurate to assume that trade credit is free. But considering that it is easier to get approved, is always renewable, and is available from competing sources, trade credit has many benefits not offered by other working capital financiers.

Companies sell to other companies on open account for many reasons. In some industries, frequent sales are made for low-ticket items. Think about an automotive repair shop that is working on all kinds of cars every day. The shop will order a dizzying selection of parts several times a day to keep the work flowing. Having to transfer payment on each sale would make conducting business less efficient and more expensive.

Other businesses sell to clients, such as a commercial laundry service or a beverage sales supplier, that need small deliveries to multiple locations. Collecting payments and accounting for them at each delivery stop would be impractical and burdensome. Trade credit allows these suppliers to send one invoice for several days' or weeks' worth of deliveries with a full accounting and be paid with one check from the buyer.

Companies trying to increase revenues or that are targeting a specific new account will sometimes use trade credit as an incentive to win the business. Depending on the company's own capitalization and profit margins, trade credit is a strong incentive to attract new business while increasing the target client's purchasing power.

It's important to note that trade credit must be maintained according to the terms offered by the seller. Habitually being late or not adhering to other terms could cause the credit to be cut off without notice, which could possibly leave the business in dire straits. Likewise a catastrophic event at the seller's business could shut off credit and make the buying business vulnerable to replacing the purchases quickly and with credit. It's a good idea to maintain multiple suppliers and a good contingency plan.

Creating Cash Out of Thin Air

Sometimes the best place for owners to look for financing is where they don't expect to find it. To get a better sense of where that is, it is helpful to expand the definition of the word financing beyond the notion of someone handing over a check. Only then is it possible to see how easy it is to access financing.

Lower Cash Needs

Too many entrepreneurs produce grandiose business plans that boost their egos but make no economic sense. Fancy offices, too many employees, or expensive benefits are symptoms of misplaced focus. These plans may propose an operation that spares no expense to create the owner's fantasy of a dream job, but shorts the prayers needed to actually make it work financially.

Most often these business plans hide the owners' unwillingness to earn their way into a business with this vision by throwing their first capital dollars at the instant gratification of their useless costs (and usually spending someone else's money). This kind of carefree spending rarely produces an economic benefit to the owners, who only multiply their risk of failure. Too many of these kinds of expenses are incurred for unsound reasons that do not generate revenue or profits for the business.

Owners should think twice about permitting their creative brain to get too far ahead of their practical brain. They should be cautious when permitting words like *atmosphere, vision,* and *upscale* to play a disproportionate role in creating the business plan. The Ritz Carlton was not built in a day.

Take Trade Discounts

The first half of a popular business phrase begins "cash talks." Many trade creditors offer significant discounts for a business if the owners pay cash on delivery (COD).

There are plenty of rewards owners can negotiate with immediate payment or even prepayment, which lowers the costs and risks to suppliers. Terms may vary per industry but are certainly negotiable with most vendors. A typical trade term may be quoted as 1 percent 10/Net 30. This translates into a 1 percent discount offered for invoices paid within 10 days of delivery. The full balance is due in 30 days.

As a business grows, discounts can be an important way to improve profitability. Managing the cash cycle more tightly can be a profitable exercise by taking advantage of such cost savings. In fact owners can probably negotiate better terms than cited in the previous paragraph by offering reliable, fast payments for all invoices.

Should owners borrow money to take advantage of such discounts? Only if they can negotiate a discount that is twice as large as the cost of borrowing the cash. Maintaining a line of credit to take advantage of these discounts may dilute savings, but if over the course of the year the owners are really lowering their costs, they should do it.

As owners accumulate cash profits in the business, they should begin to pay for these goods out of working capital to lower costs with discounts from suppliers.

Sometimes Giving Means Getting

Earlier in the chapter, the utility of clearing a business of unusable assets was described as a possible source of cash. But what about those items that just can't be sold?

Maybe there is an old desk that no one is willing to pay for because of the difficulty of moving it. Or maybe there are uniforms, phone systems, or office dividers that can no longer be used. Owners should consider contributing these kinds of items to a charitable enterprise. These items don't generate cash today, but they can be a deduction to earnings that can lower tax liabilities tomorrow.

Many charities, such as Goodwill Industries, operate thrift stores for furniture, appliances, clothing, and even vehicles. Some of these groups will even send a truck and crew to pick up large items that the organization will repair and resell. Deductions on charitable contributions are limited to 10 percent of taxable income and may offer some unique business advantages for gifts, such as computers for schools or shelters. It may be the last resort, but contributing excess assets does not cost business owners a dime and might actually save some cash.

Don't Be Shy

Some people have trouble accepting gifts, free samples, or even acts of marketing kindness from others, particularly in business. They should get over it. It's perfectly acceptable and normal behavior for vendors, bankers, financial planners, and even accountants to take business owners out to lunch to pitch their products or services. At trade shows, free meals, drinks, and entertainment are staples to get face time with prospects and, as a result, become someone's prospect.

Referral fees are fairly common in a number of industries for assistance in identifying new business for other parties. Volume rebates, overrides, and discounts are financial strategies used to recognize, earn, or grow valuable relationships. Business owners should be open to accepting these various sources of revenue without hesitation. There is no compromise in selling attention or time. Even if the value to an owner is only the price of a lunch, as the owner, it's one of the few tax-free benefits available.

Shop Till It Hurts

We are living in an age of unprecedented competition and innovation. Technology is simultaneously getting faster, easier, more functional, and cheaper, and we have to keep our eye on the price as well as on the deal. Big-box retailers have seemingly lowered the cost of everything.

Depending on how much owners use or rely on particular goods, it's a sound idea to keep someone tuned in to the costs and sources of what is needed. Planning ahead, surveying the landscape before purchasing, and knowing the pricing patterns of several sellers provides a better chance of lowering costs and saving money.

It is also important for owners to know their importance as buyers. If the company is a large consumer according to the supplier's standards, the company should be able to sell some semblance of loyalty for a price—paid for with tangible discounts. If the business is the largest account for someone, the company should benefit from that status or find another source that would love to get the business.

Owners must be cognizant of the fine print and terms of their deals. They must make smart choices, being fully aware of the obligations that better pricing places on them. For example, most cellular rate packages require a two-year service commitment. It is important to analyze these deals and make choices based on what provides the best deal, accounting for the entire commitment.

Owners should track these time commitments so that they will know when to shop around and review the market for renewal. These deals change constantly, and it behooves owners to know what it costs to modify any commitment. They may be able to negotiate a much better deal elsewhere, and the new seller may provide a credit equal to any penalty costs the owners may have to pay.

Business owners should watch for coupons, quantity purchases, and even Internet specials, because managing inventory in such a way as to take advantage of larger purchases can get better discounts. It is important for owners to take advantage of free delivery and always compare sales with the competition.

Employee Benefits

Benefits remain one of the most difficult costs to contain because owners must factor in the competition for talent when hiring new employees. Depending on the industry and the job positions, negotiations to lower benefits can be harder to deal with than annual salaries.

But the reality of the cost structure is that in the past 10 years, the earnings base for social security withholding taxes has increased more than 20 percent. That represents a tax increase to the business for every employee it has, and health-care benefit premiums have risen even faster.

Owners must weigh these costs against their ability to pay them with the profits they produce. In some instances, they may have to modify the benefits they offer to reflect what they can realistically afford to pay. The possibility that the benefits offered tomorrow will not be as good as they were yesterday is a problem not isolated to a given company.

One way to control or reduce benefit costs may include using a cafeteria-style benefit plan that offers more options tailored to the needs of employees. The company fixes its benefit contribution per employee, and employees can spend the contribution as they see fit.

Rather than reducing or eliminating health insurance coverage for employees, owners should first offer to lower the company's share of the expense. This option will permit the employees to set their own financial priorities. The company may be paying for 100 percent of the insurance coverage today but, due to premium increases, lowering that contribution to 70 percent may be better than lowering or eliminating coverage.

Another idea is to explore smarter benefit plans for employees. Many people feel that medical insurance should pay every dollar of their cost without regard for the cost or need for the services they expect. Higher benefit reimbursements require disproportionately larger than necessary premiums.

A better idea to contain cost is by raising benefit deductibles and adding copayments to insurance coverage. Sharing the costs, particularly the first few hundred dollars (deductibles) and a smaller contribution for doctor visits and pre-scriptions (copayments), lowers the potential cost to the insurer. More important, eventually it will also make the insured person a better health-care consumer. Rather than trotting off to the doctor for a non-serious illness, such as a cold, maybe employees will try to resolve their illnesses first with something over the counter.

Medical insurance should be more about covering catastrophic medical costs and less about paying for a habit of fighting minor ailments with a doctor and hundreds of dollars of wonder drugs. Raising the deductible from $1,000 to $1,500 is a great way to lower premiums substantially. It might even be that the company could save enough on lower premiums to contribute all or part of the deductible expense for the employees by self-insuring the front end of coverage.

Benefits are important, but having a job is more important. Owners should communicate with their employees frankly and honestly if changes are necessary to keep sufficient working capital in the company.

Examine the Costs

Sometimes getting the best price for a regular expense stops too short of how far it is necessary to go to control expenses. Periodically owners need to assess all operating costs and determine whether they are necessary or could be eliminated.

Spending choices and priorities are made for a number of reasons, but process and conditions are constantly changing. It is common for processes to be rendered obsolete by technology, but no one looks backward far enough to cancel a spending practice that was needed at an earlier date.

An occasional review of the general ledger may remind owners that they are spending money unnecessarily. The company's lobby may be filled with stacks of glossy magazines, but is anyone reading them now that the business has installed a widescreen television?

Are the owners benefiting from memberships in trade associations or the chamber of commerce affiliation? What about networking groups, leads clubs, civic organizations, and other community groups that require paid memberships? Is the staff taking advantage of these memberships or has the person who used to benefit from them left the company?

These are minor examples of how owners can get into the habit of paying for things they don't need. They can result in lower profits and may also be symptomatic of other expenses of greater consequence that cost the company money. Without a regular review such costs grow and become harder to find.

Owners should review their telephone costs, credit card merchant statements, supplier contracts, payroll records, and other places where larger dollars are spent to ensure they are getting what they paid for or at least still want. This is also a good practice to ensure they are benefiting from the deals they cut and are not being overcharged.

It is critical for owners to evaluate the cost details at least annually and not to hesitate to eliminate those that don't directly contribute to the well-being of the enterprise.

Guard Against Fraud

No business is too small to be a victim of fraud. There may not be millions involved but certainly no owner wants to be victimized for small amounts over time that ultimately become a proportionally huge loss to the business.

It bears repeating that many small enterprises fall victim to telephone solicitation for office supplies. An anonymous caller may telephone to offer a deal on copier toner, print cartridges, or some other specialized supply item. As innocent as that sounds, the caller gets the person who answers the phone to reveal the model number of the relevant piece of office equipment in order to send a price list.

Questions that prompt the employee to reveal the name of the purchasing agent or check writer are: Who makes these buying decisions? and To whom should we direct this information?

Four weeks later, a package arrives with a dozen off-brand goods that are priced about 20 percent higher than what the business normally pays for recognized brands. And there's an invoice that indicates that the order was placed by the name given to these fraudsters on the basis of the innocent-sounding telephone call.

No problem? Just don't pay for it? Well, it's not that simple. If the company recognizes that these are goods that were not ordered, returning them immediately becomes a hassle due to the lack of an address or the need to get authorization. That authorization is always denied, of course, without payment of a large cancellation penalty and the cost of return shipping. Meanwhile there is a lot pressure for payment of the invoice.

Using the individual's name as proof, the scam then employs a collection agency to bring additional pressure to bear through harassing phone calls and threats to report the failure to pay to the credit bureau and Dun & Bradstreet. The company may even get a letter from an attorney. Many small businesses will just pay to be done with it.

Too often the company's check writer isn't the person who orders supplies, and the company may not use purchase orders. So the cartridges are put in the supply room, and the invoice gets paid. That fraud may cost the business a few hundred dollars for inferior goods.

And, of course, a steady stream of shipments starts, with each arriving every six weeks. This is sometimes the beginning of a long, unintended relationship. Over time the outrageously priced goods could result in thousands of dollars of overcharges. Who knew?

Another fraudulent scheme is where callers represent a fundraising effort to benefit a legitimate group, such as the local fraternal association of firemen or policemen. The caller seeks a charitable contribution to support some innocuous fund to benefit widows and orphans.

What the caller doesn't reveal is that for the fundraising effort, 95 percent of the proceeds are skimmed off the top, and the caller contributes a paltry sum to the organization used as the hook for the scheme. While technically legal, these schemes lead people to believe their hard-earned money is going to a worthwhile cause rather than to some sleazy boiler-room operation.

In such a case, the caller may apply pressure and come close to saying that the business may not be provided with fire and police protection if it doesn't make a contribution.

This is the time for the business owner to hang up the phone. If the owner has caller ID, she should report the call to the local police. Owners should not give callers of this type any money because they will call again with a different charity. If owners want to make charitable contributions, they can find worthy organizations that represent their priorities.

Sometimes Spending Saves Money

Contrary to the idea of just refusing to write checks, sometimes the smart employment of cash actually goes a long way toward preserving future cash requirements or can buy permanent reductions in potential costs.

Owners should consider independent payroll processing. Our employment taxation system is a tedious process of overlapping taxes, altering deadlines, and progressive schedules. The federal tax rules change at least annually, and deciphering the rules can be very difficult for the limited staff of smaller companies.

There are many payroll processing companies that perform these services as simply as filing basic information. All owners have to do is confirm employees' work schedules, and a complete set of payroll checks, company records, and payroll deposit reports are delivered on schedule. The payroll company provides an automated service that would require a full-time employee to perform inside the company.

Owners should also think about the volume buying of various goods and inventory. If they have the storage space and discipline, often they can negotiate larger buys at great prices if they can manage the volume of inventory. Buying more can cost less.

Or owners should consider maintenance contracts for important equipment components that must operate with consistency. Rather than put the uninterrupted service of the business at risk, maintenance contracts ensure that the machinery is serviced according to the manufacturer's specifications, and they lower the risk of a surprise breakdown during crucial work periods.

These contracts should not be confused with short-term warranties. Today, most electronic products offer a warranty for a cost of about 20 percent of the product. This warranty probably offers to repair for free or replace the item if it fails within two or three years.

Owners should not buy any such warranty. Manufacturers know that selling five 20 percent warrantees earns them the retail price of another new item. Obviously they know that one item in so many will fail. Owners can rest assured that the performance rate is much better than one in five.

Replacement warranties are very high-priced lottery tickets. If owners never buy them they may end up replacing a 90-day-old electronic product someday. But that will be much cheaper than increasing the price of all electronic purchases by 20 percent. The business should self-insure against these sorts of small loses.

Manage Money Better

Every day banks across the country make millions of small loans at extraordinarily high interest rates: they pay checks on overdrawn accounts. Nonsufficient funds

(NSF) advances are made on the good faith of the bank to pay a business's checks when the account does not have collected funds to cover them.

For relationships that the bank assesses as an adequate risk, it will cover a business owner's calculation or timing mistakes by advancing the amount of the check(s) for a fee. But at least the owner didn't have to apply for the loan. These charges range from $30 to $40 and are not altered for higher or lower check denominations. This means that the same fee applies for a $5.00 and $505 check.

These costs are so unnecessary. Either people need to do a much better job balancing the checkbook or they need to stop living hand-to-mouth with their money. Managing money better means writing out checks only when there is enough money to cover them.

NSF charges are a very high cost of irresponsibility. Accidents happen, but so many businesses actually accumulate thousands of dollars annually for the service gladly provided by the bank.

And these fees don't improve an owner's relationship with the bank. The bank tracks the performance of the business's account and has the right to arbitrarily stop such conveniences without notice. Better cash management will prevent such obscene costs and keep the banking relationship on better footing as well.

Thinking More or Less

There are thousands of ways for business owners to increase cash flow, produce incremental sources of funds, reduce costs, or eliminate expenses. It only takes the willingness to study the business operation on a regular basis. Owners must accept convention while believing it will change.

Owners should explore different ways to do things and realize that they can live without many creature comforts for the good of the business. They should visit competitors or businesses in the industry who aren't competitors to see what they do differently. In this way owners can get ideas for how to improve their business.

Profitable Revenues Are Still the Best Financing

This chapter has jumped among many ideas and strategies for producing cash or for lowering the need for it in a variety of ways. It shouldn't end without confronting the most reliable way to finance a venture: through growing profitable revenues. Creating and retaining profits is the lowest-cost, lowest-risk source of financing over which owners alone control access.

This is easier said than done, but if owners have the fire in the belly to have ventured into business in the first place, they know that selling their product, idea, or self is what it is all about. Sales can be a relentless, endless job to search out opportunities, open relationships, and negotiate transactions. And tomorrow, it starts all over again.

Owners cannot stop. It's the reason the business is in business in the first place. If owners want to be the experts, the managers, the specialists, or the consultants, maybe they should have stayed in corporate life. If they want to be entrepreneurs, they are essentially in the sales business.

So what to do? Reading a finance book is probably the last place to turn to for the best sales advice. There are more gurus writing sales and marketing books than can be counted, and they must be pretty good, for they keep selling. But there are some fundamentals that bear repeating, since this source of financing is so vital to the health and sustainability of any business.

- **People do business with people they like.** Simple but true, people do business with people they feel comfortable with and like. Make an effort to be nice and build a sales force that shares that same frame of mind.
- **Don't wait for clients to find you.** Opportunities don't rush to your door, so you have to be aggressive to get out there and find the business sales for your enterprise. They may be closer than you realize, and they're worth funding for the sale.
- **Be obvious; set yourself apart.** Being in sales is no place to be a shrinking violet. In a crowded marketplace with plenty of competition you have to set yourself apart. Make it obvious that you are the best at what you do—the expert and the opinion leader. Build a social network, write articles, and make speeches. Make sure people think of you when they think of your industry.
- **Wants, needs, features, and benefits.** The fundamental strategy of selling is to listen to your client's wants and needs and answer them with your features and benefits. Selling is a two-way conversation, and you will be more successful if you shut up and let the clients tell you what they want.
- **Price sells cars.** It's amazing how many people who cannot afford a $50,000 car will sign an $800 per month lease on a $50,000 car. All dealers understand the game and break the price down to the level that is accessible and is easier to calculate. Make sure you know how to price your business for your clients.
- **ABC—always be closing.** Some people are ready to buy faster than others. Don't interrupt people's agreement to your terms by continuing to convince

them about what they have already decided. Always be closing and always know when it's time to have your client sign on the dotted line.

Don't Get a Quick, Ill-Advised Loan

In banking, the request to rush a loan draws a reply something like, "If you need an answer right now, it's no." Not to be hurried, banks, commercial finance companies, and leasing companies need time to assess proposals and make an unhurried judgment based on their deliberate consideration.

But sometimes businesses need money fast. Whether it's an emergency, an opportunity, or just tomorrow's payroll, owners will drop everything in a frantic search for cash. After having the door slammed in their faces at the usual sources, they turn and look at the remaining choices, the lenders of last resort. These sources can usually be counted on for something, but only with significant costs.

Owners should resist this temptation.

Of course I am talking about personal finance companies, hard money lenders, title lenders, and pawn brokers. These lenders charge a lot more money because they seem to take more risk. And after a while owners learn that these entities really don't take more risk. As a situation becomes less attractive to mainstream financing, the cost of capital rises in part because there are fewer options. Here is a quick synopsis of how these lenders operate, which hopefully will make working with them more distasteful.

Personal Finance Companies

These companies are consumer-driven lenders that make smaller loans (generally $25,000 and less) in the form of short-term (12 to 42 months) installment loans. They will generally take more risks, be tolerant of lower credit scores, and tack a lien onto anything as collateral without all the hassle a bank might engender. Sometimes owners can even score unsecured credit if they have a good credit score and obvious positive credit history.

Why are personal finance companies so reasonable? Owners will pay upward of an effective 30 to 40 percent interest in some states for these loans. Through myriad consumer finance laws that vary from state to state, their use of fees, discounts, late charges, and penalties easily drive the borrowing costs up beyond the stated rate.

Hard Money Lenders

These lenders offer very restrictive financing against the equity owners may have in real property or other assets that are relatively easy for them to convert to cash. Make no mistake: these lenders do not take risk. To provide liquidity for the strong equity position of the owners, they get very high interest rates for relatively low exposure to loss.

Essentially hard money lenders provide a narrow extension of credit based on a reliable evaluation of the asset value. Typically they are positioned to earn more money if the deal fails than if it's repaid. Normal cost for hard money loans is in the 18 to 24 percent range.

Title Lenders

These lenders offer the same kind of credit as is offered by the hard money lenders except their business licensing is the same as a pawn broker. In other words they can charge significant fees to pawn a car title that may equate to a 20 to 30 percent interest on the dollars borrowed. (See the next section for more information.)

Pawn Brokers

These companies lend dollars amounting to an assessment of what they will advance on the value of steeply discounted assets they hold as security. They charge a service fee for each month the advance is outstanding, and if the assets are not redeemed before the prescribed date, they are entitled to sell them to recoup the advance.

These operations are not licensed or supervised by banking regulators but rather by the local police precinct. Their service fees are extremely high and vary state to state. For example, in Georgia, brokers can assess fees up to 25 percent per month on their advances for three months, followed by 12.5 percent per month afterward. For a one-year advance, that would amount to 187 percent interest.

Part 5

Best Sources for Equity Capital

13

EQUITY FINANCING

One of the most commonly misunderstood sources of financing for small business enterprises is equity capital. Equity is funding contributed to the business by its founders and other parties in exchange for an ownership interest, usually without a maturity, rate of return, or legal requirement of redemption. Starting any business requires capital and the more the better.

Cash contributed to the business by its owner is frequently called seed money. These funds are most at risk because they are used to organize everything from scratch, launching the enterprise prerevenue and preprofit. But like any seeds, their success may depend on later fertilizing and watering. Growth often brings on the need for additional funds to expand. Where do those funds come from?

That's the magic question every entrepreneur must answer in order to bridge the divide between dreams and success. Finding the equity may take weeks, months, or years, depending on the specific ideas, experience, and luck. Other factors will include persistence and salesmanship.

One objective in this chapter is to define the various equity sources available with the context of what kind of business profiles are actually fundable. The cold hard reality is that a majority of businesses are not going to attract angel investors, venture capital, or private equity investments.

Beyond the personal contribution of seed money from the owners, there are five categories of equity financing that may or may not be tied to the particular stage a business is in:

- **Friends, family, and fools** (conceptual stage, $100,000 to $300,000)
- **Angel investors** (start-up or early stage, $500,000 to $2,000,000)

- **Venture capital** (emerging stage, $5,000,000 to $15,000,000)
- **Private equity investors** (growth stage, $20,000,000 to $50,000,000)
- **Initial public offerings** (expansion stage, $20,000,000 to $100,000,000)

Learning whether a business is a serious contender to attract equity from any of these categories will primarily begin by assessing how the business looks in the eyes of the prospective investor. These are some of the various factors that will drive an investor's interest in the business deal:

- **Industry.** Private capital generally wants to invest in opportunities that reflect innovation that can leverage technology or other factors to disrupt the marketplace and create fast, profitable growth. But owners should not think that technology companies corner the market—they only represent about 20 percent of the Inc. 500. It's the growth potential that attracts equity capital. A new iPhone application can be grown much greater and faster than can a day-care center.

    Innovation is not limited to technology but can be a new way to deliver a mature product or service. Devising a way to aggregate more business volume with a lower cost or unique delivery scheme can reinvigorate a very docile industry. It's these kinds of ideas that will appeal to investors.
- **Location.** While angel investors are more evenly distributed around the United States, the venture capital market is primarily based in California (37 percent), Silicon Valley (29 percent), New York and Boston (25 percent), and the Raleigh–Durham, North Carolina–Atlanta area (6 percent). Where a business is located may determine what kind of capital it can attract and the cost of access to prospective investors. It will also possibly impact the success of the business's launch, which will be crucial for subsequent financing rounds.
- **Management team.** Investors are seeking individuals who can provide leadership and exceptional performance. They will assess the skills, experience, style, and goals of the management team, all of which will weigh heavily in the funding decisions. There is no room for mediocrity, so make sure the entire business team is capable and that any social issues are dealt with ahead of entering the search for capital.
- **Business stage.** The funding sources listed above for companies in various stages of growth are not definitive. Most angel investors fund start-ups, but most venture capitalists generally do not. Private equity funds generally require that the company already be well into revenues with profits in the foreseeable future. Most equity investors are looking for a realistic time

frame during which their capital can push the company's progress forward toward a defined exit event.

- **Scalability of business.** To attract equity funding the business plan has to be scalable into real growth. Cool technologies can go viral and grow very large very fast, but a dry cleaner cannot. The realistic growth prospects in a relatively short period (three to five years) will draw attention from equity investors.

  Equity investors are seeking returns that can only come from businesses that can grow exponentially or that will be attractive as targets for other businesses to acquire due to their product niche, similarity, or aggregation value in the acquirers' horizontal or vertical growth strategy.

- **Prospective return on investment.** Equity investors are aiming to make an annual 25 to 30 percent return on their portfolio. Since they recognize that several of these ventures will fail, they aim to yield about 60 percent on each investment to compensate for the averages.

  Business owners must recognize that the investment return for equity investors is not about how much income can be grown over the long term, but rather how high and fast the company's valuation can be grown on a shorter time line. Investors aren't as interested in dividends as in contributing to an enterprise whose value will vault quickly into a liquid security that can be sold to others for a very rewarding profit.

- **Accredited investors.** Investors who provide the funding for angel capital, private equity investments, and venture capital are required to be accredited investors, meaning that they must attest to the qualification of an annual taxable income exceeding $200,000 for the past two years and the current year ($300,000 for joint tax returns) or a minimum net worth of at least $1 million, not including their personal residence. Only 5 percent of the U.S. population qualifies to be an accredited investor.

  Despite these barriers investment capital is alive and well notwithstanding the recent crisis in the capital markets. There are more than 250,000 angel investors and just fewer than 900 venture capital funds in the United States. In 2010 there were approximately 61,900 angel investment deals totaling over $20 billion and 2,750 venture capital transactions contributing another $22 billion of equity.[1]

- **Compliance.** Later-stage investors will have a firm grasp of the laws that regulate raising equity capital through the sale of securities, but in the event

---

1. Angel Investing—An Overview, a program of the Ewing Marion Kaufmann Foundation, 2006–2011

that owners are soliciting funds from friends and family, it's likely that no one will think about the rules to engage. Depending on how much money is being raised, it's likely that owners are exempt from registration but nonetheless are subject to security regulations. Owners should be aware of some basic information to ensure that their activities are not in violation of the law.

Two major compliance issues are:

1. **Registration.** Registration is not desirable due to the cost burden and extraordinary disclosure required, particularly relative to smaller transactions. The best course of action is to determine how to be exempted from registration and follow the rules to the letter.
2. **Antifraud protections.** Even for small investments, if owners are approaching multiple prospective investors they should provide a written prospectus of the proposed security sale. This prospectus should contain the exact financing terms being offered, with full disclosure of any material risks or information about the company or its management.

Regulation D of the Securities Act of 1933 provides safe harbor rules under which security sales may be exempt. While rules 505 and 506 provide for inclusion of up to 35 nonaccredited investors, the disclosure rules to do so are burdensome and frequently passed over for only accredited investors.

a. **Rule 504.** Security offerings for up to $1 million in a 12-month period are exempt from registration and the number of investors is not limited, and they do not have to be accredited. These offerings are not exempt from state registration and cannot be advertised.
b. **Rule 505.** Security offerings for less than $5 million in a 12-month period with an unlimited number of accredited investors and no more than 35 unaccredited investors. These securities do not have to be registered with federal regulators but are not exempt from state registration and cannot be advertised. Disclosure documents must be provided to all nonaccredited investors.
c. **Rule 506.** Security offerings without value limit but must exceed $5 million. No more than 35 nonaccredited investors can be involved and all must be sophisticated, meaning that although the investors may not qualify as accredited, their business and financial experience provides them with the knowledge to make good investment decisions. These offerings cannot be advertised or solicited to unknown parties.

- **How to navigate?** Equity investors are more focused, experienced, and perhaps more demanding than lenders. After all, it's their money on the line and they would prefer not to lose it. Accordingly, they are quite selective about where it goes. Underwriting their deals may take more time, since they are making a much more subjective decision and do not have the second or third source of repayment lenders get from collateral and personal guarantees.

While angel investors are more personally attached to their funds and to the investments they make, equity investors and venture capitalists pool their funds with contributions from many other investors to invest. Their emotional attachment is not as strong as that of angels, and they tend to have a different kind of incentive involved: they have to place the funds from their pools within a certain time frame or risk having to return the money to their investors.

But owners should expect the same fundamental questions when approaching any equity investor: Why does this deal make sense? Do you have the capacity to make this deal happen? What kind of return can I get on my investment? How much funding do you need?

The most common mistake for owners is to not have a reasonable value figured out for their exit strategy. Funders will have their own ideas, and if owners are too aggressive in figuring out the value of the prospective deal, they will walk away. It is very important for owners not to just agree to any deal to get funding. Preinvestment valuation of shares obviously affects the postinvestment valuation. If set too high up front, those investors will get seriously diluted as more money comes in from more sophisticated investors in later rounds.

Since valuation in the earliest stages is a very difficult challenge, many investors choose to use convertible debt to finance seed/start-up companies with equity options or kickers, so to provide protection for the investment, with an option to convert to equity when a clearer view of the valuation is available. (Read more about convertible debt and valuation later in the chapter.)

When preparing to meet investors, it's important for owners to have figured out the math and at least have a term sheet available to set forth what they believe the deal should look like. Where feasible they should have a subscription agreement drafted ahead of time to get the deal documented faster if the investors bite.

Until owners are involved in a public sale of registered securities through a licensed investment bank, every offering is a private placement, meaning it is not offered to the general public, is not registered with a regulatory agency that has approved its disclosure, and is limited as to the dollar amount, number of investors, or composition of investors.

While the legal requirements are certainly relaxed in a private securities sale, owners should expect to pay a minimum of $20,000 on legal expenses to prepare for selling securities to others, whether family or angel investors. These costs prepare documentation, like a subscription agreement, which is needed to protect all parties for these investments.

Of major importance for owners to understand is that they must offer everyone the same deal. They cannot negotiate the share prices, terms, or preferences differently with different investors unless they disclose all of these terms to all parties in writing ahead of the actual collection of funds. The subscription agreement lays out the investment in plain terms.

When owners arrive to the venture round or private equity funds, these investments may not use a private placement memorandum approach, but rather will issue term sheets that must be negotiated with legal representation and will drive these costs higher. Should the deal be a much larger investment ($10 million or more) with a private equity firm that is driven by a broker dealer, the actual legal costs will be significantly higher.

Once an investment is agreed to, most investors do not transfer the entire sum on day one. Funds are generally not all needed on closing day but rather over time. Investors prefer to schedule funding in tranches with the timing tied to specific milestones, which will be negotiated accomplishments planned for the business that must be achieved ahead of subsequent funding rounds or installments. In some angel investments, owners may have to continue raising money after the first tranche without a clear idea of who is funding subsequent rounds.

What follows is an in-depth look at these various equity capital sources and what business owners will face when seeking investment from them. Owners must be prepared to speak with and pitch to many, many investors. Many people will listen if only to satisfy themselves that they really don't want to invest in the deal—investors turn over a lot of rocks to find something that interests them. Owners will make their pitch to many encouraging people who will ultimately not be interested—that's to be expected. When moving on to the next pitch, owners should ask the disinterested investor for feedback so as to strengthen the next pitch or at least for advice on how the deal could be made more palatable to other investors.

Friends and Family

These prospective investors include the people on this earth who know the owners, believe in them, and are willing to show that affection by enabling the enterprise with their money. These investors will fund the concept stage of the business that gets it up and running to produce revenue. This category can usually be counted on to raise the first $100,000 to $300,000 and are generally less concerned about the due diligence that other investors would insist on.

In return they will bear the most risk, usually be totally unobservant about the success (or failure) of the business, and often be diluted and shut out of the future upside by subsequent rounds of financing. On the other hand, they will always continue to be around after the deal is history. Owners have to see their mother much more often than they do a former angel investor after losing $25,000 of her hard-earned savings.

If the business is targeting a local market, the owners' personal network is an excellent source of financing. Figuring out how much money is needed and who to get it from may be simple. More complicated is to provide at least an idea of how those people will be rewarded for their trust and when they will get back their capital.

The best advice for owners is to be sure they have a good business plan and not to take advantage of the goodwill involving these investors. Business failure is an awful topic to be reminded of at Thanksgiving for the next 25 years.

Investment in this stage of the business should be common stock. A simple percentage of ownership is easier, particularly considering that owners are generally working with less sophisticated investors in the earliest days. If an investor demands too many assurances or too many restrictions, that investor may not be suited to investing. If the business has a real shot at attracting later-stage capital, the owners will lower their prospects by tying up all opportunities with a complicated capitalization schedule.

Angel Investors

Angel investors have been around forever, but the name is newer, probably appearing sometime over the last 20 years. Comprised of a mostly unaffiliated market of accredited, entrepreneurial investors, these investors focus on small, start-up, or growth-stage businesses and provide funding to augment the thin resources of the business owner.

Only about 5 percent of the U.S. population are accredited investors, only 5 percent of that number are angel investors, and only 5 percent of those investors join angel investor groups. There are about 170 angel groups nationwide, but there are no universal terms, strategies, or investment criteria, although a majority of angel investors make investments along with other angels, not necessarily as an organized group.

Angel investors generally put in $25,000 to $50,000 per deal that contributes to a total deal size that ranges from $300,000 to $2 million. The most common deals are in the $500,000 to $1.5 million range. Presently angels fund an average of 16 percent of the transactions they personally review, though most might only contribute to two or three deals per year.

The importance of angel investors to the small business sector can't be overstated, having completed 2010 funding in excess of $20 billion. Angel investors are the front line for equity capital and can contribute to growth in other ways as a mentor and director to the enterprise.

Typical angel investors have accumulated wealth during a career as a successful businessperson or professional themselves. Typically they will make good advisors for the investment company, particularly when grouped with other investors who may have different skill sets. Investors who have more to contribute than money are an added feature of angel funding, particularly at the early stage of a business.

How does a business qualify for equity financing from angels? Owners should consider these investors to be partners. Unlike a banker, they are putting up their own money and are not restrained by regulators or loan committees. They listen to a proposal, read the business plan, perform their due diligence, crunch their own numbers, and make an offer—or not.

Where Are Angels?

The first step is to find them. Angel investors are generally accessible, particularly if owners are referred to them by someone they know. Unlike venture capitalists, who like to remain more anonymous, angels are easier to find because they are looking for smaller, earlier-stage deals. A good source for finding angel investors may be through referrals from a banker, a lawyer, or an accountant.

There are also some networking organizations in different markets that provide introduction events for owners and investors. While these events generally have mixed results, they are probably a good place for owners to expand their network and may eventually lead to identifying investors. Another good place to inquire is a local business incubator.

To get started, owners must develop a good "elevator pitch" that can summarize the deal in three or four paragraphs. Once angels have heard that, they will indicate whether or not they want to hear more. With that pitch owners have to work the phones and the crowd. They have to get face or telephone time with every person identifiable as an investor and let the deal speak for itself.

Approaching most investors is more of a serious conversation than a beauty contest. They are less interested in business plans than in getting to know solid business people (though owners still need a good business plan if only to sharpen their command of where they are heading with the business idea).

Angels will spend considerable time discussing the deal, listening to plans, and the owners with regard to the proposed investment. If owners can produce a good plan and solid numbers, they will work to figure out a deal that makes sense for everyone.

The investment strategy for most equity investors is not about how much income can be grown over time, but rather how high and fast the company's valuation can be grown. Investors are not interested in waiting for management to retire to cash out, meaning that the job security and happiness of the owners is not their focus.

Rather these investors want to employ capital that will move the company along a defined growth path. This process is designed to scale the business size and value along the way to a subsequent round of financing. At the end, angel investors want an equity interest that will become liquid and can be sold to others for a sizable profit.

Valuation

The investment decision will come down to whether and how much the business has the potential to significantly increase its value at a projected point in the future. Valuation is a complicated estimation of how much a business could be sold for at a future date. There are several ways to place a value on the enterprise, but for investors this valuation has to be done in advance—often before the business has customers, revenues, or products.

One method employed by some investors is to use an informal comparison method. They will assess several components of the subject enterprise, like the caliber of management, the competition, the idea, or the technology protection and likelihood of revenues. By comparing these features to those of a similar venture with which they have familiarity, they will try to assess the future value of their subject business to produce a valuation. This method is obviously very subjective.

A more straightforward approach to employ when there are some actual metrics available is to use a discounted future value approach. Based on a mutually agreed formula to derive the future target value, investors will determine the price of their investment based on their earning target as a percentage of the estimated future value.

For example, assume the following components of particular investment negotiation:

- Company will produce $4 million EBITDA in the fifth year of operation.
- Investor and owner agree that valuation should be 15x multiple of EBITDA.
- Investor requires a 10x return on investment in five years.
- Investment required is $2 million.

So in this scenario,

Company target value = 15 × $4 million EBITDA = $60 million
Investor target return = 10 × $ 2 million = $20 million
Return / Value = $20 million / $60 million = 33%
Therefore, investor requires 33% equity for $2 million investment

Convertible Promissory Notes

Sometimes very early-stage investors will use convertible notes as a way to document their investment transaction. The reason is simple: there is no credible way to value the company in its prerevenue stage without financials or a track record. Promissory notes are less expensive to prepare and execute and represent a promise to negotiate the equity division at the next round.

These notes sometimes carry a provision for a mandatory conversion of the loan to equity at the next financing round, but not always. Sometimes the promissory notes are expected to be repaid from the proceeds, but the investor/lender will get equity options, or kickers, to acquire common and/or preferred shares in the next round at the then-determined valuation.

Due Diligence

Due diligence in any transaction is a two-way proposition. Questions should be expected and welcomed by seasoned investors. Investors will appreciate that owners are not just handing the door keys over to anyone and should be willing to provide information about themselves before owners disclose their most sensitive information.

Owners should ask investors for references, particularly with regard to bankers, attorneys, and other companies in which they have invested. Owners will not be verifying account balances, but rather listening for these persons to confirm that these investors are serious, capable, and experienced. If angels can't or won't let the owners speak with others who can attest to their good reputation, owners need to ask why.

Termination or Exit Event

When the business arrives at the point where it has achieved the goals set with the angel's investment and it's time to graduate to a higher level of investment, this is called the termination, or exit event. There are several ways for the business to proceed through the exit, depending on the industry, opportunity, and stage of scaling to its long-term goal.

Angel investors prefer for the business to be sold to an equity investor or to roll up into a larger business that needs the capacity of the subject business. In this way the angel is cashed out and can lock in any gains as planned. Alternatively, graduating into the next equity financing round may permit the company to generate more funding while buying out the angel investor's interest. This kind of transaction meets the objectives of the company and the investors.

Less desirable for angels is for the company to graduate to venture capital. Venture capitalists generally don't like for their funds to be used to cash out earlier investors. The attraction of this potential funding leaves the angels vulnerable to being crammed down, or diluted, with their preferences reduced or eliminated, since the venture capitalists may negotiate for a better share price.

In any case, angels know these risks and take them into account before they invest in the first place.

Private Equity Sales

Another source of equity capital is a private equity sales offering. This financing is raised by investment bankers through a securities offering limited to their client investors rather than the public at large. Any private share sales exceeding $1 million cannot include more than 35 nonaccredited investors and more often than not is exclusively sold to accredited investors.

These offerings are often sold to investors who are not dedicating as much time to investing as an angel investor would and may seek a more diversified portfolio of securities. These securities are offered in smaller minimum units, meaning that the investors may purchase as few as $5,000 or $10,000. This makes the investment more attractive to investors who are relying on the due diligence performed by the bankers, since their exposure is limited and they can spread investments to more deals.

Companies electing to raise equity in this manner are reliant on an exemption from registration under Regulation D, described earlier in this chapter. The resale of shares purchased through private sales are restricted to conditions described in Rule 144 and generally cannot be sold less than two years after issuance.

Private sales can be conducted directly by the company if no sales commissions are paid for the funds generated, but this would be unusual given the burden of disclosure and restrictions on promoting the sale. These placements cannot be advertised to the general public and, according to the regulations, the seller agent is supposed to have a preexisting relationship with the customer and is therefore prohibited from making cold calls to other parties to solicit these sales.

Venture Capital

Venture capital is the financing stage that can take a proven company with more potential and provide financing to move it from a $50 million sales enterprise to a $500 million enterprise, all for a very healthy cost derived from shares bought or promised at a very low value. There are fewer than 1,000 active venture capital funds today.

In a shift from the go-go days of the 1970s and 1980s, venture investors rarely fund start-up companies or even companies prerevenue or preprofit. They are searching for safer investments that do not need as much hand-holding and management oversight but those that have all of the components in place to be on track for a larger transition to either an IPO or ownership by a much larger concern. They make later-stage investments out of necessity, because the business valuations need to be in line with the large investments made by the venture funds.

Venture funds are comprised of larger units of capital that are pooled to form funds ranging from $50 million to $100 million. These funds are raised by a group of partners that will serve as the principal investors for the group and generally will reflect a healthy contribution of their own money.

The pools may take two to four years to fully invest, but since each investment may only average $2 to $5 million, there is considerable work to do to find and negotiate a series of good deals. And they do have an obligation to invest the money, so there is some pressure to identify deals and get the money placed. After the fund is depleted the partners will set out to raise another pool and start the process over with another round of investments.

The availability of funds for each fund depends on where it is in its own life cycle. Venture funds are cognizant of the economic conditions and accordingly are more cautious during recessionary periods. During the latest economic cycle beginning in 2008, venture funds have been harder to organize due to the lack of returns for committed funds. Reportedly some venture investors have been trolling the angel market to buy out deals.

Like angel investors, venture funds are seeking average returns in the 20x to 30x range. Most of their investments do not score that well, but they do well enough to assure their investors handsome returns far exceeding the S&P or Dow Jones Industrial Average. Venture investors may include an assortment of well-heeled individuals, publicly owned mutual funds, pension funds, and even successful private or public companies.

More commonly, venture investments are made in companies that have survived well past the start-up and emerging stages and have established a good market for their products or services. They have arrived at the last checkpoint on the path of potentially becoming a really large company. They need a healthy round of financing to expand their production capacity, enlarge their distribution network, acquire more territory, or implement a grander strategy that carries the promise of multiplying their success.

To get past this last frontier these companies need an infusion of money that no bank will provide. Funding from a venture capital fund may range from $5 to $20 million, although these sums generally involve several funds contributing monies in a syndicate to achieve their goals but lower their risk.

Venture capital investors are usually focused on particular industry sectors where its partners have a depth of experience. That experience is likely to have been gained not only from investing activities but also from years spent in the industry as an executive managing a real company. As a result, they invest only in what they know best. This focus will also define the business stage they are interested in and a specialization in moving their investments through a familiar strategy, whether that be taking it through an IPO or selling the business to a Fortune 1000 company as an exit strategy.

More often than not venture capital funds are investing in technology. They are targeting companies that are market makers, whose innovation defines a new direction and brings with it the prospect of larger rewards. They may even be ripe for deals with a shorter horizon, like mobile applications, because the successful conversion to a high-value company requires a fast investment to capture a market that is always susceptible to change. Venture funds can move quickly.

Venture investors do not buy into businesses that require operating support or ongoing cash injections. They invest in operations that are self-sustaining with earnings and have a growth trajectory that will be fueled by the injection of venture financing to grow markets and lead to higher revenues and profits.

If the venture investors do suggest that specific managers be employed, they will typically be financial specialists, operational specialists, or other experienced executives who can immediately contribute to the long-term strategy. Owners will find venture capital to be focused on the company's long-term goals in every phase of participation.

Private Equity

Many venture firms are really private equity funds or merchant bankers, meaning that they buy into emerging companies with the idea of holding them for an open-ended period while the company seasons or while the market for its product matures, increasing the value of the company. These investors do not run the businesses but are certainly active investors, holding their management teams accountable on a much closer basis than typical shareholders.

These investors generally are buying more traditional businesses to aggregate their revenues and allow them to input efficiencies to increase profits. Rolling up is a strategy to consolidate similar companies and positions the larger enterprise for acquisition. The exit strategy for companies owned by equity investors is more often through a sale to a competing or similar company seeking to acquire its growth in business volume or range of products.

Where Is Venture Capital?

Venture capital firms are not hard to locate, but it may be hard for business owners to get their attention. Since these firms focus on a narrower business sector, it's likely that if they are interested in a specific business, they will find it. They rarely talk with walk-ups and develop a deep sphere of trusted advisors to refer business to them. Beyond attorneys and accountants, they will reach through industry and banking sources to let others know the profiles they want to see.

Serious referrals to venture funds are not based on just who the owners know. It is really based on who the owners are—meaning whether their business is similar to the profile of a company the investors are seeking to invest in. Venture investors may require some effort to approach, and their answer will probably be that they are not interested.

But owners should consider this fact: venture funds are typically busy searching for them. If they have not found the business, it may be for a reason. These investors make themselves somewhat hidden because they do not make money by listening to every grand scheme out there. Since they are usually well-focused on specific industries, the venture funds that invest in a business will most likely be aware of the business before the business is aware of them.

If a business is like the businesses described above, it's likely that its owners will have good professional representation. Obtaining venture funding through those sources will probably be more productive. Owners should not bother with cold calls; calling without an introduction is usually a mistake. These investors often prefer anonymity and rely on their network to screen potential transactions and help them to source deals.

A better strategy for owners may be to work with angel investors, who are easier to find. If the deal is really too large for them but is an obvious fit for venture capital, angels will recognize that and make the necessary introductions.

Initial Public Offerings (IPOs)

Perhaps the ultimate equity financing dream of every entrepreneur is to employ an internationally known investment bank that can unleash a cadre of seasoned salespeople onto every Main Street in America with the company's shares to sell. Short of Warren Buffett writing a personal check, it's just hard to imagine how it gets better. IPOs are one of the transitional moments that define a successful business.

But owners should know that it's also a very long road and takes lots of dollars to get to the point where many bankers will be willing to invest any effort on their behalf. It takes years of strong operations; a seasoned, exceptional management team; being in the right industry at the right time; and having survived a few rounds of financing to greatly dilute ownership.

Owners must understand that going public is a grueling process that takes years to accomplish and requires a lot of fire in the belly. As with any business funding, owners may always be waiting longer than it seems it should take, and they should expect disappointment along the way. If the day arrives, though, owners have to go for it or possibly miss the only chance they'll get.

As with any money sourced for the business, the more digits the owners want, the more expectations investors have. Wall Street can be brutal. The good news about being public is that stock is liquid—an international market is created to buy and sell shares of the business. The bad news is that liquid stock can be dumped, and its value can sink quickly for the silliest reasons.

Shares are subject to being valued almost minute by minute in a market of traders who could care less about the business or the value it creates. They are looking only to make money, and shares of the business are just product subject to their speculation.

The company also becomes open to scrutiny by federal and state regulators to ensure transparency to investors. Quarterly audited financial statements and disclosures must be filed, and there are analysts waiting to interpret them for the world. Every decision owners make is second-guessed by some financial geek whose acumen (or hysteria) can make shares soar (or crash) in a matter of minutes.

The average reader of this book will not be in a serious pursuit of an IPO, and when considering life in a publicly owned company—the costs, scrutiny, and pressure—probably wouldn't want to be. It's not a cakewalk, and there are plenty of pitfalls to getting there.

If owners really want to go down that path, they must be sure to understand what they are getting into before planning their life in that direction. They should talk to other entrepreneurs who have been through the process and find out what life is like on a road show, what it's like to go through an SEC audit, and whether they would ever do it again.

Part 6

Best Sources for Debt Capital

14

BANK FINANCING

The most common source of small business capital financing is the local commercial bank. From start-up enterprises to expanding operations to maturing businesses, owners can find a sympathetic ear at the local bank. That is, so long as they can meet the mysterious, evolving, and intangible requirements defined as the banker's Five Cs of credit (see Chapter 3).

Banks are regulated institutions monitored by sometimes inconsistent overseers using murky regulations. Most of the regulators are well-versed on the science of banking but have personally never made a loan. Despite regulation and the growing evolution of competition, banks still provide about half of all commercial business financing in the United States. Commercial lending continues to be the largest source of income for banks with less than $5 billion in assets.

Banks should be the starting point of the search for business capital, even though it may prove to be disappointing in this postcrisis environment. Since 2007, hundreds of banks have failed and hundreds more have been consolidated or are ailing with deficient capital. But if owners choose a healthy bank and the business qualifies, bank loans can be a readily available source of funds. Banks are businesses too, and they depend on revenues and profits to thrive and grow.

Banks need to make loans in order to generate both income and deposits. Banks are generally less expensive than most other financing sources and quite willing to consider a broad range of industries, localities, and business stages for their portfolio. Banks conduct due diligence to determine their exposure and will generally be more imposing on documentation and previous history than early-stage equity investors will be.

Banks are averse to repayment risks, however, and in that regard they will need to be assured that owners are capable of repaying their loan from at least one of three sources:

- The profits and cash flow of the business. These profits and cash flows may be historical or projected, but the reliability of either set of numbers will be integral to loan approval and will determine how stringent the loan terms will be.
- Liens on assets that secure the loan. The bank will require collateral, preferably real estate equity or tangible assets that can be readily sold. They will advance loans only against a discounted fair market value of these assets to lower the exposure to loan losses.
- The personal guarantee of the owners of the business. If the business and the collateral can't repay the bank, the bank will turn to the owners' guarantee to pay off the loan.

Banks are in the business of lending money. Loans are advanced in relatively conservative business opportunities and are expected to be repaid over a defined period through regular monthly payments. Interest charges are applied for the time the money is actually employed, and most banks add fees to cover the expense of originating, underwriting, and servicing the loan.

Most of the money banks lend is generated from the various deposit accounts of other bank customers. Good banks generate a constant cycle of new deposits and loan payments to fund a steady stream of new loans. Banks earn a spread between the interest paid on the deposits and the rate of interest charged to owners.

The loan portfolio risk underwritten by commercial banks is regularly audited by a variety of overlapping state and federal bank regulators to ensure the banks' stability and sound operations. Plus, virtually all bank deposits are insured at some level by the Federal Deposit Insurance Corporation (FDIC).

Severe loan losses could threaten the financial footings of some banks and eventually require the FDIC to step in to cover the depositors' accounts. For this reason, the FDIC is one of the most aggressive regulators of bank performance.

Banks may not be the most aggressive source for financing but they do provide financing relatively inexpensively. Unlike equity investors, who get ownership in a portion of the business in exchange for their financing, banks simply charge interest and fees.

Most banks don't narrow their range of business or restrict financing by industry. While some banks occasionally slow lending in certain sectors where they find the risks become too high or where they have a concentration in their portfolio, generally speaking, banks will look at everything.

Most bankers tend to be generalists—in small business, lending banks will rarely have expertise in any particular industry, unless geographically their market area has a concentration of some particular industry. Agriculture, mining, manufacturing, high technology, and resort housing are some of the possible exceptions in which specific expertise may develop in local banks due to the nature of the local economy.

If owners find that one local bank does not have a sufficient level of interest in the deal or that it does not have enough expertise to handle the deal, chances are that the owners will have many more banks to consider. Even with the rise of alternative financing sources and the recent wave of bank failures and rollups, the market is still ripe with a choice of banks.

If owners qualify for financing at one bank, chances are they qualify at other banks. For that reason, understanding why the company qualifies can help owners maximize any available financing. Such insight will also help owners negotiate better terms.

When preparing to apply for commercial bank financing, owners should bear in mind that banks are fairly selective by necessity. They require different and more thorough due diligence than equity financing sources do, and that includes considerable disclosure of personal financial information in addition to information about the business.

Owners usually must provide personal financial statements, permit banks to obtain personal credit reports, and submit personal as well as company income tax returns. Owners must also have a healthy personal financial status, a positive credit history, and be fairly current in settling their income tax liabilities.

While such personal scrutiny is generally not evident with other financing sources, regulated institutions have tougher requirements and a lower tolerance for risk. And if owners misrepresent themselves in order to meet the bank's requirements, they will face the wrath of the federal government.

Standard Approach to Conventional Debt

To obtain financing from a commercial bank owners generally have to fit in a box. That is to say, the deal should be a standard, no-frills financing request from a standard, no-frills company with a standard, no-frills track record.

For the most part banks don't like big, new ideas. They don't want to bank showboats or pioneers. They avoid the kinky, trendy, headline-grabbing, sexy, or fresh businesses that set a new pace. Banks like very profitable, boring, and dependable businesses.

Box manufacturers thrill bankers. Website designers are not as appealing. Banks want to finance big warehouses. They do not like to finance ore deposits. Conventional bankers sleep well putting money into a new envelope-folding machine; they get nausea just reading the word dot-com.

Limited by the risk parameters imposed from regulators, their source of funds, and a traditional history of safe, prudent investing, conventional bank lending is typically restricted to more conventional businesses per se. Owners should not expect to wow anyone with a fancy business plan outlining intentions to change the world.

Owners should go to the bank for standard financing needs: a larger building, another machine, or a vehicle. They should not expect bankers to do the extraordinary, but rather expect them to manage standard needs well. That's why they are called conventional.

Commercial banks are organized quite differently today than they were a generation ago. Years ago each bank had one office, one president, and one commercial lending department. There is a whole new industry out there now.

While there are many banks with offices in nearly 50 states, owners can conduct business at millions of ATMs or online without ever shadowing the door. As many bank logos cross state lines, there are still smaller boutique banks resembling a mall of financial services, and they are happy to accept deposits, sell insurance, or manage investment portfolios.

Commercial lending at larger banks is organized in a dizzying array of business groups designed to place credit specialists in every major area of business financing: real estate, equipment, asset-based, small business, leasing, and more. This concentration permits banks to serve particular customers better, once the right department is located (which can be challenging sometimes).

The search for business capital may require some effort just to get around inside one banking organization, much less consider all of the competition. Hopefully the bank representative has a good understanding of the product lines offered by the bank.

Another dynamic for owners to be aware of in the banking environment is the banks' goal of providing services to relationships. While banks cannot legally make loan approval contingent on owners' maintaining a checking account with them, they can modify the terms of financing in consideration of other accounts to provide plenty of incentives to bank with them.

Banks want owners to deposit their funds there and use their credit cards, wire services, cash management services, safe deposit boxes, and a long list of other offered products. In exchange, they may offer modest preferences in pricing and benefits.

Relationships are much more profitable to banks. Obviously if owners maintain strong deposits with them then their loans are in part sourced from the owners' own money. Plus, with the right type of offset, a bank could have marginally better protection with the ability to use the owners' deposits to reduce borrowings should things go really bad, really fast.

Real Estate Financing

Commercial banks are an excellent place to finance conventional real estate loans for seasoned companies or real estate investors. With decent leverage, fair amortization, and good interest rates, it's hard to beat a commercial bank for a company's standard real estate needs.

While there are better alternatives for single- or limited-purpose properties and smaller businesses needing long-term financing assistance, commercial banks offer conventional real estate owners exactly what they need: low rates. Commercial banks can generally provide fixed-rate financing for real estate loans for 10 or sometimes up to 20 years.

Banks generally prefer to finance multiuse properties: generic buildings that can be used for a multitude of commercial, retail, office, or industrial purposes. They prefer the improvements to be those adaptable to dozens if not hundreds of different business uses. The reason is obvious: in the event of default, multiuse buildings will attract a longer list of prospective buyers than single-purpose facilities will. The more prospects, the easier a property is to sell and therefore the lower the risk of financing such a property.

If such a property is to be used by the owner and the owners business has a strong operating history, a bank will loan the owner as much as 75 to 80 percent of the cost of the property. If the property is to be leased out to other tenants, the bank will generally loan the owner as much as 70 to 75 percent of the cost of the property. The final leverage offer for an owner-occupied building may be determined by the appetite of the bank (some banks do not want to finance any owner-occupied buildings), the track record of the owner, and the specific risk presented by the property.

Real estate financing is universally based on the lender advancing a loan for a certain percentage of the value of the property. This percentage, or leverage, will always be based on the *lower* of the cost or appraised value. While many factors may contribute to why a building can be appraised for a higher value than it is ultimately sold for, prospective owners can rarely borrow against the phantom equity created by the difference. Lenders will use the lower valuation figure in order to ensure the soundness of their decision.

Banks traditionally favor shorter-term loans. Their business model is to provide financing for a term representing a safe business cycle, with a window to exit should operations not look promising. This pattern is rooted in the nature of their deposits rarely being committed beyond three to five years.

A typical bank real estate loan may offer amortization (the calculated repayment period) of 15 or 20 years, but there will be a balloon payment or call provision made that permits the bank to force the loan to be repaid at a much earlier date, generally on the third-, fifth-, or seventh-year anniversary.

Due in part to the short-term loan commitments, lower cost of funds, and a more conservative appetite for loans than most all competitors, banks are able to offer the lowest interest rates of any small business lending source. A bank's source of funds includes demand deposits, which are mostly available at no charge to banks.

Another prominent reason for banks having lower rates available is that many other nonbank lending sources (leasing, working capital, etc.) rely on bank financing in part to provide them with funds to lend. Naturally these alternative sources have a higher cost of funds to calculate than commercial banks do.

Construction Financing

Banks are also good sources for construction loans used to finance the construction of new buildings. These loans require special handling and are disbursed gradually on a progress-billing, or as-built, basis. As various components of the construction project are completed, loan advances are made to pay the costs. In other words, the lender will provide enough funds to pay for 20 percent of the construction costs only after 20 percent of the construction is completed.

Using the contractor's trade credit and owner's equity to start building, the lender's money comes in last. The lender's oversight ensures that funds are not advanced to the contractor ahead of work being completed. The bank wants to know that all bills are paid as per the budget and contract, as evidenced by written claim waivers from all parties that delivered site materials or performed work on the job.

This type of lending carries extraordinary risks due to the involvement of a third party, the general contractor, who is responsible for management of the project. The contractor has to get work started and keep it moving among an army of subcontractors, each of whom contributes a specialized component to the project such as foundations, framing, plumbing, electrical, etc.

Keeping these parties on a schedule that is often mutually dependent (the floors can't be tiled before the rough plumbing is in place), ensuring the work is done right, and keeping the bills paid between loan advances takes a good business manager. Contractors typically have to use their own working capital or trade credit from suppliers and subcontractors to get the job started.

Basically the lender is advancing loan proceeds to a third party (general contractor) engaged to make improvements who is not liable to repay the money. The liable party (the borrower) will be held accountable for repayment of the loan whether or not the final building is suitable or finished.

To sort through the byzantine maze of architectural plans, material costs, building codes, and zoning laws, the lender needs the help of a professional engineer. Bankers must ensure that the proposed structure can be built in compliance with applicable laws, within the plans provided, the contract agreed to, and the negotiated budget. The engineer reviews the building plans, specifications, and cost breakdown before the loan closes in order to assure the lender that the project is feasible, legal, and within budget.

Lenders manage construction loans tightly and generally insist on structured loan advance procedures. The risk posed by the general contractor is as high as the repayment of the loan by the owner. For this reason, banks prefer that owners deal with successful contractors who have a solid track record in their trade evidenced by professional and financial references.

A chief concern of the lender will be the general contractor's financial condition and business track record. If the general contractor doesn't have sufficient capital or trade credit, he cannot finance the project between loan draws. The project stops if the contractor has drawn all of the loan funds available but cannot continue to the next stage of the project.

Worse, if a contractor has lost money on a previous job and is still trying to finish it, she will sometimes try to take funds from the next job to settle up. This dishonest maneuver will also leave her short on the subsequent project and presents a financial risk to the borrower and bank.

For these reasons, seasoned construction lenders will be firm with general contractors and enforce strict procedures when advancing loan funds. Adherence to rigid guidelines is often based on some very expensive lessons learned from past loans.

After loan closing, the lender will use a construction inspector to monitor the project. For each requested loan advance, or draw, the inspector reviews actual progress on site and calculates the percentage of completion of the project using the actual construction budget. The inspector protects the lender's interest in the project site by ensuring that loan proceeds are advanced only after the work is completed.

Equipment Loans

Banks also provide financing for the acquisition of equipment assets. Like real estate loans, where the leverage and repayment terms are going to be conservative, banks also provide very well priced equipment loans based on a more cautious approach than some nonbank lenders.

Banks prefer to finance standard, no-frills equipment that is durable, such as fork lifts, front-end loaders, injection molding machines, generators, and lathes. Banks may not be as enthusiastic about specialized components that are susceptible to technological obsolescence or that have a short lifespan.

As part of their culture of prudent financing, banks like to finance commonly used machinery that may be employed in a broad number of uses and industries. The more specialized an asset is, defined by the limited number of different applications in which it can be used, the less attractive it is for a bank to finance. Obviously, commonly used, durable equipment can be liquidated more easily if problems arise.

Banks generally advance 100 percent of the purchase price of equipment assets but will apply more aggressive underwriting on the company. They will want to see that the existing cash flow can service the proposed debt without regard to the projected uptick in revenues created by the equipment.

Lines of Credit

One of the essential needs of virtually every business enterprise is working capital. Regardless of the source, businesses need cash to pay salaries, buy materials, keep the lights on, and make the telephone ring. Nothing happens without working capital.

Working capital is the phrase used to describe the cash on hand or the available funds in a demand deposit account for the needs of the day-to-day operations of a business. Daily sales produce cash and checks that are deposited into the bank. Credit card sales are deposited into the account a few days after the sale. Some clients pay advance deposits for future delivery, while some buy on credit and pay in 30 days. These are all sources of working capital.

Most businesses pay their employees at least every two weeks. Some suppliers have to be paid upon delivery. Utilities are paid by the month, and the mortgage or rent is generally due on the first day of the month. These are all typical uses of working capital.

Most successful owners carefully manage their cash cycles, the normal time required to recover their money invested to produce with proceeds from their sales. Their management can be measured by evaluating the company's working capital adequacy.

Working capital will vary from business to business due to a number of factors:

- Industry, standard payment terms, average sale size, and trade credit availability.
- Business capitalization. How much capital is available at the outset influences the amount of working capital available for future operations and growth.
- Success in creating revenues and profits from the capital invested in the enterprise.
- Seasonality, which refers to whether revenues are concentrated in particular periods or spread evenly during the year.

The cash cycle may be out of sync with the normal cycle of the industry or size category. Since each business is unique, there can be many reasons why the business either has plenty of cash or is just getting by day-to-day.

Banks finance working capital for small businesses with a variety of loan products, based on the size of the businesses, their industry, and their normal cash cycle. These attributes define what kind of money is available and on what terms. The three most common working capital products offered by banks are discussed below.

Revolving Line of Credit

Traditionally, banks have been the largest source of revolving lines of credit for small businesses. These credit facilities are essentially a loan with an annual maturity that can be drawn down and paid up several times during the year to meet cyclical working capital needs. Interest is billed monthly.

Revolvers are based on the idea that owners can provide to the banks an annual budget that projects operating results and describes the cash cycle expected from the normal flows of expenses and revenues. The credit line is there to provide cash to cover the gaps between when the business has to pay expenses and the timing of when cash receipts are paid. Owners draw from the credit line to cover expenses and then pay down the credit line with the revenue.

These loans are for the companies with good operating histories—no start-ups need apply—and those with capable and credible bookkeepers who are disciplined enough to keep their cash working. The cost of a revolving line of credit is typically an annual fee based on the total commitment and a negotiated interest rate for the actual outstanding balances.

These credit facilities are not intended to fund losses or substitute for growth equity. Lenders generally monitor results closely and will cut off the money if owners are reporting poor trends that are draining resources. Generally, businesses are expected to be able to leave the account paid off for at least one 30-day period each year.

Asset-Based Lending

Some banks make a market in lending working capital in a credit facility that is referred to as asset-based lending (ABL). This type of credit facility is discussed in greater detail in Chapter 18, but ABL financing is a credit line where the lender is involved day-to-day with the management of a business's cash position.

ABL lenders advance loan funds against the company's outstanding account invoices generated from sales and collect the payments directly through a lockbox on the company's behalf. The receivables must meet specific guidelines to be eligible for financing.

These credit lines serve businesses that are capital-intensive and sell to other businesses with credit. As sales grow, the need for cash to support the cost of goods grows. Essentially the growth is financed by advances on new invoices to manage a constantly swelling cash cycle.

Credit Card Accounts

Another reliable source of working capital for small businesses through commercial banks has been the aggressive employment of credit card–based lines of credit. Quite simply, these are credit cards issued to business owners based on their personal credit scores; they are personally liable for the credit. These accounts are unsecured by personal or business assets, and, accordingly, are riskier to the issuer. Higher risk will mean higher interest charges for their use.

Credit card lines of credit are important to very small businesses because they provide credit facilities in smaller increments ($5,000 to $50,000) than banks would normally distribute business credit. Additionally, they provide businesses with a way to distribute corporate spending authority to several persons in small increments to conduct company business, such as business travel, entertainment, or supply purchasing.

Revolving credit lines are expensive to administer as well as costly to underwrite. Trying to provide credit lines to smaller companies is cost prohibitive, except by using this consumer credit approach. Credit cards became a natural vehicle for banks to permit qualified consumers to access credit for unlimited uses.

For such small loans, businesses do not have to produce business plans or financial projections or go through the standard commercial underwriting treadmill. These loans are simply scored on the strength of the credit history of the owners. Used within the lender's terms, such loans can be a virtually permanent source of financing to cover a multitude of purchases and expenses and allow maximum flexibility for repayment over seasonal cash flows and economic cycles.

Pricing is usually determined by the owner's credit scores at the time the account is opened. With recent federal regulatory changes, cardholders are not as vulnerable to sudden rate spikes and changing terms as they had been in the past. Now, lenders must provide an easy-to-read notice of proposed term changes and allow cardholders to opt out. If they do not agree to the new terms, cardholders simply notify lenders, stop using the account, and pay off the current balance as scheduled. Lenders cannot arbitrarily raise the interest rate on the unpaid balance.

Payment terms are fairly stringent. Most account billing provides a 20- to 30-day notification before payment is due, and it's always best to ensure payment is there on the due date or earlier. Missing the payment deadline by even one day or more may have implications according to the cardholder agreement.

Business owners should treat these balances like a true line of credit. They should pay them off in full each month if at all possible to lower costs and maintain maximum credit availability in the future. One of the features of the recent regulatory changes is required disclosure of how long it will take to repay the balance if the cardholder only makes the minimum payments. The results are eye-popping and provide plenty of incentives to pay off balances aggressively.

If business owners are distributing cards to their employees, they must be sure to maintain strict oversight to prevent abuse in unauthorized or personal expenses. It is incumbent upon them to ensure that the company pays the invoices and does not rely on employees sending in payments, lest the owners get punished for their lax performance. If owners get into disputes with employees over card charges, they must remember that they, not the employees, are liable to the bank for the charges.

Owners must be sure to keep good records of the account card numbers that they distribute to others. If the cards are lost, stolen, abused, or disputed, the owners (and the owners alone) have the authority (and motivation) to contact the bank and suspend the cards in question until the problem is solved. Owners should get something in writing from each employee that will allow the owners to offset any fraudulent charges against future compensation.

One other feature owners should explore is the cash back and reward programs offered by many banks. These features provide incentives for the continued use of the cards, which generates income for the issuer from merchants where customers spend money. Paid in the form of cash rebates or points, these incentives can result in tangible benefits that lower costs or offset them with spending credits applicable for travel or retailers. If a business has several employees with business credit cards, the reward options multiply.

15

GOVERNMENT-GUARANTEED LOANS

Despite the rise of many alternative sources and products to provide financing to the small business sector, most small enterprises will find financing difficult to access during their start-up phase. And for the financing that is available, low leverage and short repayment terms sometimes aggravate the efforts of companies to generate sufficient working capital to expand and grow the business.

Understandably, higher leverage and longer repayment terms present significantly more risks to the lender of loans to younger enterprises. Banks are discouraged by their regulators from underwriting these kinds of risks on any business, much less those that are less mature. But smaller companies need more leverage. Without always having the capital available from personal resources, larger loans are an important source of financing the launch or expansion of many young businesses.

Long-term financing is also important to newer businesses or those with a small capital base. By stretching the repayment period, payments are lower, conserving vital cash flow that is essential in the early stages of any business. Just as with purchasing a home, tying the repayment period of an asset purchase loan to the useful life of that asset makes economic sense.

But more than just start-up businesses, other valid small business concerns need financing that falls outside the parameters of the commercial banking system for one reason or another. Geography, industry, and even typical customers present certain risks that may be beyond the ability for regulated banks to fund.

To bridge this gap, the federal government introduced financial assistance programs for small businesses more than 70 years ago. Using the full faith and credit of the U.S. government in partnership with entrepreneurs, the U.S. Small

Business Administration (SBA), U.S. Department of Agriculture (USDA), and the Export-Import Bank of the United States (Ex-Im Bank) have provided assistance to millions of small enterprises.

Far from providing a handout or corporate welfare, these agencies give a credit enhancement to encourage banks to finance the small business sector. Participants pay a healthy guarantee fee for the service, which are pooled with fees collected from the participating lenders to provide a fund to repurchase defaulted loans under the program.

The results have been clear: hundreds of millions of jobs have been created or preserved, the environment for small businesses is stronger in the American economy than anywhere else in the world, and access to small business financing continues to grow. There are many high-profile corporate success stories that received early-stage financing assistance from SBA, including FedEx, Microsoft, and Intel.

The regulations governing all of these loan programs are subject to change from time to time. However, this chapter provides a broad perspective of each program to determine eligibility for assistance. It defines the programs offered by the three abovementioned agencies in an effort to expand the funding choices available to appropriate, qualifying businesses.

SBA Loan Guarantee Programs

SBA was established in 1953 to assist small business enterprises. Arguably its most important programs are for loan assistance, which provide incentives to private sector commercial lenders (banks and certain licensed nonbank lenders) to extend long-term capital financing to qualified, eligible, small businesses.

The two primary loan guarantee programs that are currently offered by the SBA for small business financing are the 7(a) Loan Program and 504 Loan Program. They are governed by different regulations and are distinguished by eligibility standards, restrictions on the use of loan proceeds, repayment terms, and the borrower's approval process. Both programs are explained in detail below.

7(a) Loan Programs

The 7(a) loan program is SBA's flagship loan program for helping start-up and existing businesses, providing funds for a variety of general business purposes. SBA does not make direct loans. Instead, it provides a credit enhancement to participating lenders in the form of a long-term loan guarantee. The cost of reimbursing banks for loan defaults is paid for from fees collected from participants that get loans and the lenders that fund them.

Small businesses can obtain financing for acquisition or improvement of assets (real estate, equipment, operating business concerns, etc.), refinancing existing debt, or working capital. Repayment terms are determined by the use of the loan proceeds according to limitations imposed on each purpose:

- Loans used to purchase, construct improvements on, or refinance real estate can be extended for up to a maximum of 25 years.
- Loans used to purchase equipment can be extended for up to a maximum of 15 years (though usually limited to 10) or to the expected useful life of the equipment, whichever is shorter.
- Loans used to acquire an operating business concern can be extended for up to a maximum of 10 years.
- Loans used to fund business working capital can be extended for up to a maximum of 7 years.

Currently participating lenders are guaranteed repayment by SBA for 75 percent of the total loan amount up to $5 million (80 percent for loans under $250,000) for a maximum loan guarantee of $3.75 million.

Eligibility to participate in the 7(a) program is limited by one of two factors: either the borrower's average annual revenues or average employment. SBA determines eligibility for financing assistance by specific limits it has set for each NAICS sector.

Generally most businesses that have an average total revenue over the previous three years of $7 million or less or have no more than 500 employees are eligible for SBA assistance. However, there is a wide range of limitations based on industry. Average revenues can range from $750,000 to $35.5 million, and the average number of employees can vary from 50 to 1,500. For the power-generation industry, small means producing less than 4 million megawatts of power. While there are definitive qualifications for each industry, only one factor—revenue or employment—is used to measure whether a company is a small business or not.

One of the most attractive features of the 7(a) program is that the repayment terms provide for the full amortization of the loan proceeds. In other words, the borrower can repay the loan proceeds over the economic life of the asset being financed over a reasonable period provided to repay borrowed working capital.

By arranging for fully amortizing terms in the initial loan, the borrower can better focus on growing business revenues and profits without the worry of changing terms. The borrower can also avoid having to refinance the debt several times before repayment due to uncontrollable market conditions.

Lenders are restricted on the interest rates they can assess on 7(a) loans. Interest is generally negotiated between the borrower and lender based on the lender's cost of funds and analysis of the transaction risk. However, SBA imposes rate caps on the interest the lender may charge. Rates can be fixed or variable. Variable rates may be pegged to the prime rate as published in the Wall Street Journal, to the one-month London Interbank Offered Rate (LIBOR) plus 3 percent, or to the optional peg rate that is published quarterly in the Federal Register.

(The prime rate and LIBOR are defined in Chapter 4. The optional peg rate is a weighted average of rates the federal government pays for loans with maturities similar to the average SBA 7(a) loan. This rate is determined and published by SBA quarterly in the Federal Register.)

Variable interest rates may be adjusted at virtually any frequency negotiated by the lender and borrower, but most are reset either monthly or quarterly. SBA lets the lender decide so long at the change term is clearly defined in the promissory note.

✳✳✳

The SBA Express provides more flexibility to lenders that make these smaller loans by abbreviating the guarantee application, by loosening collateral requirements, by allowing lenders to use their own loan documents and procedures and charge higher interest rates, and by promising a 36-hour guarantee decision turnaround when lenders request authorization. In exchange, the lenders receive only a 50 percent loan guarantee.

Express loans offer small borrowers a flexible revolving or fixed-payment loan structure, depending on the lenders' requirements, for a total of a seven-year term to repay the loan in full. Borrowers can repay the loan in full faster without penalty if they choose to amortize the loan from the beginning over seven years. Loans under this program are limited to $350,000.

The SBA Express has proven to be very popular with lenders and borrowers and has become one of the most utilized financing options offered by the SBA.

Community Advantage Program. Approved mission-focused lenders can get authorization to adopt SBA's most streamlined and expedited loan procedures to provide a unique combination of financial and technical assistance to borrowers located in the nation's underserved communities.

Communities that are eligible include SBA's Historically Underutilized Business Zones (HUB Zones) and those communities identified as distressed through the Community Reinvestment Act (CRA). To encourage small business start-ups, loans of $250,000 or less are eligible for Community Advantage Program loans regardless of where the small business is located.

Because the SBA knows that the success of its loans to disadvantaged communities rests in large part on the technical assistance it renders the borrowers, the lenders have to document this assistance. Borrowers using one of these loans have the option of using SBA's Small Business Training Network (SBTN), as well as such resources as Small Business Development Centers, SCORE (Service Corps of Retired Executives), Women's Business Centers, and Veterans Business Outreach Centers.

The Community Advantage Program offers borrowers loans that have the same attributes of typical 7(a) loan terms, such as interest rate restrictions.

Patriot Express Program. If the business owner is a veteran, this program may offer the best loan available. The Patriot Express Program is designed for small businesses that are 51 percent or more owned by veterans or members of the military community. The maximum loan under this program is $500,000, and the guarantee follows the standard 7(a) percentages. This program combines many of the features of the other Express programs.

Borrowers under the Patriot Express Program must be eligible for SBA financing with every typical financial and personal qualification but in addition must be 51 percent or more controlled by:

- A U.S. military veteran (other than dishonorably discharged)
- Active-duty military, a potential retiree within 24 months of separation and discharge, or an active-duty member within 12 months of discharge (TAP eligible)
- A reservist or National Guard member
- The current spouse of the above or of a service member or veteran who died of a service-related disability

The Patriot Express Program offers borrowers a seven-year revolving line of credit for up to $500,000 with other typical 7(a) loan terms such as interest rate restrictions (except for loans under $50,000). Lenders can use their own forms and are not required to have collateral on loans less than $25,000. For loans up to $350,000 lenders may use their own collateral policy, but larger loans must take available collateral.

❋ ❋ ❋

Since more than 70 percent of all U.S. exporters have fewer than 20 employees, the SBA has placed a high priority on providing financial assistance to help them develop or increase their export activities. There are a number of programs designed to serve these small businesses.

Export Express. The SBA Export Express Program provides exporters and lenders with a streamlined way to obtain SBA-guaranteed financing for loans and lines of credit up to $500,000, and the guarantee follows the standard 7(a) percentages. This program combines many of the features of the other Express programs.

The Export Express Program offers borrowers a seven-year revolving line of credit for up to $500,000 with other typical 7(a) loan terms, such as interest rate restrictions. Lenders make the credit decision, can use their own loan documentation forms, and are free to use their own collateral policies, such as those on non-guaranteed loans.

Export Working Capital Program. SBA's Export Working Capital Program (EWCP) loans are targeted for businesses that export and need additional working capital to support these sales. Participating lenders review and approve applications and then submit the requests to the SBA Export Assistance Center in the exporter's geographical territory.

Exporters can get up to a $5 million revolving credit facility through this program, which can be extended for up to 12 months. Loans carry a 90 percent SBA guarantee up to $4.5 million, and for larger loans there is a companion guarantee that may be available from the Export-Import Bank for the difference. The fixed or variable interest rate is negotiated between the lender and borrower.

The credit decision for these loans is made by the SBA, although lenders may use their own loan documents for the transaction. The loans require all export-related inventory and receivables be pledged as collateral as well as the personal guarantees of all owners of 20 percent or more of the business.

International Trade Loan Program. The International Trade Loan Program offers term loans to businesses that plan to start or continue exporting, or have been adversely affected by import competition. Borrowers receiving these loans must use the funds to enhance their competitive position. The program offers borrowers a maximum loan of $5 million.

Funds may be used for the acquisition, construction, renovation, modernization, improvement, or expansion of long-term fixed assets or for the refinancing of an existing loan used for these same purposes.

The maximum guarantee for this program is higher than other 7(a) programs, with borrowers able to get a 90 percent loan guarantee, which equals $4.5 million ($4 million for working capital).

The fixed or variable interest rate is negotiated between the lender and borrower, but the program restricts the maximum rate to prime plus 2.75 percent for loans with a maturity of seven or more years. As with most SBA programs the lender makes the credit decision, but the loan must be fully secured with collateral to the extent possible.

❊ ❊ ❊

There are several special-purpose loan programs under the umbrella of the 7(a) program that enable borrowers to qualify under certain conditions that may not otherwise be available. These special initiative programs are primarily intended to encourage and assist the private sector in accomplishing specific public policy objectives approved by Congress.

Rural Lender Advantage Program. The Small/Rural Lender Advantage (S/RLA) initiative by the SBA is designed to accommodate the unique loan-processing needs of small community and rural-based lenders, many of which make very few SBA loans. It's part of a broader SBA initiative to promote the economic development of rural communities, particularly those facing the challenges of population loss, economic dislocation, and high unemployment. S/RLA encourages small community and rural lenders to partner with SBA by simplifying and streamlining loan application processes and procedures, particularly for smaller SBA loans.

Key features of this program include:

- Streamlined loan application and processing for SBA loans of $150,000 or less, with limited additional information and analysis required for loans above $150,000
- A simplified SBA loan eligibility questionnaire to help small or occasional lenders meet SBA eligibility requirements
- Loans centrally processed through SBA's 7(a) Loan Processing Center
- Lenders' ability to transmit applications via fax or online

Loans in this program are limited to $350,000 or less, and the standard 7(a) guarantee percentage applies. The interest rate may be fixed or variable and is negotiated between the lender and borrower, but the program restricts the maximum rate at prime plus 2.75 percent for loans with a maturity of seven or more years. The lender makes the credit decisions, but the loan must be fully secured with collateral to the extent possible.

Since this program is limited to lenders that averaged fewer than 20 SBA loans annually over the previous three years, the SBA reviews all loans for eligibility and credit underwriting.

CAP Lines Program. This is an umbrella loan program designed to help small businesses with short-term and cyclical working capital needs for up to $5 million (less in the case of a small-asset-based line). It offers five different types of credit lines:

- **Seasonal line.** The borrower must use proceeds from this line of credit to finance seasonal increases of accounts receivable and inventory in the business (or in some cases associated increased labor costs). The loan can be revolving or nonrevolving, but the borrower must repay it in full by the end of business cycle.
- **Contract line.** This line of credit finances the direct labor and material cost associated with the borrower's performing assignable contract(s). The loan can be revolving or nonrevolving, but associated borrowing from this line should be repaid with the final payments from each associated contract.
- **Builders line.** This line of credit is for small general contractors constructing or renovating commercial or residential buildings. Proceeds can be used to finance direct labor and material costs. The project's real estate will serve as collateral for the loan, and the line of credit can be revolving or non-revolving. As with other lines, the borrower should use the proceeds from the building sale to repay the associated borrowing in full.
- **Standard asset-based line.** This line of credit is a traditional asset-based revolving line of credit for businesses unable to meet credit standards associated with long-term credit. It provides financing for cyclical growth, as well as recurring and/or short-term working capital needs. The borrower repays it by converting accounts receivable into cash, which is then remitted directly to the lender.

  The business continually draws from the line of credit based on its receivable borrowing base and repays the line as its cash cycle permits. This line generally is used by businesses that sell goods to other businesses on open invoice. Because these loans require continual servicing and monitoring of collateral, additional fees may be charged by the lender to cover the extra costs.
- **Small asset-based line.** This line of credit is an asset-based revolving line for smaller businesses and is limited to credit of up to $200,000. It operates

like a standard asset-based line except that some of the stricter servicing requirements are waived, providing the business can consistently show repayment ability from cash flow for the full amount of the outstanding balance.

Employee Trusts Loan Program. This program is designed to provide financial assistance to Employee Stock Ownership Plans (ESOP). The employee trust must be part of a plan sponsored by the employer company and be qualified under regulations set by either the IRS as an ESOP or by the Labor Department as an Employee Retirement Income Security Act (ERISA). Applicants covered by ERISA must secure an exemption from labor regulations prohibiting certain loan transactions.

Pollution-Control Loan Program. This program provides financing to eligible small businesses for the planning, design, or installation of a pollution-control facility. This facility must prevent, reduce, abate, or control any form of pollution and includes recycling. This program follows the guidelines of the 7(a) program with the following exception: loan proceeds must be used for fixed assets only.

Military Reservists Loans. The Military Reservist Economic Injury Disaster Loan Program (MREIDL) provides funds to eligible small businesses to meet necessary operating expenses that the business can't meet because an essential employee was called up to active duty in the military reserves. These loans are intended to help bridge the financial gap until the military reservist is able to return to the company. The loans are not to cover lost income or lost profits. MREIDL funds cannot be used to take the place of regular commercial debt, to refinance long-term debt, or to expand the business.

These loans are underwritten with the full expectation of being repaid. Interest rates are fixed at 4 percent, and the loans are expected to be fully secured to the extent collateral is available. Repayment is limited to a maximum 30-year term, but the SBA establishes the term based on its assessment of the installment payments the borrowers are able to repay. These loans are limited to $2 million, but the SBA has the authority to waive this limitation.

Microloan Program. If the borrower is a small businesses with a need for a small short-term loan to be used for working capital or the purchase of inventory, supplies, furniture, fixtures, machinery, and/or equipment, the borrower can apply for SBA's Microloan Program. SBA makes funds available to specially designated intermediary lenders, which are nonprofit organizations with experience in lending and technical assistance. These intermediaries then make loans to eligible borrowers in amounts up to a maximum of $50,000. The average loan size is about $13,000.

Applications are submitted to the local intermediary, and all credit decisions are made on the local level.

The CDC/504 Loan Program

The CDC/504 Loan Program is a long-term financing program of the SBA specifically authorized by Congress to foster economic development, create or preserve jobs, and stimulate economic expansion. To be eligible, the borrowing small business must create or retain one job per $65,000 provided through the program (except in the case of manufacturers, where the goal is one job per $100,000). The 504 Program provides small businesses requiring brick-and-mortar financing with long-term, fixed-rate financing to acquire capital assets for expansion or modernization.

A Certified Development Company (CDC) is a private corporation authorized by the SBA to support and facilitate economic development in its community. CDCs work closely with SBA and private sector lenders to provide financing to small businesses through the 504 Loan Program. There are about 270 CDCs nationwide, and most are restricted to specific geographic areas.

Typically a 504 loan transaction will be structured to include:

- A loan secured from a private sector lender with a senior lien covering at least 50 percent of the total project cost.
- A debenture secured through a CDC (backed by a 100 percent SBA guarantee) with a subordinated junior lien covering up to 40 percent of the total project costs.
- An equity contribution from the borrower covering a minimum of 10 percent of the total project costs; however, if the borrower is a new business or special facility owner, it will probably be asked to contribute at least 15 percent.

The loan terms for both the senior loan and CDC loan are usually 20 years for real estate loans or 10 years for equipment, with a fully amortizing repayment schedule. The senior debt might be issued with a shorter 10-year term on real estate loans, however, depending on the lender's preference.

Generally the CDC works in cooperation with a participating lender to determine eligibility, qualify the borrower, and structure financing for the applicant's financing. Proceeds from 504 loans are more restricted than other SBA financing programs and must be used solely for fixed-asset projects, such as:

- Purchasing land and improvements, including existing buildings and related development costs (grading, street improvements, utilities, parking lots, and landscaping)
- Construction of new facilities or modernizing, renovating, converting, or repurposing existing facilities
- Purchasing capital machinery and equipment (assets with an expected long-term useful life)

Proceeds from 504 Program financing cannot be used for working capital, inventory, consolidating, or repaying or refinancing debt.

To be eligible for a CDC/504 loan, the business must be operated for profit and fall within the size standards set by the SBA. Under the 504 Program, the business qualifies as small if it does not have a tangible net worth in excess of $7.5 million and did not have an average net income in excess of $2.5 million after taxes for the preceding two years. The CDC also has the option to use the size standards of the 7(a) program if it chooses to add flexibility to facilitate financing. Loans cannot be made to businesses engaged in speculation or investment in rental real estate.

The maximum SBA debenture for a typical project is $5 million for loans that meet the job-creating criteria or a community development goal. The job-creation requirement can be waived on all public policy and community development loans provided that the CDC has met its average job-creating goals. Job creation can also be waived on loans to small manufacturers that are not using the higher debenture amount.

The public policy goals that permit the job-creation requirement to be waived include:

- Business district revitalization
- Expansion of exports
- Expansion of minority business development
- Rural development
- Increasing productivity and competitiveness
- Restructuring due to federally mandated standards or policies
- Changes necessitated due to federal budget reductions
- Expansion of small business concerns owned and controlled by veterans (especially service-disabled veterans)
- Expansion of small business concerns owned and controlled by women
- Reduction of existing energy consumption by a minimum of 10 percent
- Increased use of sustainable designs to reduce environmental impact

- Upgrades to renewal energy sources
- Expansion into market with labor surplus
- Expansion of manufacturing jobs

Small Manufacturers. The maximum 504 debenture for small manufacturers is $5.5 million. A small manufacturer is defined as a company that has its primary business described in the NAICS (North American Industrial Classification System) classification sector 31, 32, or 33 and all of its production facilities located in the United States. To qualify for a $5.5 million 504 debenture, the business must meet the definition of a small manufacturer and:

- Either create or retain at least one job per $100,000 guaranteed by SBA, or
- Improve the local economy or achieve at least one public policy goal

Interest rates on 504 loans are pegged to an incremental spread above the current market rate for 5-year and 10-year U.S. Treasury issues. Interest rates are fixed, since the source of funds is from long-term debentures sold to investors. While that protects borrowers from an environment of rising interest rates, it also means that the rates will remain fixed if the market rates fall.

There is a prepayment penalty to pay off a 504 loan ahead of maturity based on a yield maintenance calculation that is a function of the net rate paid to the investor. Applicants should seek clarity by asking the CDC to project that rate ahead of moving forward with loan.

One obvious point to make is that fixing rates in a low market is a good opportunity. Even the prepayment penalties are much lower, reducing exposure to rising rates. Fixed or variable interest rates on the senior financing must be negotiated with the participating lender.

Maturities on 504 loans can be 10 or 20 years, depending on the use of funds. The SBA guarantee fee, CDC fee, and underwriting fees will total 2.15 percent and are included in the debenture balance. Other closing costs (attorneys, appraiser, etc.) for the 504 loans will be fairly constant but harder to quote as a percentage of the loan without identifying the size of the loan. These costs may be financed within the loan depending on policies of the CDC, which may vary.

Generally, the project assets being financed are used as collateral, and other personal assets may be requested if the financed assets plus borrower's equity do not provide sufficient protection to the lender. This decision will usually depend on the historical financial performance of the business, the management track record of the business, and the strength of the business plan. Personal guarantees of the principal owners are required on all loans.

✳ ✳ ✳

Now that you have read this summary of the major loan programs available through the SBA, here is a brief description of how the basic loan process works.

In light of seemingly contradictory and often overlapping state and federal banking regulations, it's doubtful that the private sector would fulfill the demand for small business financing without assistance from the SBA. Lenders seek to make transactions with as little risk as possible, and banking regulators encourage this behavior in many ways. Nothing is as financially risky as a start-up small business concern that can leverage its capital in the 80 to 90 percent range.

The SBA provides a solution to private sector lenders in the form of a credit enhancement that permits them to extend credit to small businesses that would otherwise be considered too risky. By absorbing 40 to 80 percent of the risk of the deal, SBA gives lenders assurance that their exposure to business catastrophe is limited to an acceptable level.

Lenders provide the funding for these loans and always have direct exposure for a constant percentage of the outstanding principal balance—in other words they will have enough skin in the game to exercise good judgment. The lender will be the primary contact for the borrower in servicing the loan account.

Unless the loan is not repaid as agreed, the borrower will never be aware of SBA's presence in the transaction after loan closing. If the agency pays the guarantee off to a non-preferred lender program (PLP), the SBA may initiate loan collection efforts directly with the borrower.

Since the agency rarely meets the borrower and never visits the business, SBA must rely on the written application from the lender to approve the guarantee. The requirements for this application include an extensive list of information designed to ensure the borrower's compliance with the financial, regulatory, and business qualifications intended to reduce the lender's exposure to loss and adherence to program rules.

These loan guarantees are available to small business owners, regardless of age, gender, or ethnicity. When approved, the guarantee is provided under a standard SBA authorization agreement executed by the lender and SBA, similar to the lender's loan agreement with the borrower.

SBA program borrowers are not more susceptible to extraordinary attention from any other federal agency unless the borrower has not paid income taxes or child support payments, in which case extra attention is probably warranted.

Any federal or state chartered bank is capable of participating in the SBA loan guarantee programs. In addition, there are 13 SBA-licensed nonbank lenders (SBLCs) that have the capability to make SBA-guaranteed loans.

All of these lenders have many benefits available to them through participation in the loan guarantee programs. For example, the financial guarantee permits lenders to enter into transactions with noncredit risks that otherwise might prevent them from lending. These risks might be longer loan terms, industry (such as recreational facilities or convenience stores), or collateral used to secure the loan (such as single-purpose real estate improvements or specialized equipment).

Eligible Businesses

Most every type of business and industry is eligible for SBA financing assistance as long as they meet some basic qualifications:

- The business is operated for profit.
- The business is engaged in or proposes to do business in the United States or its possessions.
- The owners have a reasonable level of equity to invest.
- The owners use alternative sources of financial resources, including personal assets, before seeking financial assistance.

Some businesses and individuals require special consideration due to certain circumstances:

- Franchises are eligible except in situations where a franchisor retains power to control operations to such an extent as to be tantamount to an employment contract. The franchisee must have the right to profit from efforts commensurate with ownership.
- Recreational facilities and clubs are eligible provided: (a) the facilities are open to the general public, or (b) in membership-only situations, membership is not selectively denied to any particular group of individuals, and the number of memberships is not restricted either as a whole or by establishing maximum limits for particular groups.
- Farms and agricultural businesses are eligible. However, if the borrower runs such a business, the borrower should first explore the Farm Service Agency (FSA) programs, particularly if there has been a prior relationship with FSA.
- Fishing vessels are eligible. However, those seeking funds for the construction or reconditioning of vessels with a cargo capacity of five tons or more must first request financing from the National Marine Fisheries Service (NMFS).
- Medical facilities (hospitals, clinics, emergency outpatient facilities, and medical and dental laboratories) are eligible. Convalescent and nursing

homes are eligible provided they are licensed by the appropriate government agency and services rendered go beyond those of room and board.

- An Eligible Passive Company (EPC) is an entity that does not engage in regular and continuous business activity, but is established by its owner to own assets for tax, estate, or liability protection, for the exclusive use by a second company with the same ownership. These are eligible for SBA financing provided the EPC uses the loan to acquire, lease, and/or improve or renovate real or personal property that it leases to one or more operating companies for conducting that company's business. The EPC has a lease in writing that is subordinated to SBA, and the operating company must qualify as an eligible SBA borrower. Any owner of 20 percent or more of both the EPC and the operating company must personally guarantee the loan.

- If the business changes ownership and benefits from the change, the borrower may be eligible for an SBA loan. In most cases, this benefit should be seen in promoting the sound development of the business or perhaps in preserving its existence when the former owner is retiring or changing careers. Loans cannot be made to help the borrower purchase part of a business in which the borrower has no present interest or part of an interest of a present and continuing owner. The SBA discourages loans to effect a change of ownership among members of the same family and it will scrutinize such applications more carefully.

- Legal aliens are eligible for SBA loans. However, the SBA will look at the borrower's status (e.g., resident, lawful temporary resident, etc.) in determining the degree of risk relating to the continuity of the applicant's business. Excessive risk may be offset by full collateralization. The borrower can discuss the various types of visas in more detail with the local SBA office.

- Probation, parole, or indictment. The SBA won't accept applications from firms where a principal is currently incarcerated, on parole, on probation, or under indictment; is a defendant in a criminal proceeding; or whose probation or parole is lifted expressly because it prohibits an SBA loan. On the other hand, if one of the principals has formerly been in prison but has served the sentence, the business would be eligible. Judgments concerning applicants who detail prison time on their personal history statement are made on a case-by-case evaluation of the nature, frequency, and timing of the offenses. If any owner answers a question on Form 912 in the affirmative, that owner will have to submit fingerprint cards with the application.

Ineligible Businesses

There are a few types of businesses that are ineligible to receive financing assistance from the SBA. In general these business activities include those based on a passive investment, those engaged solely in financing third parties, or those operating a purely speculative business activity.

Ineligible businesses include those engaged in illegal activities, loan packaging, speculation, multisales distribution, gambling, investment, or lending, or where the owner is on parole. Specific types of businesses not eligible include:

- Real estate investment firms when the real property will be held for investment purposes.
- Firms involved in speculative activities that develop profits from fluctuations in price rather than through the normal course of trade (for example, wildcatting for oil and dealing in commodities futures).
- Dealers in rare coins and stamps.
- Firms involved in lending activities, such as banks, finance companies, factoring companies, leasing companies, insurance companies (not agents), and any other firm whose stock in trade is money.
- Pyramid sales plans where a participant's primary incentive is based on the sales made by an ever-increasing number of participants. Such products as cosmetics, household goods, and other soft goods lend themselves to this type of business.
- Firms involved in activities that are against the law in the jurisdiction where the business is located. Included in these activities is production, servicing, or distribution of otherwise legal products that are to be used in connection with an illegal activity. If the borrower is running a business selling drug paraphernalia or operating a motel that permits illegal prostitution, the SBA will not guarantee the borrower's loan.
- Gambling activities, including any business whose principal activity is gambling. While this precludes loans to racetracks, casinos, and similar enterprises, the rule does not restrict loans to otherwise eligible businesses that obtain less than one-third of their annual gross income from either the sale of official state lottery tickets under a state license or legal gambling activities licensed and supervised by a state authority.
- Charitable, religious, or other nonprofit institutions; government-owned corporations; consumer and marketing cooperatives; and churches and organizations promoting religious objectives.

USDA Business and Industry Loan Program

The U.S. Department of Agriculture (USDA) provides assistance to small business owners in rural areas through its Business and Industry Guaranteed Loan Program (B&I). The purpose is to focus on job creation and retention in rural areas, which is vital to provide goods, services, and a supporting economy to the USDA's prime audience, agricultural business interests.

The B&I program is very similar to the SBA's 7(a) program in that it provides a financial guarantee to a lender to extend long-term capital financing. While limiting the program's reach to rural areas, in many respects the B&I program is much more flexible and has some very appealing features to enhance its functionality to borrowers and lenders.

Like SBA, this program requires borrowers to qualify financially and through ownership to avoid abuse and fraud. Lenders retain a healthy portion of the exposure to encourage borrowers to act in their own best interest. This section will chiefly describe the differences between the B&I and SBA programs to delineate many advantages for lenders and borrowers.

Loan Guarantee

The B&I program does not have a minimum loan amount and can generally provide a guarantee for up to a $10 million loan. However the program administrator can approve larger guarantees for up to $25 million in exceptional circumstances.

Lenders get an 80 percent guarantee for loans up to $5 million, 70 percent guarantee for loans up to $10 million, and 60 percent guarantee for loans over $10 million. However, the program administrator may grant an exception to allow a guarantee of up to 90 percent for loans of $10 million or less.

Loans can be made for a wide range of uses and have generous repayment terms to benefit borrowers. These terms can be up to 30 years for real estate purchases or development, 5 years or to the useful life of equipment, or 7 years for working capital and loan transaction costs. Lines of credit or revolving credit facilities are not eligible for B&I participation.

The program can be used for construction financing. As with any financing, no construction should begin prior to the financing being approved and closed. B&I construction loan applicants may be required to submit a notice to the Regional Clearinghouse servicing their area to initiate an intergovernmental review of their project.

One very notable difference is that the B&I program can be used to finance construction or renovation of commercial lease projects such as retail centers, office buildings, and industrial facilities. These projects do not have to be owner-occupied but must have enough committed tenants to break even. Property ownership transfers or refinancing debt are not eligible for these properties, since there are no job benefits.

Debt can be refinanced with a B&I loan, but it must be to create new jobs or preserve existing jobs. These loans will be evaluated for the cash-flow benefits and how that will relate to the company's ability to add or retain employees.

Underwriting for the B&I program will be focused on the repayment ability of the project—the strongest applications are those that can show at least three years' profitability and cash flow adequate to service the debt.

Applicants need to demonstrate repayment ability with realistic financial projections supported by detailing the assumptions used to prepare them. New business loan applications will rely heavily on a feasibility study or business plan that is required to be part of the application package.

The department delegates its state offices to approve guarantees for up to $5 million, but larger loans must be submitted to Washington, D.C., for review. Unlike the SBA, lenders only get a conditional guarantee approval ahead of the loan closing. Once the loan is closed and USDA verifies that conditions are met the guarantee is issued.

Eligible Lenders

A distinct difference in the B&I and SBA programs is that the B&I program can be used by a broad range of lenders: banks, S&Ls, Farm Credit System, Bank of Cooperatives, a bank holding company's mortgage company, credit unions, and insurance companies. And the regulations provide that any commercial lending company with experience and financial strength may apply, even if not regulated.

Lenders probably find the program much more flexible than SBA because they can use their own documents and security instruments. There are no interest rate restrictions, so participating lenders can negotiate directly with the business to arrive at a mutually acceptable rate of interest and fees. The lenders cannot set balloon payments but may structure the deal to have lower payments in the first three years.

Eligible Borrowers

Most types of commercial businesses qualify for financial assistance under the B&I program whether manufacturing, retail, wholesale, or service. New start-up businesses can also be financed with this program. What is very different from SBA financing is that the B&I program can be used by co-ops, trusts, nonprofit enterprises, Native Americans, and public bodies. One restriction is that government employees or military employees are restricted to less than 20 percent ownership.

Like SBA, all business owners with more than a 20 percent interest must personally guarantee the financing. An existing business must have at least a 10 percent tangible equity position post-transaction (20 percent for new businesses). The loan must have adequate collateral to cover the entire loan with the program defining maximum leverage to be used by various assets (80 percent for real estate, 60 to 80 percent chattels, etc.). All collateral assets must be insured, and key man life insurance is a common requirement.

What Is Rural?

The B&I program is limited to rural communities, meaning those outside any city with a population of 50,000 and that city's urbanized periphery. For many years the department held a narrower definition of the term rural and deemed that it meant the program was limited to businesses located in counties with a population of no more than 50,000. That made many counties around large urban areas ineligible due expanding suburban and exurban growth.

More recently the department has broadened its definition to provide for measuring the population restrictions on other determinations of what constitutes a rural community. Using a matrix based on census tract data, the department predetermines areas eligible for assistance in order to make financing more easily accessible to lenders and businesses alike.

Ineligible Borrowers

The B&I program cannot be used by businesses similar to those disqualified from SBA loans. The program cannot be used for owner-occupied or rental housing (although housing site development may be eligible), racetracks, gambling facilities, lending companies, investment companies, or insurance companies. Unlike SBA, golf courses are not eligible under the B&I program, and loans exceeding $1 million that involve the relocation of more than 50 jobs are also not eligible.

Production agriculture financing is very limited under the B&I program, since the department encourages those activities to use other programs.

❊ ❊ ❊

The B&I program is a great alternative for businesses located in areas eligible for participation. While the processing time is not as predictable and the lender has slightly more risk to assure issuance of the guarantee, the program's broader project acceptance and higher loan limits are very beneficial.

One limiting reality is that program funding is often lower than the demand for participation, which means the program frequently runs out of money before year end and all eligible loans are processed. This backlog frequently means that a high demand rolls over into the next fiscal year, accelerating how fast funding gets absorbed year after year.

Export-Import Bank of the United States

The Export-Import Bank of the United States was established in Franklin Roosevelt's administration to encourage exports of U.S. goods and therefore promote domestic job growth. By guaranteeing payment of U.S. company sales abroad, the Ex-Im Bank provides a means for these companies to get credit from domestic banks for production. The program benefits small and large businesses with the most prominent beneficiary being the Boeing Company for aircraft sales.

Using a variety of program tools, such as export insurance and working capital guarantees, the Ex-Im Bank helps small business owners expand the market for their products through financing and risk management. Risk on foreign exports includes the problem of ascertaining the integrity of the buyers and their willingness and ability to pay when they are in another country. Other factors, including those both political and economic, often exacerbate the risk of payment default.

Loan Guarantees

Financing assistance is provided through both loan guarantees and direct loans to importers of U.S.-produced goods. Unlike most government finance programs, the Ex-Im Bank provides term financing guarantees for foreign companies and countries that are purchasing American products, if competitive financing is not available locally. These guarantees allow these buyers to obtain one- to two-year term financing when comparable market-priced alternatives are unavailable.

This financing assistance enables many international buyers of U.S. products to obtain loans when there may be none other available. The guarantee covers 100 percent of the commercial and political risks of the transaction and offers flexible financing options and repayment terms. There are no transaction size limits, and medium-term and long-term financing options are available.

Ex-Im Bank's credit guarantee of an international buyer is generally used to finance the purchase of capital equipment and services, but another eligible use includes financing for refurbished equipment, software, and even transaction closing expenses (banking and legal fees) and certain local costs and expenses for the buyer.

Military or defense items and other sales to military businesses are generally not eligible, and all goods financed must meet Ex-Im Bank's foreign content requirements. These goods must be shipped from the United States to an international buyer, and if the transactions are in excess of $20 million, they must be transported on U.S. flagged vessels.

Ex-Im Bank can do business in most markets but is limited or unable to offer financing in certain countries and under certain terms. The bank will review all financing proposals to evaluate their respective economic impact and environmental effects.

Program Features

As with any government guarantee program, there are specific guidelines that define the limitations of the assistance. Here are some of the significant terms provided by the Ex-Im loan guarantee:

- **Size.** There are no minimum or maximum size limits to export sales that may be financed with Ex-Im Bank's loan guarantee.
- **Coverage.** Ex-Im Bank's loan guarantee covers up to 100 percent of principal and accrued interest on any amount. The level of Ex-Im Bank support will be the lesser of 85 percent of the value of all eligible goods and services, or 100 percent of the U.S. content in all eligible goods and services in the U.S. supply contract. Ex-Im Bank can also provide a medium-term insurance policy to support financings up to $10 million with longer repayment terms.
- **Cash payment.** Ex-Im Bank requires the foreign buyer to make cash payment to the U.S. exporter equal to at least 15 percent of the U.S. supply contract, which may be borrowed.
- **Repayment terms.** Generally the repayment term of a transaction is determined by a number of variables, including the borrower's financial condition and common market repayment terms for the products, industry practices, country conditions, and the product's useful life.

  Repayment terms may be granted up to five years for exports of capital equipment and services. Ten-year terms may be available for transportation equipment and exports to large-scale projects.

- **Fees.** Guarantee and other fees vary based on the transaction and term. Since some of the supply contracts can take many months or more than a year to fulfill, the guarantee commitment may be in place for an extended period while the supplier fulfills the contract. In such instances, there may be applicable commitment fees or a facility fee paid to compensate Ex-Im Bank for the outstanding obligation.

  Additionally, Ex-Im Bank assesses an exposure fee at variable levels depending on the tenor, country risk, and buyer credit risk.

Guarantee Approval

Ex-Im Bank approval of the guarantee on any contract is confirmed by issuance of its Final Commitment document. Buyers or lenders may formally apply for this commitment once the contract has been awarded.

Those seeking Ex-Im support or confirmation of eligibility ahead of a contract's being awarded can request a Letter of Interest, a nonbinding letter containing Ex-Im Bank terms for the specific transaction. This document is valid for six months and is renewable.

In exceptional cases, Ex-Im Bank may accept an application for a Preliminary Commitment, a nonbinding expression of interest from Ex-Im Bank stating that the borrower's needs generally meet Ex-Im Bank's financing requirements.

16

MICROLOANS

A relatively recent financing product developed to provide assistance to small enterprises with limited access to capital is known as microcredit. Inspired by the first modern microcredit operation, Grameen Bank, founded in Bangladesh in 1976 by Nobel laureate Muhammad Yunus, microcredit has steadily gained popularity across the world.

Microcredit was created as a tool to empower people to escape poverty with entrepreneurship. Microloans are smaller loans made with liberal terms that enable people to create or grow their own business enterprise. In its original form, loans of $100 to $250 were not unusual, given that developing economies were easy to enter with much less capital. Some of these programs also required a microsavings component that helped recirculate funding dollars to support lending growth.

In the United States microloans have grown out of a variety of sources, funding models, and targeted audiences. Ranging from hundreds of state and local economic development agencies to international nongovernment organizations (NGOs) like Grameen Bank and ACCION, microloans play a critical role in providing an important source of funding to aspiring entrepreneurs. Of necessity, the loan amounts are much larger in the United States, with some lenders providing as much as $100,000 in financing. More commonly the maximum loan ranges from $10,000 to $50,000.

Many microlenders are made available from municipal, county, or state agencies charged with assisting the development of a more robust small business economy in their jurisdictions with the seeds of microfinance. On the federal level, the U.S. Small Business Administration funds microloans through hundreds of local partners that administer these activities on the SBA's behalf. This funding helps people create jobs for themselves.

Microloans are not grants. They are responsibly underwritten loans with liberal terms. The phrase *liberal terms* is not intended to imply that risk parameters do not apply or that everyone will be approved. Rather, microloans are made with some flexibility that comes from the lender having a clear understanding of each client's situation, goals, and capabilities.

These loans can be custom fit to clients, rather than a one-size-fits-all approach. Microlenders are usually nonprofit enterprises with socially responsible missions. Their operations are funded with a combination of private donations, corporate and foundation support, and government grants. They get more involved with clients as mentors and technical advisors, which in turn gives them a unique perspective when fielding funding requests.

Microloans are provided to many budding entrepreneurs who often may be best described as those without a track record, positive or negative. Most micro-lenders are more focused on the business plans and individuals who don't have several years of financial records and credit scores. They work with prospective business owners within guidelines to assist these entrepreneurs in exploiting an opportunity to create a business that can provide full-time employment for themselves.

There are many microlenders, and each one is unique with regard to focus and criteria. To determine which could be most helpful, it's a good idea for owners to do some homework to learn which lenders service their area (many are restricted geographically) and to visit them online to inquire what kind of loan programs they have.

Here are some of the common guidelines from among several lenders surveyed:

- **Credit scores.** Few microlenders require a minimum credit score, but for those that do it's probably going to be set at a low threshold (575 range), which is more of an effort to screen out those who may have had a recent negative credit event. For those with negative events, such as foreclosure or bankruptcy, some microlenders require a minimum waiting period before they would be eligible to apply for financing.

  More important to most lenders will be establishing that applicants are current on all of their obligations. It's not intended that the microfinancing be used for personal obligations but strictly to fuel a business opportunity with capital.

- **Maximum business income.** Ranges from $250,000 to $500,000 to unspecified.
- **Maximum household income.** Ranges from "less than $100,000" to unspecified.
- **Current financial condition.** Most microlenders require that borrowers already have a stable household cash flow that can support their current monthly loan payments and the costs of the microloan payment. If that is not present at the beginning of discussions, they will probably work with borrowers to improve cash flow, but they will probably not fund a loan until the situation is stabilized.
- **Eligible enterprises.** Microlenders will fund only for-profit business enterprises, with the exception of many microlenders that will make an allowance to fund nonprofit child-care centers.
- **Ineligible uses.** Most microlenders prohibit use of loan funds for businesses that manufacture or sell alcohol, firearms, or pornography, or that promote gaming, and that acquire, develop, or rehab real estate.
- **Collateral.** Some microlenders require available collateral, even if it's of nominal value and only provides partial coverage of the loan. This requirement may be a condition of the funding the microlenders receive to create loan pools.
- **Cosigner.** Most microlenders are willing to consider a cosigner for entrepreneurs who cannot qualify alone.
- **Technical assistance.** Before loan approval some microlenders require that borrowers accept technical assistance, which sometimes continues throughout the life of the loan. Experience shows that the time that technical advisors invest in conducting training workshops for business owners pays off handsomely in fostering successful business outcomes.

17

LEASE FINANCING

Leasing is a unique financing option for the use of certain assets. In a lease transaction the asset owner (the leasor) agrees to lease, or rent, it to another party (the leasee) for its exclusive use for a specific time at a specific cost. It's directly comparable to leasing an apartment or office: the leasee enters a contract to use the space for a predetermined number of months or years at an agreed upon monthly cost.

When a leasee is using someone else's asset, the leasee has no ownership or equity in the asset; therefore, it's not reflected on the leasee's balance sheet as an asset, nor is the lease obligation reflected as a liability (with the exception discussed below). The cost of the lease payment made is charged as an expense against revenues in the income statement.

Most lease equipment agreements are written with an option for the leasee to purchase the asset at a predetermined residual value at the end of the agreement. Depending on the type of lease and term, it may be for as much as 40 to 50 percent of the asset's original cost, or it may be a nominal value like $1.

There are two basic types of leases, the open-ended lease and the closed-ended lease. The principal difference between them has to do with the asset disposition plans at the conclusion of the financing period.

- **Open-ended (operating) lease.** With an open-ended, or operating, lease it's expected at the beginning of the lease that the asset ownership will remain vested with the leasor at the end of the lease term. This lease may have lower payments that reflect the asset's residual value and that will benefit the leasor, who can liquidate the asset later.

Generally the leasee will still have an option to purchase the asset for the residual value at the conclusion of the lease. This type of lease is good for the leasee's cash flow, since the leasee is essentially deferring the decision of whether to buy the asset but still gets the benefit of its use.

- **Closed-ended (capital) lease.** With a closed-ended, or capital, lease it's expected at the beginning of the lease that the asset ownership will be transferred to the leasee at the end of the lease term. This lease may have higher payments that reflect the asset's lower residual value and that will benefit the leasee, who can acquire it for a nominal sum later.

Generally, in a capital lease the leasee is relieved of the requirement of a down payment that may be required with ownership. But if the residual value at the end of the lease is less than 10 percent of the original value of the asset, the lease must be capitalized, meaning the corresponding values must be reflected on the leasee's balance sheet as an asset and liability, respectively.

According to GAAP, such a low residual value recognizes the transaction as an alternative purchase financing vehicle and requires that the leasee disclose its obligation to pay for the full value of the asset.

Leases are most commonly used as financing for virtually every kind of equipment and for ancillary assets, such as cranes, trucks, trailers, forklifts, hotel furniture, hospital beds, dialysis machines, and even software. There is no real limit as to what kinds of assets can be leased, tangible or intangible, so long as the owner of the assets can amortize their value through depreciation or depletion. The business decision for leasing vs. owning should be determined by three questions:

1. How long does the business plan to use the equipment? (shorter term vs. longer term)
2. What is the business's working capital position? (larger payments vs. down payment + small payments)
3. What is the risk of asset obsolescence? (high vs. low)

To distinguish the unique characteristics of leasing business equipment compared to owning it, here is a profile of how a company might acquire use of a forklift.

Owning

If the company were purchasing a forklift, it would need to pay for it with cash or a loan (which would likely require a cash down payment or contribution toward the purchase price, determined by the lender). The title to the forklift would be transferred to the company with a lien in favor of the lender. Monthly payments would be required to pay off the loan over a specified term, and the company could depreciate the purchase cost over the useful life of the forklift.

Generally the financing term would be shorter than the depreciation period, meaning that the company would have to repay the loan well ahead of the forklift's breaking down. Only the interest portion of the loan payment is considered an expense, although the loan principal portion of the payment would be offset somewhat more slowly by the depreciation expense.

When the loan was fully repaid, the lien would be released, and the company would have no more monthly payments. It could continue using the lift as long as it lasted. Depreciation would end once the company had fully amortized the cost of the asset.

Advantages:

1. The company would have full use of the lift for its entire life for a fixed cost plus costs of capital financing (interest).
2. The useful life might be extended less expensively with maintenance and repairs rather than replacement.
3. The investment in the lift might be a hedge against the higher cost of a lift in the future.

Disadvantages:

1. The company would have to tie up capital in an asset well ahead of its use of the lift or benefits of ownership.
2. The selected lift might have severe operational or maintenance problems beyond the warranty at the expense of the company.
3. As with any equipment, there is obsolescence risk as machinery ages and new technology evolves.

Leasing

If the company were leasing a forklift, it would sign a lease agreement with a leasing company, a financial company that probably bought the forklift immediately before entering into the agreement to lease it. The lease would be for a specified term and might not require that the company pay more than the first and last month's lease payment of the agreement up front.

The forklift would be titled in the name of the leasing company, which would depreciate the cost of the lift over its useful life. The company could expense the entire monthly lease payments against earnings. At the end of the lease, the company would return the forklift to the leasing company or have the option to purchase it at a predetermined price.

Advantages

1. The company can lease the lift with only the first and last month's payment due up front, preserving capital in the business.
2. The term of the lease is specific, meaning that the company can deliver the old lift back to the leasor at the conclusion of the lease. Then the company can acquire a newer model for future use.
3. If the company needed the lift only for a specific job, such as a two- to three-year construction project, it could return it to the leasor without any risk of losing capital.
4. Depending on the lease terms, any maintenance or operational issues belong to the leasing company.

Disadvantages

1. The company might face escalating costs of using the equipment in the future, since the lease fixes the price for a limited term.
2. Unless it exercises an option to purchase, there is no residual benefit for the investment made in leasing the lift for the term. For example, if the useful life of the lift assumed that it would be used 2,000 hours per year, but it was used only 1,500 hours per year, the leasee would still have to pay for the 2,000 hours and could not redeem that overpayment without buying the lift.

Captive Finance

Many large equipment manufacturers own a financing division whose mission is to provide financing for their equipment. These sources are generally easier to negotiate with, since they were created to help their parent company sell more equipment. Selling equipment is not encouraged with stringent credit requirements, so it's fair to say they are more lenient that most banks.

Helpful too is the fact that they understand the value of the equipment better, have a vested relationship with the original profit margin in the asset, and support a strong network of used equipment in their brand. For these reasons, captive leasing programs are generally very aggressive, and the pricing will also reflect the best in the market (through subsidies paid from their parent, essentially shaving some profit margin).

Owners should not overlook captive financing alternatives when purchasing assets from manufacturers that offer that benefit.

Lease Factors

A lease is an agreement to use an asset, not to purchase it. The funding inherent in the transaction is where the third-party owner acquires an asset and rents it to a business. Accordingly, there is no interest charge accrued for the financing. However, in recognition that the transaction is essentially a financing transaction, there is certainly a cost calculated by the leasor for the time value of money invested in the asset.

Rather than interest, leasors use a lease factor, which is a number calculated to generate the leasor's financial return for using the asset and to determine the monthly payment. Lease factors are not interest rates and are never expressed in such terms, since legally a lease is not a loan. Therefore, the true cost of funds when comparing a lease to traditional bank financing is not as apparent, but it can be calculated easily.

To determine what the underlying interest rate on a lease factor is, divide it by 2,400. Conversely, to get the lease factor from a cited interest rate, multiply the rate by 2,400.

18

WORKING CAPITAL FINANCING

All business enterprises have an essential need for working capital. Businesses use cash to pay labor, buy materials, pay the utilities, and find the next sale. No business can continue to exist long without sufficient working capital.

Working capital is the phrase used to describe the funds available to meet the needs of the day-to-day operations of businesses. Daily sales produce cash and checks that are deposited into the bank. Credit card sales are deposited into the business account a few days after the sale. Some clients pay in advance for future delivery while some buy on credit and pay in 30 days. These are all sources of working capital.

Most businesses pay their employees at least every two weeks. Some suppliers have to be paid upon delivery. Utilities and the rent are paid by the month. These are all typical uses of working capital. Comparing the timing of the need to spend these monies to the timing that revenues are actually received—converting those operations into cash—is known as the cash cycle, discussed in Chapter 10.

Most successful owners carefully manage their cash cycles to assure that adequate funds are provided from revenues and collections to meet all of the expenses needed to continue operations without interruption. But managing this cycle is challenging due to constantly changing factors in the business environment that businesses cannot control.

Working capital will vary from business to business due to a number of factors, such as the industry and its standard payment terms, seasonality, average order size, and whether trade credit is typical. Of course, how much capital businesses start with and whether they have accumulated earnings also influence working capital, as does profitability.

Cash cycles may be out of sync with the cycles normal in the industry in which a given business operates or with size category. Since each business is unique, there can be many reasons why it either has plenty of cash or is just getting by. Many well-capitalized companies need working capital financing to meet gaps that arise or exist between receipts and expenses in the cash cycle. Revenue growth will put even more pressure on working capital by enlarging business expenses ahead of revenues.

For these kinds of situations, there are a variety of working capital solutions. Debt financing can be employed from several sources and is designed to meet the gaps in cash requirements based on the recognition of the profits from business operations. The following sources highlight some of the most readily available sources of working capital.

Trade Credit

One of the easiest lines of credit for businesses to negotiate is from the companies that supply goods or services to them. Just as companies may resell to other companies on open invoice, many of their suppliers will sell to them on terms. These companies are not banks, and while their approval may be easier to negotiate, they also will be quicker to cut businesses off if their invoices are unpaid.

Trade credit is one of the best financing sources, even if used temporarily for 30 to 45 days to delay borrowing from more costly lines of credit. Trade credit is interest free; the motivation of suppliers is to incentivize businesses to purchase more goods from them, so they will often give 30 days to pay. They are generally forgiving when that time turns into 45 to 50 days, just as long as businesses keep buying.

The suppliers' return on these financing terms is built into the profit margin of whatever they are selling. They are seeking volume and loyalty—and to be positioned to grow along with the revenue growth of the businesses to which they sell.

While there may be other places from which to source purchases, the industry reputation of businesses will suffer if they habitually pay their invoices late. Other suppliers will learn of these difficulties and be hesitant to advance anything on open account.

And if particular suppliers provide something that is more difficult to source elsewhere, being cut off from their credit may stop businesses dead in their tracks until the delinquent invoices are paid.

As mentioned in Chapter 12, business-to-business trade credit amounts to approximately $1 trillion at any given time. Reportedly, Walmart uses more trade credit than it does bank borrowing. This source of capital is the first line of external debt financing as businesses start seeking support from external sources to cover the gaps in the cash cycle.

Asset-Based Loans (ABL)

Asset-based loans are a kind of specialized lending where borrowers get funding based on the discounted value of the equity in an asset they own and which lenders value as suitable collateral. Lenders do not care what the asset is as long as they can accurately value it and control it, that is, cause its liquidation in the event of default. This type of lending may be advanced against everything from real estate to business inventory to jewelry.

The more common use of the phrase *asset-based loans,* though, is by lenders in the commercial finance sector that specialize in providing revolving lines of credit against unpaid accounts receivable. These lines provide liquidity by advancing a percentage of the sales businesses generate on business-to-business open invoices. Generally, depending on many factors, funding advances can range from 75 to 90 percent of the invoice. Of course, conditions apply, namely that the invoice be a bona fide representation of a sale that has been completed and shipped.

Additionally ABL lenders are willing to advance on good receivables but are averse to the risk of invoices that go much beyond 60 days without being collected. If customers do not pay their bills within 90 days, lenders will require that businesses repay them anyway (although some lenders do advance funds on a nonrecourse basis).

Depending on the size of the line of credit, ABL lenders usually monitor accounts on a day-to-day basis. These lenders work with the accounting staff of businesses to manage the borrowing base, which is a constantly updated calculation of the accounts outstanding and unpaid. They will add new invoices each day as appropriate and denote any payments made on outstanding accounts.

The borrowing base is the final number tabulated that reflects the eligible accounts that businesses can borrow against. It factors in all of the daily activity and credit conditions to produce a number, and businesses are able to draw a certain advance rate against that sum. Since this number is constantly changing and businesses will have to borrow constantly for expenses, it's fair to say that lenders are managing the cash and that the only decision that businesses make is to determine who gets paid with the eligible funds.

Lenders will define parameters around the kinds of invoices they will advance against, and as the invoices age these conditions may be tightened. For example a lender may be willing to advance 90 percent on an invoice when issued, but when the invoice has been outstanding 30 days, that advance may be lowered to 85 percent, meaning the business loses 5 percent eligibility on the account. When the account has been outstanding 60 days, the advance rate may be lowered to 75 percent, and at 90 days, as mentioned above, it is deemed ineligible and will not be part of the borrowing base.

The ABL borrower must utilize a blocked account, called a lockbox, which is a bank checking account that is controlled by the lender and all of the account payments made to the company go to it. In this way the lender can verify that all payments reported on the account are attributable to specific invoices, preventing any false claims by the company of payment on older, ineligible invoices that were actually payments on newer, eligible invoices.

Factoring

Another financing source for working capital is known as factoring, and it also involves accounts receivable. With factoring, rather than advancing a loan against an eligible receivable, the factor actually buys it at a discounted value. Rather than focusing on the creditworthiness of the client company, the factor looks at the value of the underlying account.

The factors can help collect an account and will participate in the collection activities once an account ages beyond expectation. Payments are invoiced and directed to an address controlled by the factor that is empowered to convert the payment, although it may name the client as the intended recipient.

A factor can advance a client a negotiated amount against invoices with a reserve amount held back. The factor may also charge additional fees in the event that payments are not as timely as expected. Once payment is received the factor releases the reserve to the client, less any charges incurred.

For example, suppose a factor agreed to buy a particular client's 30-day invoice for 97 percent of its face value and required that a 7 percent reserve be held back as insurance against timely collection. Furthermore, the factor may charge 1 percent for each month beyond the 30 days that it will take to collect the invoice.

On a $10,000 invoice the factor would agree to purchase it for $9,700 but only advance $9,000 against it while holding back $700 in reserve. If that invoice is paid on the forty-fifth day after shipment, the factor would then pay over the $700 reserve less the $100 service charge based on the collection date. Net sum paid to the client would be $600.

Of note is the cost of financing with this source. In the example just mentioned the company paid $400 to finance a $10,000 invoice for 45 days. That may sound like a reasonable 4 percent of the face value, but on time-value of money analysis the effective yield is much higher. This advance covered the outstanding account for 45 days, at a cost per day of about $8.88. Multiplying that same rate over 365 days would equal $3,241, or 32 percent. On an annualized basis that is the rate of return for the factor in this example.

Usually the credit risk of a factored receivable is borne by the factor, but some factoring arrangements are purchased with recourse, meaning that the factor can hold the owner liable for the invoice obligation if the factor does not collect.

Sometimes factors and ABL lenders will impose restrictions as to what they will purchase and set discounts according to whom the client is selling, the concentration of business, and the invoice size. Recourse may be an incentive offered to get lenders or factors to purchase certain invoices they would normally avoid.

New Trends

Asset-based lending and factoring have been the operating lifeline for many businesses for decades, but given the labor-intensive monitoring and auditing required to administer, by nature they are often very expensive. And when economic cycles swing into growth, many ABL lenders will raise their minimum credit lines to push credit to much larger clients away from smaller ones, since the cost to administer larger accounts is more favorable.

Borrowing companies often faced myriad fees based on the handling costs of other companies to collect their payments, monitor their invoices, and audit their operating results to placate the risk of this kind of working capital financing. Frequently layered on top of these costs are multiple-year line agreements with high penalties to pay off early or minimum usage yields requiring companies to borrow certain minimum amounts. By adding all these costs to the stated interest rate of prime plus a spread on the actual funds outstanding, it is easy to see how lender yields climb into the 20 to 30 percent range.

One obvious feature for borrowers was that they had to have very strong profit margins to afford ABL, and it's difficult to ever retain enough profits to graduate from asset-based lending.

Technology may be changing that model in the future, as a few upstart intermediaries have entered small business financing markets to connect borrowers and lenders in an innovative approach to ABL. While most are in very early development stages, one company has been in the market for more than three years and is described here to provide insight into the kinds of advances that will be changing this financing sector in the future.

The Receivables Exchange (TRE; http://www.receivablesxchange.com/) is a New Orleans–based company that in 2008 started the first online marketplace for trading accounts receivable. Basically, the company created an electronic platform for qualified borrowing companies to offer their invoices for sale to a market of qualified institutional buyers.

Using TRE's bulletin board, the seller-buyer match is made online through an auction process where institutional buyers bid on the offered account with advance rates and fees. The buyer providing the most money for lowest costs wins the auction. TRE is the honest broker qualifying both parties through transparent screening and providing security for each respective party to ensure the transaction and participants are genuine.

TRE also routes the advances from buyer to seller and then collects the debtor payments and divides them appropriately between the parties.

This idea holds much promise for future growth with many sellers and buyers. Buyers will be attracted to the broad selection of diverse accounts, will avoid concentrations, and will reap competitive returns. Sellers will be attracted to the ease of use, the auction approach that may result in higher advances for lower cost, and lower reliance on a single lender.

More innovations are on the way. It's an exciting market for working capital financing, as technology is bringing more competition, distribution, and access to lenders and borrowers.

Purchase Order Financing

Maybe the most difficult financing to arrange is for inventory. While some lenders may include inventory in their collateral base, few are actually advancing funds to acquire goods or convert raw materials into finished goods that can be sold. The exception is called purchase order financing, where money is advanced ahead of the sale transaction and used to finance production of the company's inventory.

The reason this financing is scarce is simple enough—it's very risky. When a company acquires or manufactures products for resale, it is preparing to create transactions with a third party. The transaction risk may include not being able to fulfill the order, buyer cancellation, buyer nonpayment, or faulty production that renders the sold goods unusable to the buyer.

Most working capital financing is done *after* the sale—once the goods are created, sold, and delivered: it's much less risky to provide financing on the receivable on an account that has already been fulfilled. While plenty of risk is present, it's not compounded by the situation where the transaction has not yet closed.

A very few financiers will step into this void for a company that has good operations and a track record of success, but that also happens to be facing a steep growth curve that it cannot fulfill without financial support. For situations where the company has secured a firm order for goods, purchase order financing provides funding to purchase goods or raw materials and finance the conversion cycle to get this inventory produced and shipped to the buyer.

Start-ups or speculative sales need not apply. These financings are afforded to situations that can be verified and present a real opportunity to fund a gap that may be only 30 to 90 days. Repayment will have to be identified clearly on the other end, usually with a takeout provided by another lender advancing on the receivable that is created at the time the inventory is delivered to the borrower.

Purchase order financing is secured with an interest in the inventory goods that survives conversion and sale until repaid. Since the lender is using funds to acquire the base goods, it will have a security interest that attaches to the proceeds once the goods are sold. The succeeding ABL lender will coordinate the loan payoff to assure satisfaction of the claim, since the purchase order lien would be senior to the receivable financing if not fully satisfied.

As with receivable financing, a company using purchase order financing must have strong profit margins, since this financing is not cheap. Manufacturing usually carries fairly strong margins, but importer/resellers may not do as well. That said, purchase order financiers are really more interested in the creditworthiness of the purchaser than that of the borrower.

Financing will generally be made available to goods with an established, mature demand. In the event that the buyer did not fulfill the obligation to honor the purchase order, the financier would want to ensure that another buyer could be identified without suffering margin or a significant sales cycle.

Part 7

Declined? Where to Go Next

19

GET TO THE BOTTOM OF NO

It's rare to find any business owner who can claim to have been granted approval for every funding request ever made. Even when the deal seems perfect, financiers and loan underwriters seem to always find a way to get heartburn over something. Even the business developers at most lenders get frustrated at the many creative ways their production gets squashed by their own team.

But though a business owner may have been turned down once, the possibility of funding still exists. Next week, next month, next year, or maybe even in the next few years, the owner will have the chance to correct all of the weaknesses and objections these naysayers put forth. And with determination the owner will make a lot more money than the naysayers expected.

There are legitimate concerns lenders must protect in order to ensure a sound portfolio, and these are more acutely exercised by investors who are laying out their own money. And even if a business opportunity has some unique features, lenders still must apply a generalized set of standards to assure that they stay within their own boundaries.

Exceptions are usually difficult to justify, but they can be made. Errors are made too, as lenders overlook important information and sometimes do not give owners the chance to modify the answers to their questions.

If an owner's funding request is declined, it's very important for the owner to stop talking and listen carefully to learn why. It's in this conversation that the owner can begin learning more about the lender's perspective about the business plan and proposal. Dissecting this discussion may reveal a misunderstanding of the owner's request. It is imperative for the owner not to become combative so as to be able to return another day to address the problem.

There are many reasons that lenders might refuse a deal, and usually they would be right to do so. Lenders have listened to more proposals than can be counted. Even in the face of a great business plan, lenders have the prerogative to invest their funds in a profile of their choosing. Their economic prejudices are applied for the protection of their capital and are based on their real business experiences.

If the owner can listen to the lender's explanation for rejecting the deal and ask questions for clarity and definition without being defensive, emotional, or rude, the owner can learn a lot that could prove helpful in the next search for money.

Sometimes No Is the Answer for Now

Sometimes the lender says no—maybe even without reasons, exceptions, or encouragement, maybe even without a phone call or a letter. Regardless of all the positive conversation, the upbeat prospects, and how badly the lender seems to want to do the deal, the owner's request will always be subject to a change of heart until it's funded.

Many lending business developers expose their distance from the decision-making process or maybe their own inexperience by continually encouraging the owner until the last minute with regard to the likelihood of approval. But when the committee says no, the loan officer suddenly finds all sorts of things wrong with the deal. This scenario plays out much too often and frustrates many relationships.

No is one-half of the possible answers available to any lender, and the owner should at least half expect it. The owner should always listen carefully to this word to understand exactly how it was said among many different ways it may have been framed. An astute owner will pay close attention to the explanation offered by the lender after the word *because*.

The owner should realize that the lender will make a decision about the funding request based on business, not personality. The lender has a responsibility to make decisions based on specific, preordained parameters that must be respected. There is a certain profile for the kinds of business that will be in the lender's portfolio and to stray from that profile would not be good business.

The business owner should not get mad or defensive or feel hurt or betrayal, and certainly should not allow emotions to irreparably damage future opportunities with the lender. If the lender has a difficult time being blunt, is uneasy communicating bad news, or, conversely, is a little too matter-of-fact about an unwillingness to fund the deal, the owner should take this news the same way: *underreact*.

No matter how well or badly the lender delivers the funding decision and regardless of how well or badly the owner handles the news inside, it's important for the owner to keep a positive demeanor and be very cordial. The owner can express anger or disappointment once away from the lender. At the moment of reckoning, however, the owner needs the lender's help in order to understand why the proposal was not fundable. That assistance will never be forthcoming if the owner creates a scene.

There are as many variations on saying no as there are people and situations. It's not the answer the owner is seeking, but neither is it invaluable or irreversible. Listening to the reasoning for rejection is the key to learning how to get the proposal approved.

Don't Take No for an Answer

The final answer to the quest for business capital may be that the business does not qualify for the funding it seeks—not only with the lender that rejected it but with any lender. If the owner is turned down more than three times, there may be an inherent weakness preventing approval from any source.

If this is the case, the owner may need assistance from someone who can objectively evaluate the situation and the financing. Whether turning to a business consultant, a CPA, or a disinterested lender, the owner should be able to benefit from their direct experience and meaningful advice.

❉ ❉ ❉

This book has offered many different ways to meet financing objectives by presenting financing products and strategies from more than one source. Financing is not restricted to just raising capital or borrowing money but rather includes a diverse range of options. Some are more appealing than others, but that's life—sometimes we have to do what we have to do. Be honest with yourself to ensure that you are doing your part to move your business along, even if it's expensive, inconvenient, and difficult to do so.

Sometimes you can reduce the financing you need by covering a portion of your business plan in another way, such as by bootstrapping, by putting in place stronger management, or by tempering expectations. Maybe it is necessary to get financing from several sources simultaneously, although doing this is usually more difficult, expensive, and time-consuming than obtaining funds from a single source. Nevertheless, if you want financing, you have to get it where it can be gotten.

Maybe you are trying to get financing prematurely. Perhaps another 6, 12, or 18 months would improve your chances by demonstrating the business strategy or by being able to provide other metrics of financial success, such as revenue growth or profitability. Recognize that time is a good investment that can be healthy for the business. It may not satisfy your ambition today, but it may allow financing to be sourced later from a position of strength. An established and stable track record decreases your lender's exposure as well as your risk.

The key is to not stop thinking or looking. The resources are there for anyone willing to persevere, learn, and be creative. While these resources may not be accessible to you today, they will still be there tomorrow.

Don't take no for an answer, at least not as a final answer. Keep building on the experiences you have, use the advantages you can find or create, and examine the needs you have (and always segregate them from your *wants*).

INDEX

ABOUT THE AUTHOR

Charles Green is an authority on small business financing with more than 30 years' experience working with entrepreneurs. Currently he consults with small business owners on a broad range of business matters through Charles Green & Company and serves as executive director of the Small Business Finance Institute.

He has experience as a commercial banker, venture capitalist, business advisor, and business owner, and he founded and served as president/CEO of Sunrise Bank of Atlanta. Charles has had clients from more than 30 countries and served as corporate director for several businesses in the United States, Mexico, and Europe, including a NASDAQ-listed company.

Charles has authored several books and articles about business financing, including the bestselling *The SBA Loan Book* (Adams Media), and has been interviewed about small business financing by dozens of leading media outlets.

He earned a BS in Finance from the University of Alabama and completed the Stonier National Graduate School of Banking at the Wharton School of Business. He serves as chair of the Fulton County Arts Council and as a director of the Atlanta Medical Center. In 2005 he was named the Financial Services Champion by the Georgia District of the U.S. Small Business Administration.

Charles resides in midtown Atlanta, Georgia, and may be contacted at director@SBFI.org.